MW01028032

THE REPUBLIC OF BELIEFS

The Republic of Beliefs

A NEW APPROACH TO
LAW AND ECONOMICS

Kaushik Basu

PRINCETON UNIVERSITY PRESS

PRINCETON & OXFORD

Published by Princeton University Press,
41 William Street, Princeton, New Jersey 08540

In the United Kingdom: Princeton University Press,
6 Oxford Street, Woodstock, Oxfordshire OX20 1TR

press.princeton.edu

Jacket art courtesy of Ingram Publishing/
Alamy Stock Vector

ISBN 978-0-691-17768-7

Library of Congress Control Number: 2017962529

British Library Cataloging-in-Publication Data is available

This book has been composed in Miller

Printed on acid-free paper. ∞

Printed in the United States of America

10 9 8 7 6 5 4 3 2 1

To the memory of
Kenneth Arrow and Anthony Atkinson,
whom I got to know personally in their last years,
for their outstanding contributions to economics,
and their humanism

CONTENTS

In a strange way, this book for me marks a return to law. For as far back as my memory stretches, my ambition was to be a lawyer. There were two reasons for this. My father grew up in Kolkata, in the northern reaches of the city, in a nondescript, overcrowded home; and, when his father died prematurely, the household was plunged into poverty. My father took up tutoring children to provide for the household, and attended evening classes to acquire what was then the easiest degree to get, one in law. Knowing no one in the world of law or business, he was prepared to join the ranks of the many briefless lawyers who operated out of cubbyholes. It was therefore a remarkable turnaround when, late in life, he became one of the most celebrated solicitors in Kolkata, with his own law firm. It was taken for granted by my large clan of relatives and me that I would study law and then run his firm. The other reason I wanted to be a lawyer was my childhood interest in logic puzzles; I used to think of the life of a lawyer as one of indulgence in the joys of deduction.

London School of Economics changed it all. Amartya Sen's lectures on Social Choice and on Investment Planning, in jam-packed classrooms, with students spilling over onto windowsills, were mesmerizing. Morris Perlman, a product of Chicago University, showing us with a few diagrams and flawless lucidity how pure reason can give deep insights into society and economy, was a deep influence, as were Kotaro Suzumura, with his calligraphic mathematical scribblings on the blackboard, Max Steuer, and several others. As I was completing my master's in economics, I decided that if Amartya Sen agreed to take me on as a PhD student, I would give up the idea of taking the bar examination. With great trepidation, I broke the news of my altered career plans to my parents, telling them that it was a finalized decision, to spare them the agony of deliberation.

The first few years as a teacher in Delhi were among my most miserable. I wondered if I had made a mistake by changing my entire life's plan on a whim and also felt sorry as my father decided to close his law firm. But it was my father who, sensing my despondency, helped lift it. He said that my decision was probably the right one. As a lawyer, I would likely earn much more, but my life would revolve around 10 or 20 wealthy business houses, whereas, as an economist and a researcher, I would be free and the world would open up to me. I liked this assurance but did not at all believe in what he said. But it turned out to be right, and I feel fortunate for that.

There was another lucky break I got early in my career that merits recording. When I was finishing my PhD, I applied for the Young Professionals Program at the World Bank. I got through the first rounds of screening and was invited to Paris for the final interview. I flew to Paris in great excitement. But my interviewers failed me. A career in the Bank can be wonderful, but, given my temperament, this would have been a loss because I would never have discovered the joys of abstract analytical research.

This book has been long in gestation and short in writing. Its central concern is with some foundational questions about the efficacy of the law that I began to contend with from 1989 to 1991 when I taught a graduate course in industrial organization theory at Princeton and, in the process, read widely on American antitrust law. Law and economics became an interest of mine, and over the years I wrote on various practical matters, labor laws, child labor, price discrimination, and rent control, taking care to ignore the methodological fault lines that lie below the surface of the discipline.

During my seven years in the world of policymaking, beginning in 2009, I worked on many real-world problems of law and economics, such as corruption control and the right to food and welfare, but there was no time or opportunity to delve into methodological matters. This is one of the inevitable problems of policymaking. You have to use tools and methods that you know are debatable because the choice is often between using these blunt instruments and a paralysis of action.

The opportunity to investigate the foundational matters that had troubled me and form the bedrock of this book arose with three invitations to deliver special lectures that I received toward the end of my tenure as chief economist of the World Bank. The first was the Amartya Sen Lecture at the London School of Economics, delivered on March 3, 2015. Then there was the D. Gale Johnson Lecture at the University of Chicago, on April 13 of the same year. Finally, on June 14, 2016, by which time my broad ideas had taken more concrete shape, I got the opportunity to lecture a large audience in Aix-en-Provence in honor of Louis-André Gérard-Varet. I must also record my gratitude to audiences at seminars that I gave on this subject at the Institute for Advanced Study, Princeton, and the Indian Statistical Institute, Kolkata. These lectures were opportunities to develop some rather abstract ideas on law and economics. I am immensely grateful to Olivier Bargain, Tim Besley, Craig Calhoun, John List, Roger Myerson, Debraj Ray, Phil Reny, Dani Rodrik, and Nick Stern for the invitations and for helpful comments and criticisms.

Soon after I gave the Sen Lecture in London, I knew I wanted to write a book. But I had no time while I was at the World Bank. The actual writing occurred uninterrupted, starting on October 1, 2016, the day after I finished my term at the World Bank. Aware that I would have little time to write once I began regular teaching at Cornell from Fall 2017. I worked mostly in New York City, where Cornell's Industrial and Labor Relations School provided a perfect refuge on East 34th Street, and occasionally in Ithaca. This was a period of total absorption in the book, to the neglect of everything else, emails to answer, books to review, papers to read. It was also a time when we were moving homes, closing down Washington, and setting up residence in Ithaca and New York. The latter needed a lot of effort since we were moving to New York for the first time. I am acutely aware that I fell short in helping my wife, Alaka, with the move. What saved me was my innate propensity not to feel guilt. Now that I have thanked my father, it is time to thank my mother, from whom I must have inherited this trait. Some fifteen years ago she was visiting us in Ithaca. Alaka, who feels responsible for everything, was telling my mother about her innate guilt and asked if my mother suffered a similar affliction. My mother assured Alaka that she was exactly like her; and added that, luckily, she had never had to deal with it since she had never done anything wrong up till then. She was 83.

Given the long buildup to this book, there are several individuals, besides those already mentioned, whom I need to thank. Early in my career, when I lived in Delhi, I got some invitations to major centers of research in the world, which allowed me to nurture some of my early interest in this area, particularly related to political power and the beliefs of ordinary people. There is no way that I can express adequate gratitude to Jacques Dreze, Nick Stern, and Albert Hirschman for inviting me, when I had little scholarship to show, to, respectively, CORE in Louvain-la-Neuve, Warwick University in Coventry, and the Institute for Advanced Study in Princeton. Some of the research I did in Warwick and at the Institute made direct inputs into the research I report in this book.

The basic idea of law and economics developed in the pages that follow is abstract and, at the same time, not mathematical enough to fit traditional economic theory. Some comments from Kalle Moene and John Roemer deserve special mention because they provided me with early impetus. Over the years, I have discussed these ideas with many economists in conversation, email exchanges, and seminars and would like to record my thanks to U. K. Anandavardhanan, Karna Basu, Kalyan Chatterjee, Tito Cordella, Shanta Devarajan, Martin Dufwenberg, Devajyoti Ghose, Indermit Gill, Bob Hockett, Karla Hoff, Luis-Felipe Lopez-Calva, Steven Lukes, Anandi Mani, Ajit Mishra, Stephen Morris, Derek Neal, Martin Osborne, Jean-Philippe Platteau, David Rosenblatt, Valentin Seidler, Amartya Sen, Claudia Sepulveda, Neelam Sethi, Michael Singer, Ram Singh, Gianca Spagnolo, Subbu Subramanian, and Jorgen Weibull. Michael and Subbu read the full near-final manuscript, and their extensive comments were immensely valuable for my final round of revision.

I owe a special word of thanks to Cornell University, which provided a multidisciplinary ethos so important for this kind of work. Cornell gave me access to some of the finest theorists in the world in the areas of behavior, reasoning, and strategy. I am referring to my colleagues in the Department of Economics. But what made Cornell unusual was also the range of scholars in related disciplines who became intellectual confidants, creating an atmosphere that was both scholarly and of warmth and friendship. The list is long, but I would be remiss if I did not mention Mary Katzenstein, Peter Katzenstein, Isaac Kramnick, Elizabeth Rawlings, and Hunter Rawlings. There have been great intellectual breakthroughs in different times and different places, but I remain convinced that classical Greece is the cradle of the modern intellectual world. My fascination with this period and some of the main personalities of the time was never matched by scholarship. It was Hunter Rawlings's erudition on this that shamed me into some piecemeal reading and attempts to catch up.

Expressing thanks is not good enough; I also owe an apology. This is to legal theorists and scholars. In writing this book I have been acutely aware of my inadequate command over the legal literature. Though my concern is with the cross section of law and economics, I wish I knew the legal side of the story as well as I know the economic. Once I had decided I would write this book, I began reading the law literature but soon realized that lawyers are more prolix than economists. So it has been an effort trying to get some command over this literature, and I am aware of the caveats that remain.

There are three locales where I did short visits that deserve special mention. Lecturing to different groups and exchanging ideas with scholars with different backgrounds have always been important to me. At the end of 2016 I spent three blissful weeks, one in Melbourne, at Monash University, and two in Mumbai, at the Indian Institute of Technology. The long walks along Yarra River and Powai Lake, respectively, provided the perfect setting for contemplation (the warning signs along Powai of leopard sightings notwithstanding). Then in May 2017 I got to lecture and have useful discussions during a week's visit to the newly formed Albert Hirschman Institute on Democracy in Geneva.

Though I did not begin serious writing on this book while I was at the World Bank, I had begun piecemeal work in the nooks and crannies of a busy schedule. It was truly a blessing to have been surrounded by people who were instinctively helpful and also had a sense of humor to make the office productive and at the same time fun. Special thanks go to Laverne Cook, Indermit Gill, Vivian Hon, Grace Sorensen, and Bintao Wang. After I moved to New York and began working on the text, Grace Lee provided able assistance, and during the final lap of the writing in Ithaca I had very helpful research assistance from Haokun Sun. I am grateful to both Grace and Haokun.

Working with Princeton University Press has been a wonderful experience. When I began interacting with the Press, it was a source of some satisfaction that the press was being headed by Peter Dougherty, who, he may or may not remember, was my (young) editor when I wrote one of my earliest books in the eighties. For the present book I worked closely with Sarah Caro. Her keen interest in the project, unstinting advice at all stages, and human warmth make her a rare editor. I must also record my thanks to the two outstanding anonymous referees of Princeton University Press and Jenny Wolkowicki for their many comments, suggestions, and encouragement too.

All family members were coaxed to read and comment on various parts of the manuscript. I would like to thank Karna Basu, Diksha Basu, Shabnam Faruki, and Mike McCleary. Finally, Alaka read the entire manuscript, and many parts more than once, as I revised and reworked them. It is not an exaggeration to say that I am married to one of the most intelligent human beings I have met. While it has some downsides, when it comes to writing a book and getting comments, this is an unmitigated advantage.

A preface is a good place to give some tips on how to read the book. This is a book strung around one central thesis. The first four chapters are linear; they present the standard model of law and economics, describe the problem and inconsistencies in it, provide a brief introduction to game theory, and then develop the central thesis of the book—the focal point approach. Chapter 5 presents some applications of the new approach and analyzes the interface between the law and social norms. So to get the core idea of this monograph, one can treat the first five chapters as a slim and complete book.

The last three chapters are more speculative, and can be read selectively. They illustrate how the focal point approach can be brought to bear on diverse real-life problems, such as the prevalence of corruption, the origins and risks of totalitarianism, and the challenge of global governance and order. They provide not final answers but the groundwork. In the hope of not losing readers I

have labored to keep these chapters brief. The preference for brev-
ity comes from my interest in economic theory and its beautifully
spare character.

There is however another source for this preference, from literature. I have been acutely aware of the need to be succinct ever since
I read English poet Philip Larkin's interview in the Summer 1982
issue of *Paris Review*. He remarked that, when it came to other
people's poetry, it is wise to read rather than listen to it, since that
way you would know "how far you are from the end."

August 1, 2017
New York

THE REPUBLIC OF BELIEFS

CHAPTER ONE

Introduction

1.1 Practice and Discipline

Economists and legal scholars have had an abiding interest in the question of why so many laws languish unimplemented. But an even more intriguing and philosophically troubling question is its obverse. Why are so many laws so effective, being both enforced by the functionaries of the state and obeyed by the citizens? After all, a law is nothing but some words on paper. Once one pauses to think, it is indeed puzzling why merely putting some "ink on paper" should change human behavior, why a new speed limit law recorded in a book should prompt drivers to drive more slowly, and the traffic warden to run after the few who do not, in order to ticket them.

Traditional law and economics dealt with these questions by avoiding asking them. The purpose of this book is to take on this conundrum of ink on paper triggering action frontally. In the chapters that follow I spell out and explain the enigma, and then go on to provide a resolution. This forces us to question and in turn reject the standard approach and replace it with a richer and more compelling way of doing law and economics. The new approach, rooted in game-theoretic methods, can vastly enrich our understanding of both why so many laws are effective and why so many laws remain unimplemented, gathering dust. Given the importance of law and economics for a range of practical areas, from competition and collusion, trade and exchange, labor and regulation to climate change and conflict management, the dividend from doing this right can be large. This monograph contributes to this critical space that straddles economics and law, and is thus vital for understanding development and peace, and, equally, stagnation and conflict.

The hinterland between different disciplines in the social sciences is usually a rather barren space. Despite proclamations to the contrary, multidisciplinary research remains sparse, its success hindered by differences in method and ideology, and a touch of obstinacy.

The confluence of law and economics stands out in this arid landscape. Ever since the field came into its own in the 1960s, with the writings of legal scholars and economists showing recognition of the existence of and even need for one another, the discipline of law and economics has been gaining in prominence. The need for this field was so obvious and immense that it did not brook the standard hindrances to interdisciplinary research. Laws are being created and implemented all the time; one does not have to be an economist or a legal scholar to see that a poorly designed law can bring economic activity to a halt or that a well-crafted law can surge it forward. For this reason the confluence of law and economics was an active arena of engagement even before the field had a name. In the United States, for instance, concern about collusion among business groups dates back to the late nineteenth century. The Sherman Antitrust Act in 1890 and later the Clayton Antitrust Act of 1914 and the Robinson-Patman Act of 1936 were landmarks in the use of the law to regulate market competition and deter collusion.

As so often happens, practice was ahead of precept. While there was no subject called law and economics then, small principles were being discovered and acted upon by policymakers and practitioners. It was, for instance, soon realized by American lawmakers and political leaders that while curbing collusion was good for the American consumer, it handicapped US firms in the global space. In competing against producers in other nations and selling to citizens of other nations, it may be useful to enable your firms to collude, fix prices, and otherwise violate domestic-market antitrust protections. This gave rise to the Webb-Pomerene Act of 1918, which exempted firms from the provisions of laws that ban collusion, as long as they could show that the bulk of their products were being sold abroad. Japan would later learn from this and create exemptions to its Antimonopoly Law, exempting export cartels from some provisions.

The realization of the power of the law to affect markets was in evidence when, soon after the defeat of Japan in the Second World War, the Allied Forces quickly imposed a carefully designed antitrust law on Japan. This was the so-called Antimonopoly Law 1947. Japan would later modify it to reinvigorate its corporations.

Not quite as directly as with the American experience but nevertheless with important implications for everyday life, the *practice* of law and economics goes much further back into history. Human beings were writing down laws pretty soon after they learned to write anything. The most celebrated early inscription was the Code of Hammurabi. Written in Akkadian, the language of Babylon, these laws were developed and etched on stone during the reign of the sixth king of Babylon, Hammurabi, who died in 1750 BCE. Ideas in this code survive today, such as the importance of evidence and the rights of the accused. It also gave us some of our popular codes of revenge, the best-known being "an eye for an eye." The codes survived, but not without contestation. It is believed that it was Gandhi who warned us, nearly four thousand years later, "an eye for an eye will make the world blind."

Indeed, it is possible to argue that the idea of law existed even before we invented writing. This took the form of conventions passed on by word of mouth. And some would argue that, in this broad sense, law predates humans (see discussion in Hadfield, 2016). Laboratory experiments show that capuchin monkeys give evidence of a sense of fairness and, by extension, the propensity to punish those who play unfairly. In the present book, however, I stay away from such a broad, all-encompassing notion of law.

The origins of law and the question of what law is and why people abide by it are matters that have long been debated. Much of this discourse was fueled by the enormously influential debate for and against "legal positivism" (see Kelsen, 1945; Hart, 1961; Raz, 1980), which was in turn a response to Austin (1832), who argued that "a proposition of law is true within a particular political society if it correctly reports the past command of some person or group occupying the position of sovereign in that society. [Austin] defined a sovereign as some person or group *whose commands are habitually obeyed and who is not in the habit of obeying anyone else*" (Dworkin, 1986, p. 33, my italics). But why such commands are obeyed and how the sovereign can get away without obeying anyone else (to the limited extent that these are true) were poorly explained by not just Austin but also later legal scholars and philosophers.

While Austin and Hart were both legal positivists, Hart distanced himself from Austin's view of law as "command" to the idea of law as "rules," thereby suggesting that they may not need enforcement by a sovereign or a higher authority. There is an element of obligation naturally built in. Underlying this notion of law is an innate sense of justice and fairness.

For the purpose of this book it is not necessary to have a formal definition of law (and anyway one does not exist). It is often the case that it is possible to talk about a discipline and develop it further without having a formal definition for it. The same is true here. It is enough to note that the law consists of rules of legitimate behavior in a society, and a law-abiding society or a society where the rule of law prevails is one where members of society abide by the law. I do not assume that the law innately possesses qualities of fairness and justice. In this discourse it is just as possible to have an unfair law and an oppressive law, as a noble law and a just law. In fact, what I hope to achieve in this book is to show that some of the early debates and contentions were not necessary. Once we have developed the new approach to law, rooted in game theory, we will see that some of the debates may have been spurious, grounded in methodological flaws, and constrained by a limited vocabulary. With the rise of modern game theory, we are able to create concepts and terms that facilitate debate and remove some of the controversies that flourished because of the linguistic coarseness of discourse. It is not always appreciated that a large part of the advance of science is predicated on the granularity of grammar and vocabulary.

The new approach will give us an understanding of how a society becomes law-abiding. Gordon Brown, former British prime minister, is believed to have said (World Bank, 2017, p. 95), "In establishing the rule of law, the first five centuries are always the hardest." Gordon Brown's observation is often treated as a joke, but it is not. It makes the important point that for the law to develop roots and the rule of law to prevail requires ordinary people to believe in the law; and to believe that others believe in the law. Such beliefs and meta beliefs can take very long to get entrenched in society. This is a matter that will be important for my thesis.

By way of digression, I may remark that, while the above quote is commonly attributed to Gordon Brown, there seems to be no actual record of his saying it. The only reason to believe he did is that he has not contested the attribution. But then again, put yourself in his shoes. If such a memorable quote were attributed to you, it is not clear that you would go out of your way to challenge the attribution.

Returning to the question of origins, the law, as we know it today, took concrete form in ancient Greece. Solon in Athens and Lycurgus in Sparta are often viewed as "founders of Western legal and political thought" (Hockett, 2009, p. 14). Solon, born in Athens in 638 BCE, became chief magistrate, when the city-state was in disarray. He played a role in creating one court for all citizens but, more importantly from the perspective of this book, he paid attention to laws that made economic life possible, encouraging specialization and exchange, and taking explicit positions on trade, allowing commerce for some commodities but banning it for others, showing that not just international trade but even protectionism has a long history.

Solon's counterpart in Sparta was Lycurgus, often treated as the founder of the Spartan Constitution, the *Rhetra*. To him are attributed ideas and rules concerning social equality and even wealth redistribution. When he rose to power, wealth had become extremely unequal and, it is said, he set about devising rules to equalize landholdings. Among these important economic rules, he also slipped in some idiosyncratic ones such as the need for men to eat in public in large groups. The trouble with getting into much detail about Lycurgus is that he believed that laws ought not to be written down but held mentally as a code to abide by. An inevitable consequence of this is that many have questioned the existence of Lycurgus's laws[1]; and, to make matters worse, some historians have questioned the existence of Lycurgus.

1.2 The Emergence of "Law and Economics"

The emergence of the discipline of law and economics, luckily, does not give rise to such existential questions. There is reasonable consensus that the birth occurred in the 1960s, marked by some iconic papers, most prominently those by Coase (1960), Calabresi (1961), and Becker (1968), even though the roots of the discipline go much further back.[2] Within years it was evident that this was a hugely influential discipline. As Sunstein (2016, p. 53) recently observed, "The field of 'law and economics' has revolutionized legal thinking. It may well count as the most influential intellectual development in law in the last one hundred years. It has also had a major impact on how regulators in the United States, Europe, and elsewhere deal with anti-trust, environmental protection, highway safety, health care, nuclear power and workers' rights." It is easy to go on and draw attention to the power of law and economics in many other areas, from shaping regulation relating to finance and banking, to fiscal policy and laws to regulate the fiscal deficit. It is clearly a subject that deserves attention.

Yet there have been problems that we have encountered in applying the lessons of law and economics that should have alerted us to all not being well. One of the biggest challenges lies in the implementation of the law. A perennial problem faced by a host

1. This is in contrast to the belief often held by game theorists that the law must not just be known by all but known to be known and known to be known to be known and so on, which is referred to as common knowledge. Hadfield (2016, p. 26) makes this quite explicit. Common knowledge will play an important role in the approach to law and economics developed in this book.

2. It is arguable that the first identifiable law and economics movement goes back to the late nineteenth century, to the work of American economists grappling with the administration of interstate railroad administration and trying to promote market competition and develop antitrust regulation (Hovenkamp, 1990; Mercuro and Medema, 1997; Medema, 1998). Interestingly, this early law and economics movement, in contrast to the work in the 1960s, was much more concerned with inequality, and distanced itself from mainstream market economics.

of economies, especially emerging and developing ones, is that the law is often not implemented. In India, for instance, where the law is quite sophisticated, thanks to the country's post-independence intellectual ardor as well as its colonial history and even precolonial experience (see Roy and Swamy, 2016), a common refrain is that the law is impeccable on paper but more often than not poorly implemented. There is almost a collective looking away from the law.

The other related challenge is that of corruption. The ubiquity of corruption in many developing economies and also some advanced ones is not just distressing for civic life, but also leads to perverse and damaging economic outcomes. But what is corruption? It can take many forms but, in the final analysis, it is a form of violation of the law, perpetrated either individually or in cahoots with state officials and enforcers of the law, as happens in cases of bribery. What is it that makes some laws tick and others get violated and corrupted? The standard discipline of law and economics is unable to give a satisfactory answer.

The failure to understand corruption and, as a consequence, our ineptness in curbing it, is one of the big failures of law and economics. The chinks in the standard model were visible from the observation that those entrusted with enforcing the law are often lax or susceptible to bribery, which led to the philosophically troubling question: "Who will police the police?" This immediately leads to perplexing questions about the role of higher and higher levels of authority within the state. Quite independently of the discipline of law and economics, the economics of corruption has become a large subject today, and this book will have much to say on this once the building blocks of a new law and economics are in place.

1.3 Institutions and the Enforcers of Law

A critical counterpart of modern law is the enforcement machinery—the police, the judges, the courts. Indeed, we often draw a distinction between the law and social norms by the presence or absence of these institutions and agents of enforcement. Social norms, it is believed, are enforced without a formal machinery, whereas the modern state is a critical counterpart of the concept of law. It is the state that gives law its authority.

Some readers may perceive some of my skepticism in my use of qualifiers like "it is believed," and they will be right. These are matters that I will return to at some length. Indeed, doubts on this score were sowed in my mind by the writings of some anthropologists, who showed how sophisticated some of these social norms were and how formal their enforcement was in some so-called primitive societies such as the Barotse of Northern Rhodesia (Gluckman, 1955; see also discussion in Hadfield, 2016).

Remaining within the confines of traditional thought, it is worth emphasizing that this presence or absence of a machinery to enforce the law has been central in discussions of international law. At one level, it is indeed true that in the domain of intercountry relationships, international trade conflicts, and currency wars, we do not have the same kind of enforcers as a conflict within a nation has. There is the International Court of Justice at The Hague, but its ability to enforce codes and laws is open to question. We have tried to mimic the courts and justice systems at the global level by creating various global institutions, but their reach is limited. For this reason, nations have frequently taken it upon themselves to create institutions to penalize global norm violations. America's Helms-Burton Act of 1996 is a good example of this. The United States wanted to isolate Cuba (and thereby hurt its economy) and so created a law not just to ostracize Cuba but to punish even other nations that traded with and invested in Cuba. This was a form of taking the law into one's own hand but also an attempt to create a global jurisdiction that does not exist.

International organizations, such as the International Labour Organization (ILO), World Trade Organization (WTO), and the Bretton Woods institutions, have often been created to deal explicitly with this concern, to bring a modicum of law to bear on labor practices and international trade customs and even to manage global monetary and fiscal policies. The success of these initiatives continues to be debated, but it is clear to all that there is a dearth of globally enforced law in our rapidly globalizing world. The need for this became apparent soon after long-distance sea travel became common, starting from the end of the fifteenth century with the landings of Christopher Columbus in America in 1492 and of Vasco da Gama in India in 1498. Skirmishes in

the seas heightened thereafter, the most celebrated being the seizure of the Portuguese vessel *Santa Catarina* by the Dutch in the
Strait of Singapore, in the early morning hours of February 25,
1603. The lawyer called upon to defend the Dutch seizure was
Huig de Groot or, as he came to be better known as, Grotius. This
case led to Grotius's engagement, in 1604, with the need to codify
international law and his commentary on the subject, which may
well be viewed as the genesis of our intellectual engagement with
international law.

With globalization and new multinational initiatives, the most
important being the Eurozone and the European Union, and also
some recent cases of nations trying to get out of that union, the
subject of international law and its enforcement has acquired ur-
gency.[3] Though these are not matters that I address directly, this
monograph being concerned with more methodological issues, I do
return to some of these questions in the closing chapter.

1.4 Agenda

My interest in law and economics arose when I researched industrial organization theory and rent control and tried to understand
the reach and effectiveness of antitrust and other laws.[4] Two questions proved troubling. Why was the law effective when it was? In
brief, even though citizens may have followed the law for fear that
the police would catch them if they did not, and the magistrate
would punish them, why did the police and the magistrate perform
their duties? After all, as noted at the start of this chapter, the law
is nothing but some ink on paper, rules written down on paper by a
parliament or an inscription on a stone ordered by a king or some
digital document in today's world.

My interest in law and economics was revived in an unusual
way, from my engagement in policymaking. In 2010, as I worked
as chief economic adviser to the government of India, one problem

---

3. I have been drawn into some of these debates in my recent work in policymaking
at the World Bank, which entails multicountry engagements: see Basu (2016a), Basu and
Stiglitz (2015).

4. I discussed this briefly in Basu (1993) and developed some of these ideas in Basu
(2000). For the work on rent control, see Basu and Emerson (2000).

that kept crossing my desk was that of corruption. As one scandal after another broke, in addition to the more persistent and nagging ones that did not make the news but we nevertheless had to deal with, the subject loomed as an important one.

India has an extensive system of providing subsidized food to poor households. This is now enshrined as a "right to food." But there was widespread evidence that poor households were routinely denied this right, by either being turned away or by being asked to pay a bribe to get what was their due. There is strong empirical evidence that over 40 percent of the food grain collected by the government for distribution to poor households leaks out of the system, and is sold for profit by the stores meant to feed the poor.[5]

In many other areas there was similar evidence of people forced to pay bribes for what was their due. You have taken a driving test and performed fine, and when you are about to receive your license, the official demands a bribe. You file your income tax return, but are asked to grease someone's palm to get the final certificate. And the list goes on. While looking into the problem I learned that, according to the Indian law, namely, the Prevention of Corruption of Act, 1988, the taker and the giver of bribes are treated as equally guilty.

It was then easy to see one reason why bribery was so pervasive in India. Once a bribe had been paid, the interests of the bribe giver and the bribe taker were completely in alignment. If they were caught, both would be fined or jailed. Little wonder then that the bribe giver and the bribe taker in India collude to hide the bribery after the fact. It is this assurance that, in turn, emboldens the bureaucrat to accept the bribe. What needed to be done seemed clear to me. At least in the case where a person was being asked to pay a bribe for something he or she was entitled to—I called this a harassment bribe—we must distinguish between the guilt of the taker and the guilt of the giver of the bribe. I proposed that the 1988 law be amended by introducing an asymmetry in declaring the *giving* of harassment bribes a legal act.

Since this was within months of my joining government, with the naivety of a greenhorn, I wrote up and posted my short paper

5. See Khera (2011); also Jha and Ramaswami (2010).

on the Ministry of Finance website (see Basu, 2011b). Furor broke out, with questions asked in parliament about the immorality of my idea, and letters written by members of parliament to the prime minister and the finance minister, asking them to explain my misdemeanor.

Fortunately, I was the person entrusted with the drafting of the replies to these members of parliament. So I could stem some of the immediate crisis, but the attacks persisted in the news media and television. I have written about this in Basu (2015) and do not provide details here. But the simple upshot was I was back to law and economics, this time via a very different channel.

I had become engaged in this debate on the Indian law concerning corruption control without knowing enough of the background. So I decided that, now that I had written on the subject, it was time to read. This is what drew me into the subject in a big way. What became quickly apparent to me was how flagrant the violation of law was. It was not just bribery that led to the collusive evasion of law; I discovered a profusion of laws that existed on paper but were collectively ignored.[6] This inevitably led to the question of why some laws were followed and others overlooked. It was obvious that we did not have an answer and, more importantly, did not have the wherewithal to understand it. The discipline of law and economics has made huge contributions to modern economic life, but it clearly also has shortcomings.

This book is about a major fault line that I believe runs the gamut of traditional or what may be called neoclassical law and economics. I referred to this as the "ink on paper" problem (Basu, 1993). This book draws attention to and explains the fault line and then reconstructs it carefully. While it is true that this is major surgery, I must stress at the outset that no accusation is being made that all our achievements of the past are flawed. It is somewhat like what has been seen in mathematics. Every now and then we hit upon a flaw in the foundations of mathematics. This usually happens when we suddenly discover a paradox or a conundrum and, in

---

6. Debroy's (2000) estimate is that, between the federal and state governments, India has over thirty thousand laws, a disproportionate number gathering dust and, worse, occasionally invoked to harass and use strategically.

trying to understand it, realize that it is not caused by carelessness or a typographical error but is a reflection of some deep problem lodged in the foundations of the discipline. It is arguable that we have not seen the end of this; mathematics still has flaws lodged in its foundations. What is interesting is that this means not that we have to unlearn our education but that we will hit road bumps in the future and may realize that some of what we took to be hard knowledge is not so, that some of our understandings will have to be abandoned and some modified.

It is similar with law and economics. As the fault line is corrected, hopefully we will have a more robust discipline. Some of our traditional knowledge will cease to be valid; but we will have a richer discipline, giving us certain new insights and enabling us to avert contradictions and paradoxes that we could not deal with adequately earlier.

This book is planned such that it can be read by the lay reader with no prior knowledge of law, economics, or game theory. For this reason, I shall occasionally veer to build up some of the conceptual arguments from the basics. For the trained legal scholar or the game theorist, these excursions will be redundant or at best a little diversion, but I hope that by this ploy the book will be of value to many more readers, from the beginner to the expert, who may have an interest in seeing some familiar structures being dismantled and rebuilt.

For reasons of this completeness, the next chapter begins with a short description of the standard or neoclassical model of law and economics. I then go on to demonstrate some of the contradictions on which the model is built. Thereafter, the exercise turns reconstructive—to take the best of traditional law and economics, and build on it. Rebuilding is never easy, and I am aware that the task is unlikely to be completed in this or any single volume. But I do expect to provide a fairly comprehensive description of how we ought to amend the traditional model.

I use game-theoretic arguments, starting with instantaneous or normal-form games and moving on to strategic interactions between agents played out over time—called extensive-form games. All this will be presented with a commentary on related works. There are prominent writers, both legal scholars and economists, who have had insights into the same fault line around which this book is written. I comment on their works, pointing out the similarities and differences. Intellectual ventures are, by their very nature, group efforts.

Once this structure is in place, and occasionally alongside it, via digressions, I engage with some of the standard subtopics of law and economics, such as the differences between the Chicago school and the Yale school (see Sunstein, 2016, for a short and lucid overview of this debate), the roles of individual rationality and morality, how best to curb corruption, how to improve the implementation of the law, and so on.

Despite the effort to be comprehensive, I am reconciled to the fact that we will keep running into open-ended questions. A new model is bound to have its own open problems. I point them out as transparently as possible as we proceed, but some of these open-ended matters will have to wait for the last few chapters, where I lay them out as clearly as I can in the hope that others, more capable, will take on the challenge to complete the project.

CHAPTER TWO

A Brief History of Law and Economics

2.1 The Law and Its Implementation: Some Examples

This book has an ambitious agenda. It argues that a fault line runs through much of the discipline of law and economics, which explains why, despite several major successes, the discipline remains challenged in some fundamental ways. Its shortcomings are nowhere as visible as in developing economies, in many of which, a constant refrain is how the law is fine on paper, but is not implemented in practice. The explanation is usually left to a hand-waving reference to corruption, poor governance, and the lack of determination on the part of political leaders. The main aim of this monograph is to draw attention to a conceptual flaw that underlies much of contemporary law and economics and the way the discipline has been conceived, in order to provide a deeper understanding of how and why law influences behavior, and also why it so often fails to do so.

The big challenge, however, is not pointing to the problem, which, once articulated, is easy enough to grasp, but rebuilding the discipline once the flaw has been identified. That turns out to be a formidable task, which compels us to draw on multiple disciplines—law, game theory, economics, and philosophy—and confront some intriguing logical puzzles. But building a new conceptual outline for the discipline of law and economics is likely to yield rich dividends, enabling us to craft better laws in terms of economic outcomes and also laws that are implemented more effectively. This monograph will develop a basic structure for doing law and economics, with the fault line corrected. This opens up exciting new possibilities, some of which are explored in the book, but I am also aware that the agenda is large and open-ended and, as such, much scope will remain for future work.

As pointed out in the previous chapter, the roots of the neoclassical model of law and economics go far back into history; but the seminal steps toward a formal framework were taken in the 1960s, by, among others, Ronald Coase (1960), Guido Calabresi (1961), and Gary Becker (1968). In some specific ways, Becker's research in which he developed a full model of crime and punishment turned out to be of critical importance for both the studies and the critiques it generated, including what we are about to venture into in this book.[1] Becker was not trying to create a framework of law and economics but simply using some ideas from mainstream neoclassical economics to analyze how best to control crime, including corruption. But since his was a mathematical model, it compelled the author to lay out a formal structure, which quickly became the template for law and economics.

When I say that this monograph deals with the discipline of law and economics, the conjunction with "economics" is critical. Legal scholars and legal philosophers, most prominently H.L.A. Hart (1961), had long tried to conceptualize how the law does what it does, the basis of legitimacy, and the reasons for compliance. I comment and draw on some of these works, but my main engagement is with law *and economics*, that is, with Becker, Calabresi and Coase rather than Hart. For that reason, I present the central idea behind the crime and punishment model of economists with some care, in

---

1. See also Becker and Stigler (1974), Cooter and Ullen (1988), Baird, Gertner, and Picker (1994), Mercuro and Medema (1997), Schafer and Ott (2005), Persson and Siven (2006), and Paternoster (2010). For an excellent discussion of the broader background to crime and punishment that goes beyond law and economics to legal philosophy and ethics, see Murphy and Coleman (1997, chap. 3).

the next section. But it is useful to start with a practical problem—
that of the implementation of some actual laws.

I draw my examples mainly from my own experience as adviser
to the government of India. The country has a large program, now
backed by law,[2] to provide a certain minimal amount of food to all
citizens, the target, of course, being the poor. The program is run
as follows. The Food Corporation of India (FCI), established by the
government following the enactment of the Food Corporations Act
of 1964, is a state-owned corporation charged to execute the government's food price stabilization program and the food support
program for the poor. Each year, the Indian government announces
a Minimum Support Price (MSP), a price at which farmers have
the right to sell food to the FCI. Usually the MSP is set sufficiently
high to make it attractive to farmers to sell to the government. In
states where the collection system is efficient and there are a large
number of collection windows, the government, meaning the FCI,
buys up substantial amounts of rice and wheat under this program.
There are however states and regions where the MSP is purely no-
tional, since there are no collection windows for the grain that the
farmers may wish to sell.[3]

A part of this grain that is collected is then stored as reserve for
times of shortage in the future. But a large part is meant to be sold
to poor households that have government-issued cards identifying
them as Below Poverty Line (BPL) households. The sale to BPL
households is done through what are called ration shops or public
distribution shops, numbering roughly half a million across the nation. The FCI sells the food grain meant for distribution at below
market prices to the ration shops, with the directive that they will
then sell the grain to poor households at a prefixed price, below the

2. The National Food Security Act, 2013, popularly known as the Right to Food law,
is part of an effort to protect the poor from some of the extreme vagaries of the market, a
topic that has long been of concern to economists (see Johnson, 1976) and been a major
part of India's food grain policy.

3. Since MSP is set fairly high, the way the glut of sales to the government that would
result from this is effectively kept manageable (though no one in government will admit to
this as a strategy) is by not having windows for receiving food grain in large parts of India.
This indeed gives rise to an unlevel playing field for farmers in different regions of India
and deserves criticism, but that is not the battle I want to wage in the present book (but,
just for the record, this is something I did push for as a policymaker but without success).

free market price, and according to the maximum per-household quota specified by the government. The idea is that poor households should have the right to obtain a certain amount of essential food grain at a low price. Immense effort goes into designing this system, which is now part of a law enacted by parliament.

The problem, however, is that the law is widely violated. There are excellent studies that show that over the past decade somewhere between 43 and 54 percent of the grain meant to be distributed under this system and released by the FCI simply leaked out (Jha and Ramaswami, 2010; Khera, 2011). There are interesting patterns in the leakage. Wheat diversion is significantly greater than that of rice. Overall food grain diversion peaked in 2004–5, when more than half the grain released for poor households did not make it to those households. There has been a slight improvement since then, but only slight. These are all matters of interest and analysis, but my aim here is simply to document that this well-meaning law, which could have made a large, positive difference to Indian society, is wantonly violated.[4]

The problem is not with the intention of the law but with its design. The massive grain leakage has meant that the poor have not received the assistance intended for them, and the nation's fiscal balance has been under greater strain than otherwise would be the case. The proximate cause of this poor implementation is easy to see. The law and, prior to that, the rules of food distribution were written up assuming that government officials and functionaries, including the ration shop owners, would implement the program diligently, or robotically, that is, take the subsidized food from FCI and mechanically hand it over to the poor.[5] Unfortunately, individual rationality intervened. What many of the shop owners did in India was to take the food from FCI, sell a part of it on the open market at the higher price that prevails there, and turn away the poor who came to collect their subsidized rations saying that their

4. I have described and critiqued this food distribution in some detail in Basu (2015).

5. The connection between corruption and governance structure and even political institutions has been investigated widely (see, for instance, Mishra, 2006; Rose-Ackerman and Palifka, 1999 [2015]). For me, the experience in India was especially instructive because it was a hands-on application of what I knew from the academic literature.

supplies had run out or not arrived. There are also cases of adulterated grain being sold to the poor.

I had argued in my role as adviser that the solution, at least partially, was to be realistic about the ration shop owners and not hand over to them the subsidized food. Instead, the subsidy should be given directly to the poor, in the form of vouchers, food stamps, or plain cash, basically, as a small basic income; and then to allow them to buy the food they needed from private sellers. By handing over the subsidy to the poor and letting them purchase directly from the farmers or from private suppliers, leakages would be much less. For one, if the poor found that their street corner store was selling adulterated grain, they would go elsewhere. It is true they may not spend all the subsidy on food, but at least the subsidy would have gone to the poor instead of the ration shop owner as currently happens.

This is however not germane to my present concern, which is to point out that laws in developing countries often fail to do good not so much because their intentions are malevolent (of course, there are occasions, in rich and poor countries, where they are) but because they are not implemented by the functionaries of the state, and the way we design our interventions contributes to this.

A related debate that I got drawn into in India, which I alluded to in the previous chapter, was to do with India's Prevention of Corruption Act, 1988, which pertains to the use of bribery to circumvent the law. What is interesting about this legislation is that it is, in a sense, a meta law—a law to ensure that other laws are better enforced. It seeks to plug the scope for violating other laws by bribing government officials. The genesis of my argument was that this law could be seen to be flawed once one took a realistic view of not just ordinary citizens but also civil servants, such as the police, the magistrate, and other government functionaries in India. The problem arises from the fact that, under this law, in particular Section 12, the bribe giver and the bribe taker are treated as equally guilty and punishable.[6] If the law was amended to break this symmetry by

6. It may be worth pointing out that under Section 24 of the Act the bribe giver does have some exemptions from punishment. However, over the years, this section has effectively become an exemption only for those, mainly journalists, wanting to carry out a sting

holding only one side, in this case the bureaucrat accepting the bribe, guilty, he or she would expect the bribe giver to more readily blow the whistle; and, knowing this, the bureaucrat would be reluctant to take the bribe in the first place.[7] This law is of particular relevance here because it alerts us to the problems caused by not modeling the functionaries of the state properly.[8]

By thinking through each piece of legislation, we may be able to do better, as illustrated above with the Indian policy of trying to ensure that the poor have enough food and the Indian law meant to curtail bribery. But, more importantly, this happens because of a fundamental flaw in the way the role of law has been conceptualized in the standard, neoclassical model of law and economics, and because this thinking has permeated through the world of policy. Before I describe the flaw and suggest steps to correct it, it is useful to briefly outline the standard model of law and economics.

2.2 Traditional Law and Economics: A Very Short Introduction

Consider an individual contemplating some new enterprise, for instance, mining the earth for a valuable mineral. I shall call this activity "coal mining." To start with, suppose coal mining is a legal activity. This person has to simply decide if this venture is commercially worthwhile. The standard model of economics tells us that

---

operation against a bureaucrat to trap the person taking a bribe (Basu, 2011b). Apart from this, the bribe giver and the bribe taker are equally guilty under the Indian law.

7. The subject of bribery and the vulnerability of the law enforcer has a large literature. Some of this was discussed in Basu, Bhattacharya, and Mishra (1992), and Basu, Basu, and Cordella (2016). For recent analysis of this problem of bribery and the motivation of the law enforcer, see Pethe, Tandel, and Gandhi (2012), Abbink, Dasgupta, Gangadharan, and Jain (2014), Spengler (2014), Suthankar and Vaishnav (2014), Dufwenberg and Spagnolo (2015), Oak (2015), Dharmapala, Garoupa, and McAdams (2015), and Pani (2016).

8. Here and later, when I go into this topic in full, I stay away from the debate concerning whether the possibility of giving bribes and other forms of corruption enhance efficiency in the economy. Some economists have taken the view that they do, and there is no denying that, in an immediate sense, this may well be true. However, my own view is that bribery and corruption do so much damage to the moral fabric of society and cause an erosion in trust that they are hugely detrimental to the quality of economic, social, and political life. There is, however, no need to resolve this controversy to take on the question of how best to curb bribery and other forms of corruption.

the agent will basically calculate the probability of finding usable coal below the soil and the expected revenue that this will earn, and add up the costs of the enterprise, such as renting or buying the necessary equipment, labor costs, and so on. Deducting the latter (the cost) from the former (the expected revenue), we can calculate the expected net return or profit from this venture. Call this net return B. Standard economics tells us that if B is positive, the entrepreneur will proceed. Otherwise, she will consider it not worthwhile and abandon this coal mining project.

This standard view of rational decision making has weaknesses and has rightly been criticized, challenging the idea of selfishness inherent in it, the assumption of unlimited capacity for computation implicit in it, asking whether human beings are driven by profit alone or also by envy, stigma, and the search for status, and so on. These are important matters and have generated a copious literature,[9] but these are not the criticisms that I am concerned with here. Barring a few comments on selfishness in this section, for now I treat the rational actor assumption as valid. I shall return to some of these broader behavioral questions in later chapters.

Next, suppose the government, concerned about the environment, enacts a new law that declares coal mining illegal. It further specifies that anyone caught mining will be fined F dollars. Let us suppose that, given the level of policing and quality of governance, the probability of getting caught is p. Given this new law, the agent's or the entrepreneur's calculations and decision criteria will get changed. It is easy to see that, now, she will go for the mining project if and only if:

$$B > pF,$$

that is, if the net return from mining exceeds the expected cost associated with the illegality of the activity, or, in brief, the "crime."

---

9. There is a large literature on this, from Veblen (1899) to Sen (1973, 1997), Tversky and Kahneman (1986), Basu (2000), Bowles (2004), Thaler and Sunstein (2008), Gintis (2009), Kahneman (2011), Benabou and Tirole (2006), Ellingsen and Johannesson (2008), World Bank (2015).

This also means that, in case the government is keen to stop this crime, it has to choose p and F such that:[10]

$$B \leq pF.$$

This is the briefest sketch of the standard model of law and economics. The model has served us well in many ways, giving us some new insights and helping us get away from some of the more nebulous explanations of compliance with the law that earlier legal scholars grappled with. It tells us, for instance, that the state has two variables to act on when controlling crime, p and F. It is arguable that in most situations, raising p is costlier to the state than raising F. To raise p, namely, the probability of catching a criminal, it may need more police personnel, more surveillance cameras, more police jeeps, and so on, whereas raising F is simply a one-time decision—*once a criminal has been caught and found guilty*, he or she has to pay F.

Thus one interesting implication of the neoclassical model is that crime control is most efficient if we raise the F very high and contend with a low p. In other words, the chance of being caught is small, but, if caught, the penalty is hefty. There are however limits to how far we can go with this. For one, many nations, certainly all industrialized countries, have limited liability laws, which prevent the state from inflicting punishments beyond a certain level.[11] In poor countries, without such laws, the criminals may be sufficiently poor that they are unable to pay a penalty beyond a level. One can push the line of discussion here by moving away from F being treated as a financial punishment to allowing for torture, in which case F can be raised very high. However, in most societies this would be considered ethically unacceptable. Hence, F will have an upper bound. In that case the government has to raise p to make sure that pF is as large as B. In brief, there is a rich research and policy agenda that opened up even with this simple model; and

10. For reasons of fastidiousness I should point out that I am making the arbitrary tie-breaking assumption that a person indifferent between committing and not committing a crime chooses the latter; and I might add that I hope that is indeed the case.

11. In the absence of that we run into the kind of problem highlighted by Stern (1978).

there is an enormous literature that builds on this model, whether by way of policy design or criticism.[12]

This model has come under some straightforward criticism, which has helped to enrich it, and hidden in this criticism there is a critique that forms the basis of my main argument that I will get to eventually. It has been pointed out, for instance, that as soon as you have a penalty or a fine, you open up the possibility of bribery. Hence, the crime control equation above may not be quite as simple as it appears at first sight. A criminal, once caught, may try to negotiate a bribe with the police. So we need a theory of bribery to determine what will deter the crime in the first place. Moreover, if bribery is a crime, then surely some will pay bribes to escape punishment for the crime of bribery. So there is clearly a second-order problem here, and by the same logic, a third-order one, and a fourth, and a fifth.[13]

In brief, the agenda that opens up is large. But that need not detain us here. What I want to do more importantly is to draw out some conceptual underpinnings of the Becker model, which are often left implicit and so are accepted with little thought. The Becker model is founded on mainstream neoclassical economics, whereby people are supposed to have well-defined preferences or utility functions, satisfying standard assumptions like selfishness, captured by the assertion that each person prefers more of everything for himself or herself. In addition, it is assumed that individuals have diminishing marginal utility or, more generally, convex preferences.

Morals do not play a role in this setting. In this model, a fine is like a price.[14] If you are told that driving above 65 mph is illegal and that if you do drive faster you will have to pay a fine of $100, in the Becker model this is the same as saying that you can drive above 65 mph, but doing so entails a price of $100. What Becker demonstrated is that this is a powerful assumption, which can help

12. See, for instance, Rose-Ackerman (1975), Lui (1986), Klitgaard (1988), Bardhan (1997), Mishra (2006), Borooah (2016), Burguet, Ganuza, and Montalvo (2016).

13. This and related arguments occur in Cadot (1987) and Basu, Bhattacharya, and Mishra (1992). See also Mookherjee and Png (1995), Hindriks, Keen, and Muthoo (1999), Rahman (2012), Chernushkin, Ougolnitsky, and Usov (2013), and Spengler (2014).

14. For a critique of the use of this kind of rational actor model in law and economics, from a moral philosophy perspective, see Nussbaum (1997).

us make inroads into understanding a lot of human behavior.[15] As Cooter (2000, pp. 1577–78), contrasting the approach of economists vis-à-vis that of legal scholars, notes, "Almost all economists . . . practice moral skepticism. . . . The success of the economic analysis of law demonstrates the power of skeptical models." This is also some of the difference between the so-called Yale and Chicago school approaches (see Calabresi, 2016; Sunstein, 2016), though it is arguable that in Calabresi's celebrated paper on risk and the law of torts (Calabresi, 1961), he had the Chicago hat on.[16]

It may be worth pointing out here that, though we associate the origins of this economic approach to law with the works of Gary Becker and a few others in the 1960s, its roots go back to the research of the legal philosopher Hans Kelsen (1945), who stressed that the law was a command directed not at ordinary citizens as much as at the officials of the state. The officials were directed to carry out certain actions (punishments) in the event of ordinary people doing certain things. It is this fear of officials' action that made ordinary people behave according to the law. The criticism of neoclassical law and economics that I develop in the last section of this chapter and carry through much of the book therefore applies to Kelsen's pioneering work as much as to the papers in the 1960s cited above.

Game theory is less demanding than neoclassical economics in some ways because it does not assume the endless urge to consume more. But it does assume that each person is endowed with an exogenously given preference or utility function or payoff function and that he or she chooses actions so as to maximize this.

These founding assumptions have come under criticism from various quarters. Consider the assumption of selfishness. If it were true, the safety announcement made on airplanes to secure your own oxygen mask before helping others would be redundant.

15. The law works simply because it is an order backed by a sanction, often known as the "imperative theory of law." For a well-known review of this, see Raz (1980).

16. Citing Pigou (1920), Calabresi (1961, p. 502) refers to this as the "allocation of resources justification" and notes, "At its base are certain fundamental ethical postulates. One of these, perhaps the most important, is that by and large people know what is best for themselves." If Guido Calabresi were a neoclassical economist, that "by and large" would not have been there.

Luckily it is not. Other ideas of textbook human rationality, such as consistency, have also been questioned, for instance, in several works of Sen (see 1993) and, more recently, from the challenge of behavioral economics (see World Bank, 2015). Legal scholars have been aware of this. When it comes to paying taxes, they noted, people do not always follow pure cost-benefit analysis (Posner, 2000). It has, for instance, been noted that "whereas economic models of self-interest predict low rates of tax compliance, some countries like the United States and Switzerland, enjoy unusually high rates of compliance" (McAdams, 2000, p. 1579). I should add here that neoclassical economists need not feel deflated by such findings because in many developing and emerging economies and even some advanced ones, which are best left unnamed, individuals do display a high degree of rationality in that their tax compliance is as low as neoclassical economics would predict.

This is an important critique, and a lot of it has come from legal theorists,[17] and I shall turn to some of this in the later chapters of this book. My own belief is that the neoclassical assumption, while not always valid, has played a useful role. The main fault line of mainstream law and economics that I want to begin with has to do with internal consistency and not this assumption per se. I shall argue that parts of its analysis contradict assumptions in other parts. In other words, I am attempting a more blunt criticism. I am not questioning the assumptions but showing that the assumptions taken together are inconsistent. In other words, no matter what your ideology, what your normative stance on crime and punishment, you cannot hold on to the neoclassical model of law and economics. It is *internally* flawed.

In this spirit, until further notice, I shall retain the assumption of human rationality as in mainstream neoclassical economics. It will be argued that even without questioning this assumption of the neoclassical approach to law and economics there is reason to question other fundamental features of this approach. With this methodological comment in the background, let me illustrate the use of

17. Calabresi's (2016) recent reflective essay is a good example of this. Posner (2000, chap. 3) discusses a range of motivations beyond selfishness that motivate people to behave the way they do. Behavioral economics is of course replete with this.

the neoclassical or Chicago method by applying it to the problem of crime and punishment.[18]

What is it about the law that has the potential to change human behavior? Under the neoclassical approach to law and economics just described, a law seems to change behavior by altering the returns that individuals get from different kinds of behavior. This is, indeed, what economists and practitioners of law and economics assume (see Baird, Gertner, and Picker, 1994). To quote McAdams (2000, p. 1650), "By imposing liability or punishment on individuals, the state changes the payoffs so that cooperation rather than defection is the dominant strategy." Again, on the same page: "The first step in the causal chain by which law affects individual behavior is that the formal sanctions law imposes raise or lower the costs of behavior." In the language of game theory, the law changes the rules of the game, and since a game is described by its rules, we can say that the law changes the game people play.[19]

This is quite in keeping with the view taken by legal scholars, especially those who broke away from the natural law school and can be described broadly as legal positivists. For them, the law is associated with rules of behavior, often coming from a ruler or the state, and with possible punishments and sanctions associated with the violation of rules. Echoing ideas in the works of Jeremy Bentham and John Austin, latter-day legal scholars and philosophers, such as Kelsen (1945) and Hart (1961), gave these ideas sharper focus, often leading to further refinements, such as the distinction between primary and secondary rules in the case of Hart. It is worth stressing that Hart distanced himself from earlier writers, especially from the command theories of Austin and the sanction-based theory of Kelsen.[20] Hart's work, as several critics have noted, leaves some

18. Throughout this book I use the term "the traditional approach to law and economics" interchangeably with "the neoclassical approach" and "the Chicago approach."

19. As Robson (2012, p. 1) puts it in his book, lucidly presenting the central ideas of modern law and economics: "Legal rules influence market outcomes by altering the incentives faced by individuals participating in the market process."

20. It is, however, interesting to learn from Lacey's excellent biography of H.L.A. Hart (Lacey, 2004) that, based on Hart's notebooks, Hart worked much more from first principles than in response to earlier writers, contrary to the impression we get by a direct reading of his 1961 classic.

ambiguity about whether or not there is a distinction between behaviors induced by law and by social norms. This is a subject that will be addressed later in the book.

The view of law as a specification of the rules of the game may also be attributed to some earlier schools of thought, on the ground that there are serious scholars who have resisted the sharp distinction between legal positivism and earlier theories, such as the natural law (see, for example, Starr, 1984).

Before I proceed any further, it may be useful to introduce the reader to the basic idea of a game and the equilibrium of a game, since these are concepts that I have been and will continue referring to, and it is important to rule out ambiguities as much as possible.

2.3 Game Theory: A Very Short Introduction

Game theory is the analysis of interactive rationality. There is clearly a difference between making a rational decision when the other party is nature or a mechanical device with no ability or intention to outsmart you, and a situation where the other party is also rational like you and trying to guess what you may do. Thus when you study the weather forecast and take a decision about whether to carry an umbrella, you do not typically have to worry about whether nature will change its decision concerning rain depending on whether or not you carry an umbrella. But when John F. Kennedy in 1962 strategized what he and the United States should do in light of the Soviets having placed ballistic missiles in Cuba, he thought a lot about what Nikita Khrushchev was thinking, and no doubt also thought about what Khrushchev was thinking about what Kennedy was thinking. This is a typical game-theoretic problem.[21] In Aumann's words, "'Interactive Decision Theory' would perhaps be a more descriptive name for the discipline usually called game theory" (Aumann, 1987, p. 2).

In a game-theoretic context the biggest mistake you can make is to not take account of other players' rationality. Some years ago,

---

21. I should clarify that even the decision concerning what to wear given the weather forecast may be thought of as a game-theory problem, though in a trivial sense. Basically, it is a one-player game and, in this sense, standard individual decision making is just a special case of game theory.

writing for *Scientific American* for an audience possibly not familiar with game theory, I used the following tale I had heard in India
to illustrate this central idea of game theory (Basu, 2007). A hat-
seller walking from one village to another felt sleepy; and so, setting
down his collection of hats, under a shady tree, he dozed off. When
he woke up, he discovered to his dismay that all the hats were gone.
A group of monkeys had taken them to the tree top and were wearing them. In anger and desperation, he took off his own hat and
threw it down. Monkeys, as we know, are great imitators. Soon all
of them were throwing down their hats. The hat-seller was relieved.
He collected the hats and went his way.

Forty years later, his grandson, who had become a hat-seller,
was going with his wares from one village to another when he felt
like a nap. So he set the hats down and went off to sleep. When he
woke up he discovered that monkeys had taken them to the tree
top and were wearing them. He was desperate; what should be do?
And then he remembered his grandfather's story. Relieved, he took
off his own hat and threw it down. But, at that point, one monkey
clambered down, picked up the hat, put it firmly under its arm,
walked up to the hat-seller, gave him a tight slap, and said, "You
think only you have a grandfather?"

The moral of the story is the essence of game-theoretic thinking. In deciding on your own strategy be aware of other people's
rationality. A lot of government welfare programs, as we already
saw earlier in this chapter, go wrong because government designs
them without taking account of the fact that those meant to carry
out the enforcement are also agents with their own ambitions and
desires, such as the ration shop owners in the case of India's food
distribution system.

Formally, to describe a game, we need to specify three constitu-
ents.[22] First, we need to specify the set of players. Then, for each

---

22. What I am describing here is a normal-form or strategic-form game. We will briefly
encounter extensive-form games in Chapter 4, and I will describe those as we go along. A
fuller and excellent treatment of the interface between game theory and the law, which
covers extensive-forms, incomplete information, and also cooperative bargaining theory,
is to be found in Baird, Gertner, and Picker (1994). There is indeed an intriguing question
as to why cooperative game theory has not been used as extensively as the non-cooperative
one being described in this section. See Maskin (2016) for a discussion of some of the
hurdles we need to cross to change this.

player, there has to be a set of feasible strategies or actions from which the player has to choose one. And, finally, once all players choose their respective actions, each player gets a payoff or return. This is specified by what is called a payoff function. It is assumed that each player knows everybody's payoff function. The aim of each player is to make a choice so as to maximize his or her own payoff. This exercise of maximizing one's own payoff is known as rational behavior. Most of game theory is done under the assumption that all players are rational and, further, that rationality is common knowledge. Common knowledge of rationality means all players know that all players are rational, all players know that all players know that all players are rational, all players know that all players know that all players know that all players are rational, and I am sure the reader wants me to stop now. But basically all such higher-order assumptions must be valid.[23]

What will be the equilibrium outcome in a game? There are many different ways of answering this and we will encounter some of these variants later. But it is useful to introduce here what is probably the most widely used concept—that of the Nash equilibrium. A set of strategies or actions, one for each player, is called a Nash equilibrium if no single player can do better by unilaterally deviating to a different strategy in his or her feasible set of strategies.

Let me explain the concepts just introduced with the example of what is probably the best known game, the Prisoner's Dilemma. Cutting out the fable from which it derives its name, the Prisoner's Dilemma is a game with two players, 1 and 2, each of whom has to choose between actions A and B. It is a useful mnemonic, as will be evident later, to think of B as standing for "bad behavior." The payoffs they earn by these choices are displayed in the table or payoff matrix shown in Game 2.1. Player 1 chooses between rows, player 2 between columns. The payoffs earned by the two players are shown in the payoff matrix. For each pair of payoffs the number on the

---

23. It does not happen always, but the presence or absence of the common knowledge of rationality can often make a critical difference (Aumann, 1976; Basu, 1977). For some compelling accounts of what such higher order knowledge can do in different fields, see Rubinstein (1989), Morris and Shin (1998), Gintis (2010).

Player 2

		A	B
Player 1	A	7 , 7	1 , 8
	B	8 , 1	2 , 2

GAME 2.1. Prisoner's Dilemma

left is what is earned by the player choosing between rows and the number on the right is what is earned by the player choosing between columns. I refer to the payoffs generally in dollar terms, but one can think of them in units of happiness or "utils."

As is obvious, in the Prisoner's Dilemma with rational players the outcome is (B, B), since each player is better off choosing B, no matter what the other player does. The outcome of course is disastrous for both. They earn a payoff of $2 each, whereas they could have both earned $7. This is a familiar story that we encounter in many different domains and contexts of life. This, for instance, is the tragedy of the commons, whereby each person exploits the environment to satisfy his or her individual interest and collectively they do badly, such as through overgrazing. We see the same idea crop up in Runciman and Sen's (1965) interpretation of Rousseau's "general will."

It is easy to see that (B, B) is a Nash equilibrium. If player 1 unilaterally deviates to A, she will get a payoff of 1, instead of the current 2. And likewise for player 2.

The one problem with the Prisoner's Dilemma is that the Nash equilibrium is compelling to the point that hardly anybody would contest it. Since you would choose B no matter what the other person does, the game-theoretic character of the problem or the interactive nature of the decision is uninteresting. To illustrate that, let me introduce another related game, the Traveler's Dilemma (Basu, 1994b), which will also be a handy tool for some of my discussions through the book.

The Traveler's Dilemma is the fable of travelers who return from vacation on a remote island to find that the identical village artifact each of them had bought had been damaged by the airline. So they ask for compensation and the airline manager offers them the following deal.[24] Since he has no idea of the value of the strange artifact, each traveler is asked to write down an integer, from 2 to 100. If both write the same number, the manager says that he will take that to be the true price and give them that number in dollars. If they write different numbers, he will take the lower number as the true price and give them that number in dollars but with an additional reward and punishment. The person who wrote the lower number will get the lower number plus $2 (as reward for honesty) and the person who wrote the higher number will get the lower number minus $2 (as punishment). Thus, if both choose 97, each will get $97. If traveler A chooses 97 and B chooses 50, A will get $48 and B will get $52.

It is easy to see that the only Nash equilibrium is (2, 2), that is, A and B both choose 2. Clearly in the Traveler's Dilemma wherever possible it is always best to choose an integer just below what the other player chooses. Hence, the only pair of strategies from which no one can do better by deviating is if both choose 2.

The game was created in a way that virtually all rigorous reasoning with rational players and with rationality as common knowledge leads to the prediction of (2, 2). One way of thinking is to start from 100. If you both choose 100 you will get $100. That is a nice outcome (it was a very cheap artifact, after all), but it will soon be evident that if both of you wrote 100, you would be better off deviating to 99, since that way you would get $101. But then, if both of you are rational, both of you would switch to 99. But in that case you would both get $99; and further, by deviating to 98, you could do better (you would get $100). But then the other player would do the same. This logic of "backward induction" is relentless, and both would end up at (2, 2).

Another way of reasoning is the following. It is easy to see that it is never worthwhile to choose 100. By choosing 99 instead you will always do as well no matter what the other player chooses, and, in addition, for some choices of the other player you will actually do better by playing 99 instead of 100. Hence, if you and your opponent are both rational, both of you will eliminate 100 as a possible

---

24. In the original story, giving a hint of what is to come, it is mentioned that he is described by his juniors as a "corporate whiz," by which they mean "a man of low cunning."

strategy. Once you have done so, it is easy to see that 99 is dominated by 98. So you should eliminate 99. And this is a relentless process that leads to only one viable outcome (2, 2). This is the logic of "iterated deletion of dominated strategies" and, in this case, is identical to the logic behind a "rationalizable" outcome (Bernheim, 1984; Pearce, 1984).

All this is not surprising since the Traveler's Dilemma was developed so as to lead all formal reasoning to the same prediction, and this was done deliberately to precipitate a conflict with intuition (Basu, 1994b, 2007).[25] There is a large literature, experimental and theoretical, showing how the formal game-theoretic prediction is not right.[26] The backward induction argument for instance uses the assumption of rationality being common knowledge between the two players. That is, A knows B is rational, B knows A is rational; A knows B knows A is rational, B knows A knows B is rational. And so on, endlessly. We can try to contest the plausibility of this assumption. I shall have occasion to return to some of these questions later.

What is of immediate interest here is that both these games make us aware of the need for the law. The "invisible hand" of the market that allegedly leads selfish individuals to a socially optimal outcome clearly fails here and urges us to marshal the hand of the law.[27] How does one do so, at least according to the neoclassical approach to law and economics outlined above? The idea is to use the law to deflect society to a better outcome. As McAdams (2000, p. 1650) observes, "By imposing liability or punishment on individuals, the state changes the payoffs so that cooperation rather than defection is the dominant strategy."[28]

---

25. Its philosophical implications become more evident from a similar game, the Gingerbread Game, developed by the philosopher Martin Hollis (1994).

26. See, for instance, Goeree and Holt (2001), Wolpert (2008), Pace (2009), Gintis (2009), Arad and Rubinstein (2012), Manapat, Rand, Pawlowitsch, and Nowak (2012), Capraro (2013), and Morone, Morone, and Germani (2014).

27. In formal theory, the idea of social optimality is defined precisely, using a concept first developed by Vilfredo Pareto. A "Pareto optimal" society is one in which it is impossible to make anyone better off without making someone else worse off.

28. Similar ideas underlie the works of Coase (1960), Calabresi (1961), R. Posner (1977), and Schauer (2015).

Player 2

		A	B
	A	7,7	1,6
Player 1	B	6,1	0,0

GAME 2.2. Prisoner's Dilemma with Fine

It is easy to see how a legal intervention may work in the Prisoner's Dilemma.[29] Suppose the country adopts a law that says that action B is illegal and anybody who chooses such an action has to pay a penalty equal to \$2. The penalty could be an actual fine of \$2 or some time behind bars that inflicts a pain equal to \$2. This transforms the above to a game, as shown in the payoff matrix in Game 2.2. The only difference between Game 2.1 and this new one is that, whenever someone now plays B, we deduct 2 from that player's payoff.

In this new game, it is a dominant strategy to play A. That is, no matter what the other player does, you are better off choosing action A. And, this changes the outcome. The players end up with the good social outcome (A, A), which is also the Nash equilibrium. This is one of the most important objectives of the law—to deflect society, which, left to itself, would tend to get trapped in a bad outcome, to a socially superior situation.[30]

One can think of similar legal interventions for the Traveler's Dilemma. Suppose a law is enacted that says that if you choose any number n, you have to pay a penalty of $(100 - n)$. In other words, if you choose 100, you do not have to pay any penalty, but for all smaller numbers you have to pay an increasing penalty. Tack this

29. It is possible to view this as a central task of the Prisoner's Dilemma to show the role of political institutions in enabling people to realize their true interest. As Swedberg (2005, p. 83) puts it, "[The Prisoner's Dilemma may be viewed as] an example of a situation in which you need to change the existing institution in order for the actors to be able to maximize their individual interests." And he is clearly aware of the special role of the law since he goes on to add, "In this particular case, the existing institution is that of the US system of justice."

30. This is not the only objective of law. There are in fact other objectives pertaining to justice, fairness, and individual liberty, which could even conflict with the Paretian aim discussed above. One of the most celebrated examples of such a conflict is that of the "liberty paradox" (Sen, 1969). See also Gaertner, Pattanaik, and Suzumura (1992).

penalty on to the payoffs in the Traveler's Dilemma, and it will be obvious that in this modified Traveler's Dilemma new Nash equilibria, which entail choosing large numbers, get created. For instance, (100, 100) is now a Nash equilibrium.

These examples illustrate the traditional view of law and economics. What the law does is to transform the game that society plays. In the case of the Prisoner's Dilemma, the game is transformed from Game 2.1 to Game 2.2. This is what enables society to achieve a Pareto-superior outcome as in the above example, or a more just outcome or a fair outcome, whatever it is that we seek to achieve. This, in a nutshell, is the traditional or neoclassical or Chicago approach. It is the model's clarity and transparency that shot this model into prominence, and it quickly became a touchstone for doing law and economics and even designing policy. It has given law and economics the standing it has.

2.4 The "Ink on Paper" Critique and the Neoclassical Fallacy

The traditional approach has all the qualities just mentioned, but it is nevertheless flawed. To see this, consider a new law being discussed by the parliament or whoever enacts new laws in the nation. Once this has been enacted, the new law is, of course, nothing more than some words on paper, or, in today's world, some digital document. It would, typically, say something like: you are not supposed to do such and such a thing and, if you do, you will be fined or jailed, and so on.

The question that must arise is why mere words, written on paper, should make a difference to what individuals *can* do or what payoffs they earn. If everybody chose to ignore the ink on paper, and did what they did earlier, they would surely get the same payoffs as before. If, for instance, each person chooses the same action as he or she would have chosen in the absence of the law, clearly each person must get the same payoff as he or she would have got in the absence of the law, since the fact of some jottings on paper cannot affect the payoffs. Hence, given the way we usually think of the strategies open to individuals and the payoffs they earn, in brief, the game that people play, a new law cannot change these, and so cannot change the game that people play. This is what I had described as the "ink on paper" problem in Basu (1993).[31] The traditional model of law and economics clearly needs to contend with it.

To get a deeper understanding of the problem, return to the Becker model of crime and punishment. Why, in the first place, did we think that the game was altered by the new law? Presumably because, after the new law, the same act of mining, which earlier earned a payoff of B, now earns a payoff of B − pF.

So, at first sight, it does appear that the payoff function of the entrepreneur is changed. That is what must have appeared to Gary Becker when he wrote his celebrated model. But clearly the payoff changes, if it does, because the police person tries to catch the entrepreneur who does the illegal mining, and, if she succeeds, the entrepreneur is fined F dollars. However, the police person could have done the same thing even in the absence of the law. If everybody behaved the same way after the law was enacted as they did before the law was enacted, everybody would get the same payoff. Hence, the law or the fact that some ink has been smeared on paper or digital jottings made on a computer cannot make a difference to the game that people are playing. The same set of actions taken by all the players must lead to the same payoffs for all the players. The law or the ink on paper cannot change this.

Likewise, for a speeding law. Suppose a nation imposes a new speeding law whereby you are not supposed to drive above 100 km per hour and, if caught doing so, you are fined a certain amount. At first sight this seems to change the game people are playing. Earlier when you decided to drive above 100 km per hour you calculated the returns in terms of the time saved, the risk of a skid, and so on. Now on top of all those, it seems, you have to add the expected cost of a fine. But this implicitly assumes that the traffic police is a robotic creature who will impose a fine because the law says so.

The mistake in the neoclassical approach to law and economics arises because of the unwitting assumption that leaves the enforcers

31. Indeed, there are conditions where it is neither in the digital record nor written down on paper. We find a quizzical observation on this in the twelfth-century writing by Ranulf de Glanville: "Although the laws of England are not written, it does not seem absurd to call them laws—those, that is, which are known to have been promulgated about problems settled in the council on the advice of the magnate and with supporting authority of the prince—for this also is a law that 'what pleases the prince has the force of law'" (Hall, 2002, p. 2).

of the law out of the picture or treats them as robots who will automatically do what the law asks them to do.[32] If all the players in this game—the driver, the traffic police, the magistrate, the prime minister—are included in the game as players, as indeed they should be, it is clear that the law cannot change the game. If everybody behaved the way they did before the law, then everybody would get the same payoffs after the law, since the mere writing down of the law cannot change the payoffs.[33] This is the flaw in the traditional approach to law and economics, and it has sullied a lot of our analyses and hurt the policies we have crafted with this conceptual flaw in the foundation.

Let us pause and think about how the Prisoner's Dilemma changed because of the law.[34] This happened because now when someone plays the bad action B that person is charged a penalty of 2. But *who* charges the penalty? In most normal cases, there has to be *someone* who does it—a police officer, a traffic warden, a magistrate. But if there were such a person who could be marshalled to penalize what is not permitted under the new law, why was he or she not a part of the initial description of the game people play? In other words, the Prisoner's Dilemma, the two-player game described in Game 2.1, was not a full description of what was going on in society. Minimally, there is another person who has the power of inflicting penalty, and who is there waiting in the wings to act. If she were there and had the power of inflicting pain on the players, she should have been part of the description of the game.

If we wrote down the full game, with all players included, that is, by including the person with the ability to charge a penalty or impose a sanction, alongside the two engaged in the Prisoner's Dilemma, it is not clear that the new law could change the game. This

32. It is conceivable that a time will come when as soon as a law is enacted, hundreds and thousands of robots will be clicked to a different mode of behavior. But that is not the world we live in now.

33. There can be no doubt that some of this will change as we move into a more digital age. We can use computers and robots to monitor and implement some of the laws, and it may be possible to switch these machines into a special mode to carry out their altered role mechanically, at the moment of adopting a new law (World Bank, 2015). However, we are nowhere near that yet, and it is arguable that even as we enter such an age, human volition and the need for human action will never be fully obliterated.

34. Similar remarks would apply to the Traveler's Dilemma.

is because even in the absence of the law the third person could have charged a penalty. So, after the passage of the law, the three players can do all the things they could do before the law was enacted; and every time the three of them choose any triplet of actions, they will get the payoff they would have got before the law came into existence. We are back to the "ink on paper" critique of the standard view of law. If the game played by society is fully described to start with, the law is unlikely to be able to change the game.

The Becker model either was an incomplete description or assumes that the agents of the state—the police, the magistrate, and the judge—always do what the law requires them to do. But in assuming that the agents of state behave mechanically carrying out their duty, the Chicago or the neoclassical model is making use of an inconsistent set of assumptions. It treats ordinary individuals as relentlessly rational agents, doing what they do to maximize their own utility or payoff, whereas agents of the state are mechanically programmed to do what they are supposed to do. In brief, the traditional model is either incomplete or based on an inconsistent set of assumptions, assuming that people are fully rational and implicitly violating this when describing the civil servants.

In other words, once we have fully described the game, with the ordinary players and the agents of the state included, in order to justify the traditional model of law and economics, we have to make a strange assumption, namely, that all ordinary citizens are neoclassical agents maximizing their own payoffs, whereas civil servants are impartial agents waiting to carry out the dictates of the state. Since the neoclassical model is quite adamant about all agents being individual utility maximizers, this dichotomy was not deliberate. It is an inconsistency that unwittingly slipped into the model of law and economics that emerged in the early 1960s and clearly leaves it flawed. Even as I make this critique I want to emphasize the significance of traditional law and economics as developed in the 1960s. It gave us a prototype, which is valuable. As I will show in the chapters that follow, it is a good starting point even though it now needs to be set aside. Once the fault line beneath it has been corrected we can build a much richer and more consistent model. As I show in Chapter 7, such a model can be used to bring in ideas from neighboring disciplines, such as psychology and sociology, to

allow for a more realistic model of human motivation, thereby giving rigorous shape to ideas that legal scholars, from H.L.A. Hart to
contemporary ones, have emphasized.

If we are to ground this exercise in the literature on law and legal
philosophy, it can be said that what this book tries to do belongs
to what is often referred to as impact studies. As Friedman (2016,
p. 2) puts it, "What kind of impact or influence do any of these acts
within the legal system have? By *impact*, I refer to behavior tied
causally, in some way or other, to some particular law, rule, doctrine
or institutions."[35] However, I try to take this a step further than
standard impact studies do. Again, to quote Friedman (2016, p. 2),
the typical questions that impact studies ask are: "Do easy divorce
laws lead to family breakup? Do tort rules and medical malpractice
cases cause changes in the behavior of doctors?"

The present book asks these questions concerning changes in
civilian behavior caused by new laws or legal amendments, but also
asks another set of questions: Do easy divorce laws make judges
grant easy divorce and, if so, why? Why does a new speed limit law,
say of 100 km per hour, make the traffic warden stop and ticket
those who drive above this limit? Why does it not prompt the traffic warden to say, now that the speed limit law prohibits driving
above 100 km per hour, I shall shut my eyes if anybody drives at
over 100 km per hour, or even fine any driver who drives at less
than 100 km per hour? These questions give rise to a host of philosophical quandaries. The big challenge is not the delineation of
empirical regularities but the explanation of them. Why does the
traffic warden enforce the law? Why does the head of transport authorities punish the traffic warden who does not enforce the law?
Clearly, these questions lie within the ambit of impact studies, but
they are seldom asked; and, when asked, they are answered hastily
before changing the topic because of a subliminal awareness that
they take us into difficult terrains. However, by using elementary
concepts from modern game theory we can give clear answers to
them and thereby develop a new approach to law and economics.
That is what I shall do in the next two chapters.

---

35. This is a matter of great practical importance in making the law more effective (see
Bull and Ellig, 2017).

CHAPTER THREE

The Focal Point Approach
to Law and Economics

3.1 The Salience of Beliefs

The flaw in the traditional approach is compelling enough. The two founding assumptions of traditional law and economics, to wit, that people have exogenously given preferences or utility functions or payoff functions, which they try to maximize, and that a new law influences outcome by changing the payoffs people receive from actions or, what is actually the same, by changing the game that people are playing,[1] are mutually contradictory. Once we have described the full game of life, in which we include not just the ordinary civilians but also the agents of the state, the law in itself cannot change, at least not in any obvious way, the options open to individuals or the payoff functions of the individuals. In brief, the game that people in a society play, once fully described, is in an important sense impervious to being changed merely by writing down a new law or amending an existing one.

This, however, gives rise to a troubling question. How, in that case, does the law at all change behavior and outcomes? At first

---

1. This, in turn, is the same as saying, as people often do, "by changing the rules of the game."

sight it appears that the criticism that the law cannot change the game because it is nothing but some ink on paper should lead to the conclusion that the law cannot have any effect on behavior. But of course it does. We simply have to look around us to see that there are plenty of examples of laws that are effective, change the way people behave, and result in societal outcomes that are different from those that happened in the absence of the law. It is true that laws are frequently disregarded in society and often sit in legal tomes, unimplemented and gathering dust, especially but not exclusively in developing nations, as discussed in the previous chapter. Nevertheless, the fact remains that laws also often have an impact on behavior. Anyone who has been ticketed for driving above the speed limit or parking improperly knows this. In the light of the ink on paper criticism developed in the previous chapter, our challenge now is to explain and understand why and how law affects behavior. As pointed out in the previous chapter, this is a form of "impact analysis" (Friedman, 2016), but at a more fundamental level than usually conducted.

Given that the traditional answer in terms of changes in the payoff function or altered games is invalid, there seems to be only one possible way to explain how law affects behavior. The way that law can change human behavior is by changing people's beliefs about what other people may or may not do. If the law cannot change the rules of the game, and it cannot change the payoffs people earn from the same actions undertaken by all, the only way in which it can change my behavior is if I expect that the announcement of the law will change other people's behavior, and so what constitutes my optimal behavior changes. Of course, we will have to explain why the law may change other people's behavior. The discerning reader may begin to suspect that if other people's behavior changes, it must be for the same reason. Other people expect other people's behaviors, including mine, to change.

If a new speed limit law sets a maximum speed limit of 70 mph, when driving above that speed, I expect the police to stop and fine me. It is that belief that may make me decide to drive below 70 mph. But why might the police officer stop me if I drive above 70 mph? This can be because, after the new speed limit law is enacted, the police officer believes that if he does not stop and fine me for driving above 70 mph, the head of the police department will dismiss him from the job or deny him a salary increase. Of course, we will also have to explain the behavior of the head of the police. If behavior is to change, there must be an internally consistent structure of beliefs each of which is propped up by the others, which makes society shift to a different pattern of behavior.

The might of the law, even though it may be backed by handcuffs, jails, and guns, is, in its elemental form, rooted in nothing but a configuration of beliefs carried in the heads of people in society—from ordinary civilians to the police, politicians, and judges, intertwining with and weaving into one another, reinforcing some and whittling down others, creating enormous edifices of force and power, at times so strong that they seem to transcend all individuals, and create the illusion of some mysterious diktat enforced from above. In truth, the most important ingredients of a republic, including its power and might, reside in nothing more than the beliefs and expectations of ordinary people going about their daily lives and quotidian chores. It is in this sense that we are all citizens of the republic of beliefs.

The above idea, in embryonic form, goes far back into history, certainly to the mid-eighteenth century and, in particular, to David Hume. As Hume pointed out in his essay on government (Hume, 1742 [1987], essay 4, para. 6): "No man would have any reason to fear the fury of a tyrant, if he had no authority over any but from fear; since, as a single man, his bodily force can reach but a small way, and all the further power he possesses must be founded either on our opinion, or on the presumed opinion of others." What is being suggested here is that what matters are my beliefs and my beliefs about others' beliefs, and others' beliefs about my beliefs.

Another remarkable writer who grasped this facelessness of political power and the origins of it in the dailiness of life, and in the beliefs and behaviors of ordinary people, was Franz Kafka, as is amply in evidence in his masterly novel *The Trial*, in which the very existence of an overarching authority is left ambiguous.

What Hume and Kafka, with their remarkable capacity for insight, realized is exactly right, but they did not have the wherewithal to give it formal shape or structure. It may appear that in emphasizing this particular Humean insight, I am distancing myself from the philosopher who wrote much more extensively and is treated as an authority on law and the sovereign, namely, Thomas Hobbes. That impression is correct.

Hobbes's contributions were pioneering; nothing takes away from that. The distinguished political philosopher Norberto Bobbio considered him among the greatest natural law theorists of all time.[2] Nevertheless, it seems to me that Hobbes, unwittingly, fell into the same trap in the early seventeenth century that neoclassical economists would fall into in the mid-twentieth, namely, to treat the sovereign as exogenous to society.[3]

To advance Hume's insight requires ideas and concepts that come from game theory and were unknown in the eighteenth century. What we need to do is to take this essential Humean insight and give it formal structure to get a modern theory of law and economics. That is what I shall proceed to presently.[4] But before that

2. Though, having remarked on the large number of conferences held in 1988 to commemorate Hobbes's 400th birth anniversary, he points out, "More and more often conferences are organized to promote tourism" (Bobbio, 1989, p. 197).

3. This is clear from chapter 26 on "Of Civil Laws" in *Leviathan* (Hobbes, 1668 [1994]). There are however troubling ambiguities in Hobbes. As Goldsmith (1996), in analyzing Hobbesian law, points out, in *Leviathan* Hobbes treats the law as a command addressed to people who are "obliged to obey" (p. 274). If that is the case, it is not clear why we need enforcers of the law. Also, it may be clarified that in the Hobbesian formulation the sovereign or assembly that makes the law is chosen by the citizens. But, once chosen, the assembly acquires a resilience that puts it beyond the control of the citizens. In other words, it seems to evolve into an exogenous authority. Hobbes in his time stood out for being an admirer of mathematics and the use of mathematical methods. His analysis of law and the authority of the sovereign shows that appreciation of mathematics does not automatically translate into being good at logic. Coming to Hobbes from a different angle, Cooter (1982) refers to "Hobbes's theorem," and argues that it is untenable, while admitting that it is an "illuminating falsehood" (p. 18).

4. There were writers and analysts in the nineteenth and twentieth centuries who captured different aspects of this Humean idea but never the full scope of it. In recent times, there has been more work in this mold. Lukes (1974) and Havel (1986) articulate ideas concerning political power and even totalitarianism in terms of people's beliefs about one another, which led to Havel's argument that the oppressed are co-conspirators along with those who are traditionally viewed as the oppressors (Basu, 1986). Ideas related to the line that I take here, rooted in game theory, are to be found in Lewis (1969), Cooter (1998), Sunstein (1996a, 1996b), Posner (2000), Mailath, Morris, and Postlewaite (2007, 2017), and McAdams (2015). I have also discussed some of these ideas in different forms in Basu (1993, 1998, 2000). I return to some of these writings and how they relate to the present work later in the book.

we need a short primer on focal point and equilibrium, the main instruments that I use to explain how human beliefs can prop one another up.

3.2 A Primer on Focal Point and Equilibrium

Much of this section will be familiar territory for many economists, but to carry all readers into the new theory of law and economics, and to a new explanation of why some laws are poorly implemented, it is useful to elaborate on the basic idea of a focal point. The focal point is a somewhat mysterious concept that emerged from modern game theory. It is intuitively obvious but hard to define. Despite the lack of a concrete definition, it is a useful concept that can be *seen* to work and the power of which can be harnessed to solve many practical problems.

We have already encountered the concept of an equilibrium in a game. For the most part, I shall be using the concept of Nash equilibrium when I talk about equilibria. A Nash equilibrium, as we already saw, is a choice of action or strategy on the part of each individual, such that, given everybody else's choice, no individual has reason to deviate unilaterally to some other action.

An important problem with applying the concept of equilibrium is that there are many situations in life with multiple equilibria. Suppose two persons with fast cars arrive on an uninhabited island with nice highways and settle down there. (In game theory, when we consider abstract, illustrative examples it is good policy not to waste time asking how and why such a strange situation arose.) Now, each of these new residents has to decide which side of the road he or she will drive on. Let me call this the Island Game. And, I am assuming that no one likes an accident. The only strategy that each person has to choose is "Drive on the left" or "Drive on the right."

Clearly, if everybody decides to drive on the left, it is in your interest to drive on the left. And exactly the same logic applies to driving on the right. In other words, the Island Game has two equilibria—everybody drives on the left and everybody drives on the right. To see this, note that if everybody drives on the left and you, unilaterally, decide to change your strategy, you will have an accident and be worse off. Likewise, for the case where everybody has chosen to drive on the right. I may add that in games of this kind, if we allow the individuals to choose "mixed strategies," that is, a person can decide "I will drive some of the time on the left and on the right at other times," there could be other equilibria. In the Island Game if both players decide to drive on the left half the time and on the right half the time, that will be an equilibrium. It is a dreadfully chaotic equilibrium with accidents, but there is nothing anyone can do unilaterally to improve his or her well-being.

It is easy to construct realistic games where there are several equilibria (and even without allowing for the use of mixed strategies). The problem in all these cases, where there happens to be more than one equilibrium, is that even if the players are smart enough to figure out which are the equilibrium outcomes, there is no surefire way for all to converge on the same equilibrium. Consider the Island Game. It is entirely possible for some to believe that you are opting for the drive-on-the-left equilibrium and others to believe you are all headed to the drive-on-the-right equilibrium. The result will be disastrous. In brief, people can be caught in bad equilibria and also in situations of chaos where they are not able to settle into any equilibrium.

This is where the idea of focal point can play a role (Schelling, 1960). The focal point is a concept that arises from a psychological capacity, prevalent among human beings, especially those who share a common cultural background, which enables each to guess what others are likely to do when faced with the problem of choosing one from among many equilibria. Despite this somewhat mystical definition, the focal point turns out to be very useful, and indeed some have argued that the concept may have its roots in evolution (Binmore and Samuelson, 2006; see also Sugden, 1989; Young, 1993; Janssen, 2001).

In the Island Game, in case both the persons who arrive are from Germany, each person may reason that the other will use his or her historical experience and drive on the right and so choose to drive on the right. Such reasoning would, in this case, work. Basically, the focal point is a Nash equilibrium that is salient and so helps people coordinate their actions. The problem is that there is no certain way of determining which one is the focal point. If, for instance, the new arrivals consist of some from the United Kingdom and some from Germany, there may be no clear way to agree which is the focal point, especially if the journey to the island happened soon after the Brexit vote.

Despite this ambiguity, the concept of focal point is important not just for understanding human behavior but can also be put to practical use. There are many instances where a focal point can be deliberately created. The best example of this pertains to meetings at airports. Suppose two persons have decided to meet at an airport at a certain time but have forgotten to specify the place. They are then locked in a game in which each player has to choose a place to go and wait. If they both choose the same place, they meet and are happy. If they choose difference places, they are unhappy.

This game clearly has a multitude of Nash equilibria. For every location, if both choose that location, then their choices constitute an equilibrium. But a problem stems from the fact that there are so many equilibria that it seems very difficult to coordinate and make sure that both are heading toward the same equilibrium point. Fortunately, many airport authorities have solved this problem by deliberately *creating* a focal point. They do this by simply choosing any visible place in the airport and putting up a sign, saying "Meeting Point."

This works, not inevitably, but extremely well. The point where the sign is placed is treated by the travelers or players as the focal equilibrium. So if my friend and I are trying to meet up but did not agree in advance on where to meet, I will wait below the Meeting Point sign knowing that she will and, she will, knowing that I will. Why this works so well is not well understood, but what is important is that it works.

Once we are sensitized to it, we simply have to look around to see how widely the concept of focal point is used in our everyday lives. In our everyday language, for instance, we make extensive use of it. Consider a group of friends planning to meet for coffee and conversation at the local coffeehouse the next day, a Sunday. All of them say they are free on Sunday and any time is as good as any other; and so one of them says, "In that case, let us settle on 4 PM." And they disperse. On Sunday, they meet at 4 and have a wonderful time.

How did this happen? After all, what they did on Sunday was to play a game. Each person had to choose a time when he or she would show up at the coffeehouse. If they all chose the same time that would constitute a Nash equilibrium. How then did they solve the coordination problem by all choosing the same time? They managed this because the last sentence uttered the previous day created a focal point. All of them knew that all of them would show up at 4 and so it was in the interest of each of them to show up at 4. If the above were happening in Brazil or India, among friends all of them would show up at 4:30, but that in no way changes the argument. Language often prompts behavior by creating focal points.

There is no hard definition of how focal points get created; and it is not a concept without ambiguity. If, in the above story, the gathering was that of Japanese and Indian friends, there could be some confusion about whether they were meeting at 4 or 4:30.

Since the focal point is an idea that I shall return to on multiple occasions, here is another example to further clarify the concept. Two players sit across a board that has nothing but 16 squares, in four columns and four rows, as shown in Game 3.1. Each player has to choose a square. If both choose the same, they get $1,000 each. Otherwise they get nothing. I call this the Squares Game, illustrated as Game 3.1.

Clearly, this game has 16 Nash equilibria. If they play this game the chances are they will not be able to coordinate on a square and so get nothing. If both choose completely randomly, each person's expected income is $62.50, which is equal to 1,000 multiplied by

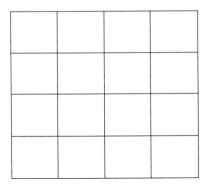

GAME 3.1. The Squares Game

one-sixteenth, the probability that the other person will choose the square I have chosen. This is a game where a focal point can clearly really help.

One way to create a focal equilibrium is to place a visible marker, say a yellow stone, in any one square. Once this is done, there is little need to say anything else. The likelihood is that this will act as a focal point. Both players will choose the square with the yellow stone and earn $1,000. Given that there is virtually nothing to distinguish one square from another, placing a yellow stone clearly marks one square out from the rest, and the human mind quickly zeroes in on it, knowing that the other player will also do so. The players will solve the coordination problem and get to the same square.[5]

It troubles some people that we do not have a hard definition of what constitutes a focal point and we still proceed to use it. Some may feel that it is not possible to put the concept to extensive use, as I do in this book, without a hard definition to identify it. My response is to point to primitive tribes that would set out to catch horses (and even actually catch them) without having the ability to define a horse. "Horse" was an important category to them even though they could not give a definition by which they could verify if the animal concerned was a horse. It still worked because of common categories in the human head that enable human beings to agree on terms without being able to define them. Of course, this can lead to mistakes. It is possible that primitive groups would end up some chasing a mule and some a horse, and so failing to catch either. Indeed, we will encounter this problem here where

5. Myerson (2004, p. 93) has drawn attention to the same idea, more colorfully, and raised a subtle question concerning fairness, with the following observation: "A group of players . . . must independently write one player's name on a piece of paper. If they all write the same name, they each get $100, except that the person named gets $200. Otherwise, they all get $0. The players have never met each other before. But just before they play, someone walks in, puts a big shiny crown on one player's head, and walks away." It is likely that this will create a focal point, namely the crowned person. This example raises some interesting questions concerning fairness and equity, since the crowned person may or may not have been arbitrarily chosen (see also discussion in McAdams, 2015, chap. 3). The problem is ethically more troubling if one of the players gets this idea and puts the crown on his or her own head (some dictators have been known to use this ploy). Everyone will be tempted to write this person's name since the person has now gained salience, even though people may resent the person's audacity and slyness.

ambiguities about what is a focal point will help us understand unstable collective behavior. As we shall see later, such ambiguities about the focal point give us important insights into lawlessness and conflicting behavior.

3.3 The Law as Focal Point

Let me now return to where I left off at the end of Section 3.1. The central idea being proposed here is that the first step toward a better-founded theory of law and economics is to recognize that the way that a law has an impact is through its effect on the beliefs of people. This can take complex forms such as influencing the direct beliefs of people or the beliefs of people about other people's beliefs and so on. But as soon as this is recognized, it is evident that the conduit for formalizing this approach is the focal point. A successful law is one that shifts human behavior by creating a new focal point in the game we all play in life, often referred to as the game of life (Binmore, 1994) and what I shall, occasionally, refer to as the economy game.

The economy game or the game of life is meant to be a full description of all the actions and strategies that individuals can choose;[6] and when we speak of individuals we mean all of them—not just the ordinary citizens, but also the police, the judges, the jury, and the prime minister. In such a game, all the individuals or players can choose any action or behavior or strategy available to them by the laws of nature. And, given all individuals' choice of action, each individual gets a payoff or utility (which we may, for convenience, express in dollar terms). This is, as we have already seen, referred to as a payoff function. The terminology is useful here because law and economics can be thought of as the study of how laws affect outcomes and behavior in the economy game.

As argued in Section 3.1, in the game of life the law cannot change the actions or strategies open to individuals, nor can it change the payoff functions of individuals. All it can do is to change individuals' beliefs about what others will do. These changed beliefs

---

6. Mailath, Morris, and Postlewaite (2017) refer to these as all the actions permitted by the "laws of physics."

can prompt individuals to behave differently and that is what can take society to a new equilibrium in which people behave differently and so the societal outcome is different. In other words, the only way the law can affect behavior and outcomes is by deflecting society to a new equilibrium or a new set of behaviors. The law is simply an instrument that gives salience to certain equilibria and certain kinds of behavior. Basically, a new law, if it is to be effective, has to create a new focal point.

We can now state one of the central claims of the focal-point approach to law and economics: *The law works, to the extent that it does, by creating new focal points in the game of life or the economy game; and, further, this is the only way in which the law affects individual behavior and collective outcomes.* It is important to stress that I am not asserting that this is a way in which the law *often* works but that this is the way in which the law *always* works. This is important to understand because there are prominent legal scholars and theorists who have made significant contributions to law and economics by using the idea of the focal point to understand ways in which *certain kinds* of laws work (see, for instance, Cooter, 1998, 2000; McAdams, 2000, 2015).[7] However, I make a more universal claim. This stems from an important conceptual difference between what the legal theorists using the concept of the focal point argue and the line that I am taking. I shall return to this later.

The claim I am making is that the enactment of a law is like the placing of a yellow stone in the Squares Game, described above. It does not change the game. The available strategies are the same, the rules are the same, and the payoffs for different possible actions are the same. But the new law can, nevertheless, like the yellow stone, affect the play and the outcome. It does so by altering what I expect the other person to do and altering what the other person expects me to do. It also probably affects higher order beliefs, that is, beliefs about beliefs. And it is worth stressing again, it is not being suggested that the law can, at times, work like this, but that this is the way the law works.

---

7. The same point is made by Posner (2000, p. 3) when he asks, rhetorically, "Can we evaluate different kinds of interventions according to the likelihood that they will enhance desirable forms of nonlegal cooperation and subvert undesirable ones?" See also Geisinger (2002).

This argument has an interesting obverse. Since the outcome brought about by the use of the law is anyway an equilibrium, that outcome could have occurred without the law. In brief: *Any outcome that is made possible by creating a law could have happened without the law.*[8] If a law prohibiting freedom of speech can curb people from speaking freely, then a curb on people speaking freely could occur without the law. It is for this reason, I argued elsewhere (Basu, 2000), that if we want to see if a certain society has freedom of speech, it is not enough to study the nation's laws because the same outcome can be achieved through informal social sanctions or the threat of ostracism. India's caste rules are not backed by the law, but in many rural Indian communities they bind behavior with as much force as the law (Akerlof, 1976).[9]

Consider a food security law, of the kind outlined in the previous chapter, in the context of India, which says that poor people should be given vouchers that they can use to buy food from privately run food stores, and the food stores can then give the vouchers to banks and exchange them for money. If this law does work in the way in which I suggested it is likely to, then, even though this sounds strange, the whole system can work even without the law. In such an equilibrium some people would print the vouchers and give them to the poor, who would then take them to markets and buy food. The food shop owners would then take the vouchers to banks and get cash in exchange. In brief, if the law is effective, and if everyone—the citizens, the police, the judge—did exactly what they did in a society with the law, then their actions would constitute a Nash equilibrium. Hence, they could have sustained that outcome without the law. If this reasoning sounds alien to us that is only because the standard view of law has, unfortunately,

8. It is not surprising that there are many instances of how groups of ordinary citizens, firms, or guilds have often succeeded in creating self-enforcing rules for monitoring their own behavior (Bernstein, 1992; Greif, 1993; Greif, Milgrom, and Weingast, 1994; Myerson, 2004; Dixit, 2004, 2015). This also explains the possibility of spontaneous order, on which there is a substantial literature (see, for instance, Elster, 1989; Sugden, 1989; Ellickson, 1991; Hadfield and Weingast, 2013).

9. I elaborate on some of these ideas in Chapter 5. At first sight this proposition may sound somewhat mystical, reminiscent of Frank Hahn's (1980, p. 289) tongue-in-cheek description of Keynesian policy: "Some economists have taken up a rather odd, not to say paradoxical, position vis-a-vis government macro-policies. The oddity consists of the fact that these policies are discussed in the context of a model where no such policies are needed."

become so much a part of our thinking and has corrupted our ability to see clearly.

To understand this better, let us return to the Prisoner's Dilemma. How can the law be used to rescue the individuals from the bad outcome? Taking society to a better outcome is one of the central motivations of the discipline of law and economics. However, in case the game (in this case, the Prisoner's Dilemma) has been rightly described and this is a full description of the game of life, the answer is simple: they cannot be rescued from the bad outcome.

However, the fact that we talk about imposing a fine on bad behavior and trying to steer the two individuals to a better collective outcome shows that we do not really believe that the game that has been described is the real game of life that is being played. After all, to impose a fine, we minimally need one more person—the police or the traffic warden who can be brought in to monitor and punish. And if such a person exists, that person should have been modeled, in the first place, as part of the game.

Let us proceed to do that. I shall create a somewhat contrived game, for the aim here is not to solve an actual problem but to explain the new approach. So let us assume there is a third person—the police, or player 3. The first two persons play the Prisoner's Dilemma, as before. But the police person gets to make a choice as well. If she chooses left, L, players 1 and 2 get the same payoff as in the Prisoner's Dilemma (Game 2.1). If she chooses right, R, they get the payoffs of the Prisoner's Dilemma with Fine (Game 2.2). In other words, the players get punished for bad behavior. Clearly, it is player 3's action that determines whether or not players 1 and 2 will get punished for bad behavior. A good way to remember the actions is to think of R as standing for "Regulation enforcement" and L as standing for "Laxity" (on the part of the police).

To complete the description of the game, we need to specify what payoff the police player gets. Since the aim here is purely illustrative, let me, for simplicity and without bothering to create a story, assume that she gets a payoff of 1 if she chooses R, no matter what 1 and 2 do. But if she chooses L, what she gets depends on what 1 and 2 choose. If both choose A, she gets 0. For all other choices by players 1 and 2, she gets 2. All this is summed up in the two payoff matrices in Game 3.2. I am assuming for simplicity that all the choices are made simultaneously. Hence, the two matrices together describe the three-player normal-form game.

I call the game just described the Prisoner's Dilemma Game of Life I because it brings in not just the players who are locked in the Prisoner's Dilemma but also others who are there—in this case player 3—and who can be marshalled into action if need be; that is what explains the reference to the "game of life." I call this Game of Life I, because there will be an alternative version, II, that will be described later. This game has two Nash equilibria. One can see this easily by examining the payoff tables. The two Nash equilibrium outcomes are (B, B, L) and (A, A, R). The two outcomes result in the following payoff triples: (2, 2, 2) and (7, 7, 1).

Suppose the game, left to itself, reaches the equilibrium (B, B, L), though it could also fail to reach any equilibrium. The players then get a payoff of (2, 2, 2). No one can do better through a unilateral deviation. But, collectively, 1 and 2 suffer in this equilibrium. This is where the law comes in. Suppose a new law is enacted that declares action B as wrong and asserts that a fine equivalent to $2 will be charged to anybody who chooses B. Implicitly, what is being asserted is that the police will usher in a world in which this punishment is inflicted on the erring individual. In other words, what is being said is that the police will choose R.

Hence, what the law does here is simply to urge society to shift to (A, A, R). According to the new approach, the law's power comes solely from its ability to make (A, A, R) a focal point, so that everybody's—the citizens' and the police person's—beliefs are appropriately changed and society actually ends up there. The law is like placing a Meeting Point sign in an airport terminal or a yellow stone on one of the squares in the Squares Game. The law, in this formulation, is mere prediction. It chooses an equilibrium, from

	A	B			A	B
A	7,7,0	1,8,2		A	7,7,1	1,6,1
B	8,1,2	2,2,2		B	6,1,1	0,0,1
	L				R	

GAME 3.2. Prisoner's Dilemma Game of Life I

among all available equilibria, and says that that will happen and, by doing so, it hopes to make that outcome focal. What the law does is to create an edifice of beliefs, such that if everybody believes in it, everybody's belief is ratified.

What is critical to understand is that there is nothing special about this game. What the law does here is all the law can do. It also follows that if everybody decides to look the other way and ignore the law, the law will have no impact. On the other hand, if it does manage to change expectations, it can have a binding effect and give the appearance of an iron fist controlling society from above, an illusion that has deceived some of the greatest minds in philosophy, and breaking out of that delusion is what distinguished Hume. The exogenous power of the law is always mere appearance. The law can do nothing more than affect the beliefs of individuals. We are all, for good or for bad, citizens of the republic of beliefs.

The law uses the language of command but is, in reality, nothing but a forecast of behavior. If you are bad, the police officer will punish you. If you are bad and the officer does not punish you, the officer will get punished by the sergeant. By pointing to an outcome, it tries to persuade people to go there. If the direction to which they are being directed is an equilibrium, once people believe that others expect this to happen, they are locked in.

It follows, and this is critically different from what happens in the traditional law and economics model, that if the game of life has only one equilibrium or, more elaborately, only one outcome that can occur under equilibrium play, the law can do nothing. If in the above game, for instance, the payoff from the outcome (A, A, R), instead of being (7, 7, 1), were (7, 7, −1), and all other payoffs were unchanged, the only Nash equilibrium outcome would be (B, B, L), and so, no matter what the law said, this would occur. Since the law cannot alter the game and the game has a unique equilibrium outcome, the citizenry would be destined to it. The law cannot create new equilibria, as supposed in traditional law and economics; all it can do is direct society to some preexisting equilibrium.[10] We may designate some individuals as functionaries of the state—as

---

10. At least not in the direct way in which traditional law and economics supposes. There are, as we shall later see, some ways in which new equilibria might get created, but the process is rather different from that of traditional law and economics.

police, judges, and prime minister—and some as ordinary citizens; but all are players in the game of life. And in the end the law's efficacy depends on all of us, the beliefs we hold, what we expect of others, and how we respond.[11]

The fact that the law often affects the behavior of citizens and the outcome reached by society shows that the game of life generally has multiple equilibria. Indeed, contrary to what many economists believe, economic life is, in all likelihood, riddled with equilibria.[12] That is what makes economic policymaking a challenge and an exciting venture. Indeed, if the economy game happened to have only one equilibrium, the law would be of no consequence since the economy would have only one place to settle. This argument is clearly articulated by Myerson (2006, p. 12): "I would argue that the right mathematical model of institutions should admit such a multiplicity of solutions, because real institutions are manifestly determined by cultural norms and traditional concepts of legitimacy, which would have not scope for effect if the economic structure of the true game . . . admitted only one dominant solution."[13]

11. In Auden's more lyrical words (from his "Law, Like Love"):
Others say, Law is our Fate;
Others say, Law is our State;
Others say, others say
Law is no more,
Law has gone away.
And always the loud angry crowd,
Very angry and very loud,
Law is We,
And Always the soft idiot softly Me.

12. For an excellent essay on the real-life plausibility of multiple equilibria, especially in the context of developing economies, see Hoff and Stiglitz (2001). A lot of this work tries to explain poverty traps and the persistence of poverty (see Bowles, Durlauf, and Hoff, 2006). What is more unusual, though it is also grounded in the notion of multiple equilibria, is the idea of an "inequality trap," whereby a society gets caught in an equilibrium with poor income distribution and also economic inefficiency (see Bourguignon, Ferreira, and Walton, 2007). It can be that publicly educated workers are all born as poor children, whereas the children of the rich get special education and thereby stay rich (Roemer, 1998). In this setup it is possible to get an inequality trap whereby overall income is lower than would otherwise be the case. What is interesting and echoes discussions elsewhere in the book is that these equilibria rely on the intersection of economics with social and political factors.

13. As in the present book, Myerson (2006) uses the idea of "focal-point effects" to explain institutions, but, interestingly, he extends the idea of focal "points" to set-valued solution concepts, such as the curb set used in Basu and Weibull (1991). If we were to pursue this route in this setup, and it is eminently suited for that, what we would need to focus

To reiterate, let me add what is at one level merely a personal belief, that an economy, as described by economists, will typically have multiple equilibria, in fact a multiplicity of them.[14] Of course, in the end, there is only one thing that happens. To assert that there are many possible outcomes that could have happened is simply a matter of realism on the part of economists. It says that what we as economists can isolate as the set of possible outcomes consists of the actual eventual outcome, and, typically, some more outcomes. A master discipline that understood not just economics but psychology, politics, sociology, and also oceanography, meteorology, and much else maybe could identify the unique equilibrium that actually occurs. But from economics alone to claim uniqueness of equilibria amounts to hubris. In other words, in most situations in life, using the tools of analysis available to us as economists, even with the aid of neighboring disciplines, such as law and politics, we have to be reconciled to the possibility of there being numerous equilibria, the outcomes to which our discipline can safely point and say that, given what we know about the world from our discipline's perspective, what happens will be somewhere in this set.

The focal point approach relies on the expressive function or suggestive power of the law and not on any human irrationality. It is purely a device that *uses suggestion* to facilitate coordination. The power of suggestion has been written about by researchers but also observers of our daily lives. As Mr. Biswas, the protagonist in

---

on is the concept of the "focal curb," that is, a curb set that is somehow salient and so all players know that this is the set of outcomes within which the game is going to end up. A new law would, in this case, take society not to a well-defined outcome but to a set of possible outcomes. I develop this more fully in Section 3.5. This idea is important because the actual game of life is so complex that a precise description of proposed behavior is virtually impossible. The law often specifies behavior for a limited number of situations. Thereafter, we have to proceed by analogy and interpretation, and extend it from one case to another. This was the thesis associated with Levi (1949; see also Swedberg, 2014, chap. 4). To formalize this, it is useful to have a set-valued equilibrium concept, which leaves room for ambiguity and maneuver. There is a suggestion of the same idea in Hardin's (1989) conceptualization of the role of a constitution. For him a constitution is not so much a contract as an aid to coordination, creating mutually reinforcing expectations of behavior in a population.

14. For descriptions of how in realistic settings there can be many equilibria, see, for instance, Basu and Van (1998), Platteau (2000), Hoff and Stiglitz (2001), Morris and Shin (2001), and Basu and Weibull (2003).

V. S. Naipaul's classic novel, quickly learned when he went to work in his relative's lucrative alcohol store in a small town, "The rum was the same but the prices and labels were different: 'The Indian Maiden,' 'The White Cock,' 'Parakeet.'" And Naipaul went on to point out with his remarkable powers of observing human frailty: "Each brand had its adherents" (Naipaul, 1961, p. 61).

Of course, in reality, there will be situations where the law, simply by giving labels to actions, can have an effect on behavior. This is what underlies some of the discussion on the expressive function of law (Sunstein, 1996b).

Let me sum up for now. It has been a conundrum in law and economics why some laws or laws in some countries are obeyed and others are routinely flouted. Indeed, this is founded in a long-standing philosophical debate. "The problem of explaining why we should obey the laws of nature—or indeed, why we should obey any set of norms—is one of the most enduring in philosophy."[15] Echoing an idea that has also had a long, parallel life, certainly from the time of David Hume, and utilizing concepts from game theory, I argue that once we recognize the social pressures we create on one another through nothing but the beliefs in our heads, we can understand why we often do what the law requires us to do even though it may not in itself be in our interest. It is the socially self-enforcing mechanism that gives law the enormous power that it often has. It is the same for social norms, and this is what gives a common basis to behavior enforced by the law and enforced by social norms. Order enforced by law and order without law (Ellickson, 1991) may not be as far apart as may appear at first sight.

3.4 The Implementation of Laws

This altered approach to law and economics gives us important insights and a deeper and more correct understanding of how the law affects economic outcomes. The move from the traditional approach to law and economics to the focal point approach is somewhat akin to moving away from a partial equilibrium analysis of the

---

15. The quotation is from the entry on "Hugo Grotius" in the *Stanford Encyclopedia of Philosophy*, https://plato.stanford.edu/entries/grotius/.

economy to a general equilibrium one. A partial equilibrium analysis works by assuming that variables outside of the particular market being studied remain unchanged even while behavior within the market changes. This is a handy model, but flawed, because we do know that changes within a market often affect variables beyond the market and these can come back to alter what happens in the market. Indeed, there are situations where the partial equilibrium results are actually inconsistent in the overall economy. In mainstream economics this shift occurred in the late nineteenth century, thanks to the contributions of many economists, most notably Léon Walras, even though the finer details of the general equilibrium model were worked out in the mid-twentieth century by Kenneth Arrow, Gérard Debreu, and others (Arrow and Debreu, 1954). Though, like all research, the project remains a work in progress, the switch from the traditional partial-equilibrium analysis to general equilibrium vastly improved the power of economics as a discipline to understand economic and social phenomena, from growth and prosperity to famines and recessions.

There is a similar potential for law and economics. The traditional approach to law and economics works by focusing attention on a *segment* of the full economy game, by leaving some vital players out of the picture and assuming that they are robotic followers of the law. What the focal point approach to law and economics does is to take on the full economy game, including the police and the judge, and then tries to explain how and why the law works. As we have seen, this shift of perspective forces us to alter the very paradigm of analysis, from viewing the law as an instrument for changing payoff functions and the rules of the game to an instrument that, while powerless to do so, can act as a catalyst for altering the beliefs of players, and, through that, behavior.

One important contribution of the focal point approach to law and economics is that it helps us understand better when and why so many laws fail to be implemented and simply languish on paper, and why this happens more in some societies, especially developing nations and emerging economies.

The first reason why some laws fail to be implemented is that they try to direct the economy to a non-equilibrium point. If you adopt a law that asks people to behave in certain ways, and it has the attribute that if everybody behaves in the way recommended, then it is in the interest of at least one person to behave differently (that is, the proposed behaviors do not constitute an equilibrium), then clearly the law will not be borne out in practice, at least not in a sustainable way. In brief, the implementation of the law must be self-enforcing with all human beings—citizens and agents of the state—being treated alike and as rational. This is, of course, the assumption behind much of mainstream microeconomics. But interestingly, traditional law and economics has assumed this strictly for all ordinary citizens and flagrantly violated this assumption for agents of the state.

If a law is enacted that tries to direct the entire society to an outcome that is not an equilibrium and hence not a focal point, then it is doomed to not be implemented. To see this in an interesting case, alter the above Prisoner's Dilemma Game of Life I a little. Change all the payoffs of player 3 in the left payoff matrix to 2. Now suppose a new law is enacted, which asks each of the players 1 and 2 to choose action A and player 3 to choose action L. This law will never get implemented because if persons 1 and 2 expect all others to follow the law, then it is not in their interest to follow the law. This law is doomed because it targets an outcome that is not an equilibrium of the game. This is because the new approach to law and economics, unlike the traditional one, asserts that a law can never *create* an equilibrium. It can simply direct society to some preexisting equilibrium. A cardinal mistake we often make is to not realize this limitation of the law, and try to overreach and direct society to some outcome that is not an equilibrium, and hence not sustainable. In such cases we end up with laws that are doomed to fail.[16]

Second, and this is widely appreciated in the mainstream literature, many governments state their laws in ways that are ambiguous or even contradictory, with different laws demanding conflicting behaviors, making it impossible not to violate the law.[17] The

16. This is not worth laboring further since what I am arguing here is a line taken by the mechanism design literature (see, for instance, Myerson, 1983; Maskin and Sjostrom, 2002; Arunava Sen, 2007).

17. As Hadfield (2016, p. 289) observes in her new book, "It's not that there are no formal legal rules and systems in poor and developing countries. Indeed, there are often so many rules and systems that no one could possibly comply with them all."

problem is more acute with the focal point approach since there is no certain way of creating focal points. Contradictory messages can occur not just by having laws that openly contradict one another but in other more subtle ways as well. This is because the law often makes suggestions through signs and signals, the so-called expressive mode. As Sunstein (1996b, p. 2021) observes, "Actions are expressive; they carry meanings. . . . A lawyer who wears a loud tie to court will be signaling something distinctive about his self-conception and his attitude towards others." These signals can contradict speech acts, thereby creating confusion.

Governments, at times for Machiavellian reasons, give such mixed signals, leaving the citizenry confused about the right course of action. But often this is the consequence of the backlog of laws, gathered over a long period, and contradicting one another. Parliaments are aware of this. That is one reason why laws are frequently stated with the caveat, "Notwithstanding any other provision of law."[18] This is of no help however when two contradictory laws are both backed up by such caveats.

The third reason for non-implementation of the law, somewhat related to the second, pertains to the generic and rather open-ended problem of focal points—namely, that it is not evident what constitutes a focal point for different groups of people. The same signal may be picked up by one set of people to be focal and be ignored by another group. We know, for instance, that players sharing a common group identity find it easier to coordinate onto a focal point (Habyarimana, Humphreys, Posner, and Weinstein, 2007; see also Boettke, Coyne, and Leeson, 2008). This, in turn, implies that when a group of people gets reasonably used to a focal point, the presentation of a new focal point can actually make the coordination problem worse.

Thus suppose in the Squares Game, a society gets used to choosing, most of the time, the top left square; that is, when two individuals are made to play this game, they are both likely to choose the

18. Here is an actual example: "Notwithstanding anything contrary contained in any other law for the time being in force, no fees shall be payable to the Central Government out of the assets of the Banking Company." This is a direct quote from India's Banking Regulation Act, 1949. It will be interesting to see a bank try to get away, citing this law, with not paying the Central Bank what some other law demands.

top left square. In brief, this is the social norm that helps these people to frequently earn $1,000. Now suppose, to be helpful, someone places a yellow stone in some other square and asks people to play this game. It is entirely possible that coordination will now get worse, with some expecting the square with the yellow stone to be focal and others continuing to assume that the old custom of the northwestern square being focal will persist.

This is not as abstract an exercise as may seem at first sight. In an important paper, Kranton and Swamy (1999) discussed the agricultural credit market in colonial India. The market was an informal one that ran on norms.[19] It worked but only moderately well, with defaults and consequent credit scarcity. To rectify this, the British rulers of India created civil courts in the Bombay Deccan. The outcome was a worsening of the market's functioning and diminution of efficiency.[20] Drawing on historical records the authors show how farmers did not benefit by this. There can be many reasons for this, including the piecemeal nature of reforms, as Kranton and Swamy suggest. But it is also possible and in fact likely that when you try to replace custom and norms with law and courts, two focal points are created. Far from helping, it is likely to worsen matters, at least for some time, until a winner focal point emerges among the contenders and acquires salience.[21] This explains why the observation by Gordon Brown, cited in Chapter 1, is so insightful. Given the self-fulfilling element in the idea of a focal point, it may take a long time before other instruments, such as custom and social norms, are put aside and people begin to treat the law as the most salient coordinator of behavior.

19. In a similar spirit, Acemoglu, Johnson, and Robinson (2005) point out how culture can be an enabler for societies to coordinate onto certain equilibria. In this sense it can do what the law does and, for that very reason, be an impediment to the effectiveness of the law.

20. A fascinating micro corroboration of this occurs in Weber and Camerer (2003), who found through laboratory experimentation that the merger of firms with different organizational cultures results in reduced performance.

21. Posner (2000, p. 4) makes a similar observation when he writes, "The desirability of a proposed legal rule . . . does not depend only on the existence of a collective action problem on the one hand, and competently operated legal institution on the other. It depends on the way non-legal systems already address that collective action problem and the extent to which legal interventions would interfere with those non-legal systems."

To take another analogy, if at Heathrow airport an official decided that instead of making people walk great distances to get to the spot with the board marked Meeting Point, he would put up two or three such boards at different places, the whole project could become a failure.

Once we recognize the focal point foundation of the law, we have to take extra care to ensure that the law becomes salient. This may require education and other forms of persuasion, and even then we may have to be reconciled to the fact that it will take time for the law to become effective. However, in the process, there is a risk. If it takes too long, people may come to disregard the law and, when that happens, the law can lose its effectiveness altogether. Indeed, as individual pieces of legislation lose effectiveness, a citizenry can come to believe that the laws are there to be ignored. It does come close to this in some developing countries where no one pays attention to the law.[22] What I am arguing is that this is fully rational. If it is known that no one at an airport pays any attention to the Meeting Point sign, it will be foolish of you to go and wait under it to meet your friend. It would be better for you to try the bookshop or the pub, depending on your friend's predilection for books and beer.

This is one problem that plagues newly industrializing and modernizing nations and developing countries. Most of them have relied for large stretches of time on social norms, feudal customs, and cultural practices to make some form of economic life possible. Simple economic functions, such as trade and exchange, require some basic norms and customs to be in place. It can be shown that they cannot function purely by the drives of individuals to maximize utility and amass wealth (Basu, 2000, chap. 4). So either through feudal pronouncements or, more likely, through slow evolutionary processes, these societies come to acquire certain equilibrium-selection norms, which are nothing but focal points, that

---

22. But it is by no means exclusive to developing countries. As Mailath, Morris, and Postlewaite (2017) point out, there are many examples even in the United States of the twentieth century. For instance, during World War II, native-born Japanese Americans had their property taken away and were imprisoned. This was in violation of the US Constitution and unlawful but was collectively overlooked by the functionaries of the state, including the Supreme Court. Acemoglu and Jackson (2015) present examples of laws in the United Kingdom and France that were collectively overlooked.

make economic life possible. More precisely, societies that exist are the ones that have these basic norms in place.

The process of modernization that is occurring today takes the form of trying to import laws and rules from industrialized nations, some of which were the rulers of former colonies, to the former colonies and other poor nations. In brief, the laws in these cases are competing with preexisting focal points determined by custom and the long history of social evolution. Dislodging those norms is not easy. Indeed, matters may get worse since these laws in many cases amount to trying to create a new focal point when an old focal point exists and can make matters worse. This is most likely the reason why in developing and emerging market economies laws are so often overlooked by all and sundry.

One finds in history interesting examples of how some colonial leaders had an intuitive grasp of this. Modern law was brought into India most prominently by Warren Hastings from 1772 to 1781, during his rule over Bengal. As Roy and Swamy (2016, pp. 17–18) observe, Hastings's effort was "unprecedented and revolutionary." His project was "to understand, reconstruct, and preserve indigenous religious codes." "The legal regime that Hastings had set in motion tried to be neither a completely new order nor a completely traditional order." His effort to draw on Hindu pundits and Muslim *ulemas* to make this transition showed his capacity for strategic thinking and awareness of the challenge of shifting traditions.

This must, however, not be confused with nobility of purpose. When Nandakumar, a senior tax officer of the *nawab's* court, brought a charge of bribery against Hastings, the chief justice of the Supreme Court turned the case around to a charge of forgery against Nandakumar and gave him the death sentence, which was carried out on August 5, 1775. The chief justice was a friend of Hastings's.

There is an important conceptual problem that underlies this discussion of focal points, and understanding it can help us create an environment where laws are more diligently followed. This pertains to the question of how to *erase* focal points, which has received very little investigation. How focal points are *formed* may not be fully understood, but it is a matter that has received a lot of attention, and we have at least a rudimentary understanding of it. But on how focal points are erased or switched off we have no understanding. Yet that is what is needed if we want new laws to be better implemented. The prior salient outcome, which allowed some behavioral coordination, however imperfect, may need to be erased from collective belief for new laws to be more effective. The reason why this is such a difficult problem is that once people get used to some kind of behavior, removing the coordinating marker may not change anything. Suppose the Meeting Point board at an airport was located just outside a prominent burger restaurant. If, after many years, the board is removed, people may still continue to use the burger shop as the meeting place. Memory, in these kinds of problems, tends to leave a residue that is hard to erase.

One thing we do know, however, is that much depends on the meta beliefs held by a society. If it is known by all that once a law is enacted everyone follows the law or is law-abiding, then that belief itself allows the law to acquire salience. In brief, the law is likely to be more effective if everyone knows that laws are meant to be followed. If that founding assumption is not there in society, then the announcement of a new law does not stand much of a chance in being effective. Hence, even before considering the question of whether it is in one's interest to follow a particular law, there is a need for a more foundational belief that laws are meant to be followed.

I am not asserting here that anyone will follow the law solely for that reason for we are still operating within the mainstream, neo-classical paradigm, whereby each person has an exogenously given preference or utility function and takes decisions to maximize this. So whether to follow the law will be decided on the basis of pure selfish optimization. Nevertheless, whether or not one has the prior belief that laws are meant to be followed is important. It is the existence of such a belief that gives the law a chance of creating a focal point. If people do not have this foundational belief, then they are unlikely to even notice and certainly unlikely to cogitate over a new law. If you live in a society in which it is not known that a red light means stop and a green light means go, you may not stop when you see red and you may allow the other car crossing your path to cross even when you see green and the other car sees red. In many developing nations, this foundational belief is weak and a large part of the non-implementation problem of the law stems from this. A signal cannot create a focal point if people do not even take cognizance of the signal in the first place.

Some of these arguments are at play in why India's food security law and its predecessor, the government instructions to supply cheap food to poor households, worked so poorly, as discussed in Chapter 2. It is possible that the law is attempting something that is not a Nash equilibrium in the first place. It is not in the interest of the ration shop owner to sell the food below the market price to poor households. This argument is valid if we assume that the police will not catch and punish ration shop owners who behave like this. In other societies, this may not happen, not because ration shop owners are instinctively law-abiding but because they fear they will be punished by the police if they violate the law. And, if this is part of a Nash equilibrium, we have to explain why the police will try to catch and punish an erring ration shop owner.

However, it is also possible that the law does point to a possible Nash equilibrium, where the ration shop owner would give out the food to the poor if he or she expected the police to punish were it otherwise and the police would punish for the police knew that otherwise the magistrate would punish the police and so on. But in this society the violation of the law is so common that people do not get the cue that the new law is focal. You know others will not treat this as focal, so you do not; and the others do not for the very same reason.

3.5 Focal Curbs

The streamlined theory of law and economics based on the concept of the focal point presented thus far can be generalized in several ways. First of all, my use of the Nash equilibrium as the relevant equilibrium concept is because of the centrality of this concept in game theory and economics and also because most other concepts are in some sense offshoots of the fundamental idea of self-enforcement underlying the Nash equilibrium.

As we carry this approach to more complicated situations there may be a case to think of set-valued equilibria, that is, the idea of an equilibrium in which each player is confined not to one strategy but to a set of strategies that he or she may use. To see the importance of this, consider Game 3.3.[23] Player 1 can choose from the strategies T (top), M (middle), and B (bottom); and player 2 can choose from among L (left), C (center), and R (right). The payoffs they get are shown in the payoff matrix. I shall throughout assume that players choose pure strategies.[24]

Clearly, this game has only one equilibrium, (T, L).[25] If player 2 chooses L, player 1 will be best off choosing T, and vice versa. But now suppose 2 says: I will choose one of C and R. It makes very good sense for 1 to commit to choosing either M or B. And if 1 does so, it is indeed in 2's interest to choose C or R. Thus, in an important sense, player 1 confining herself to the set of strategies {M, B} and 2 confining himself to the set {C, R} constitutes a self-enforcing equilibrium. This is the broad idea behind the concept of the curb set (Basu and Weibull, 1991), "curb" standing for sets that are "closed under rational behavior." More generally, for games in which individuals have a finite number of feasible strategies, a curb set is a collection of subsets of each player's feasible set of strategies, such that if each player believes that all others will remain within the specified subsets, she has no reason to want to employ a strategy outside her specified subset.[26]

In doing law and economics, set-valuedness is an important concept.[27] Indeed, as Myerson (2006) has pointed out, in understanding institutions, there may be something germane in the need to consider sets of actions rather than unique actions. To see this, suppose in Game 3.3 the two players are stuck at the equilibrium (T, L). There is clearly a case to try to use the law to take society to

23. This game is taken from Basu and Weibull (1991).

24. That is, they do not use strategies with probabilities attached to them, such as saying, "I will play T with probability three-fourths and B with probability one-fourth."

25. The game, however, has more than one *mixed* strategy equilibrium.

26. Just for the record, in games where players may have an infinite number of strategies open to them, the formal definition of "curb" is a Cartesian product of nonempty and compact subsets of strategies, one for each player, such that if each player believes that others will remain within these subsets, he or she has no reason to want to use a strategy that is outside his or her own strategy subset.

27. Not surprisingly, curb is just one example of a set-valued equilibrium. There are other related concepts that have been explored in the literature. See, for instance, Bernheim (1984), Pearce (1984), Voorneveld (2002), and Arad and Rubinstein (2017).

Player 2

		L	C	R
	T	1 , 1	0 , 0	0 , 0
Player 1	M	0 , 0	2 , 3	3 , 2
	B	0 , 0	3 , 2	2 , 3

GAME 3.3. The Curb Game

a better outcome. The trouble is that there is no other point that is self-enforcing. If player 2 chooses C, player 1 will choose B. If player 1 chooses B, 2 will shift to R, and if 2 chooses R, 1 will switch to M, which will make 2 switch to C. And this goes on.

However, even without knowing where society will settle and even if it does not settle anywhere, the two players will be better off if they can be deflected from {T, L} to player 1 committing to playing one of M and B, and 2 committing to one of C and R. In such a case, the law will have to be used to direct society not to a focal point but to what may be called a "focal curb," that is, a set of strategies open to each player, such that the ordered collection of these sets—one for each player—is closed under rational behavior.[28]

This would entail having a law that says that no one is allowed to play T or L. If players believe the law will be followed by all, it is in each player's interest to abide by the law. In a law-abiding society, we do not know exactly what will happen but behavior will be contained within {M, B} and {C, R}.

It may be interesting to see how the idea of a focal curb applies to the Squares Game introduced earlier in this chapter. Suppose each player is allowed to choose a set of strategies (from the 16 that constitute the feasible set of strategies for each player) that he may use. It is easy to see that as long as both choose the same subset the pair constitutes a curb set. And whenever they choose different

28. In the sense of no one having an interest to step outside his or her specified set in order to respond to others' choice.

subsets that pair cannot be curb. In other words, the Squares Game is teeming with curb sets, even though it also has a huge number of non-curb sets.

We can see what the law can do in this game. Start from a lawless state. Individuals have no idea what others may do and so consider all actions as equally likely. In such a state, as I have already shown, each individual expects to earn \$62.50. Now suppose a law is enacted that says that individuals are not allowed to choose any square outside the four in the northwest of the full board. This law directs society not to a *point* but to a set of actions. But what is interesting is that each player confining her choice to the four northwestern squares is a curb set. So if each individual believes that the other will confine his choice to the northwestern set, she has no reason to step beyond those four squares. The law in this case can be thought of as creating not a focal point but a focal curb. It is also interesting to see that if people believe that everybody will abide by the law, each person can ensure an expected payoff of at least \$250. If players pick randomly from among the four available strategies in the focal curb, the probability of choosing the same square that the other person has chosen is one-fourth. Hence, the expected income is 1,000 multiplied by one-fourth.

Because of the ambiguity that surrounds the language of the law, it is important to go beyond focal points to focal curbs. This creates space so essential to accommodate the inherent ambiguity of the law and the legal process. The ambiguity of the law is a large subject. As Lopucki and Weyrauch (2000, pp. 1407, 1409) observe, "In the conventional view of the legal process, courts determine the facts and then apply law to those facts to generate outcomes." And then they go on to note how "this conventional view coexists with another that sees the legal process as highly manipulable through legal strategy." The ambiguity arises not just in interpreting the law but also in interpreting human behavior to decide whether or not they are in violation of the law. Cole (2017b) has recently discussed the fascinating case of Donald Trump's travel ban. Under the law, he cannot target a particular religion. He therefore on paper directed the ban at certain countries. Nevertheless, two federal judges, in Hawaii and in Maryland, barred enforcement of Trump's order on the ground that, as

Cole (p. 5) noted, "the order impermissibly targeted the Muslim faith." The judges went beyond the literal to decide on the true intention. They took note of Trump's oft-repeated campaign pledge to prohibit Muslims from entering the United States and also the fact that, after he signed the first order in January 2017 with no mention of Muslims, he looked up and said, "We all know what that means" (Cole, 2017b, p. 6).

In this book I do not go into these matters, but they point to the fact that it may be futile to think of the law as unequivocally directing society to a focal *point*. We need to invoke set-valued targets such as the focal curb. In fact, in future research we may want to go even further, with the law directing society to domains of actions that contain equilibria but need not constitute one. There can, for instance, be situations where there are several equilibria, one in which the two players earn paltry payoffs and others where they do much better. We may want to use the law to deflect society from the bad equilibrium to a zone within which the good equilibria are located, even though the zone itself is not an equilibrium, point-valued or set-valued.

In such a case, the law directs society not to a particular equilibrium but to one of several equilibria. The law, in such cases, does not create a focal "point" but tries to create what may be best thought in terms of a "negative focal area," that is, specifying a set where society should *not* settle. In other words, instead of making one equilibrium salient, it partitions the outcomes into the negative area where we should not go and the rest where society may settle. The rest may not be a point- or a set-valued equilibrium but a more amorphous zone.[29] The hope is that, given that what is being played is the game of life, society will eventually settle in some equilibrium *within* that amorphous zone. One specific application of this idea occurs in the context of the Traveler's Dilemma game and is discussed in Section 7.2.

29. The inherent ambiguity of the law has long historical roots. As Singer (2005, p. 121) points out, it was certainly there in Kant, who "had already pointed out that applying laws to facts was far from being a routine process. Rather, it required a *capacity for judgement* (*Urteilskraft*)." It is possible to argue, though that would take me far beyond the scope of this book, that ambiguity is not just a part of the law but serves a role in making the law more effective and even fair.

I want to present here one more embryonic idea pertaining to ambiguity that may be worth formalizing and developing in the future. Contrary to what economists and game theorists model, in reality, there is often ambiguity even about the game that we are playing and will be playing in the future. The game of life allows for the fact that there may be some probability that in the future we will be playing game A and some probability we will be playing game B. The ambiguity in reality is deeper. We may not even be sure of which set of games may crop up in the future. So it is not simply a case of attaching probability to each of a set of well-defined games, one of which we know we will encounter in life. In reality, often, we do not even know the set of potential games that may crop up in our lives. This creates an interesting problem with specifying focal points in advance. If you do not know what the game you and others in your society will be playing tomorrow, how do you specify the focal point? Since the law directs society to focal points, it may in certain situations not be possible to specify the law adequately in advance.

One way of tackling this problem is to develop the idea of a "focal person" or a "focal player." Suppose n persons expect to play a game tomorrow but do not know what the game will be, nor the set of games from which the actual game to be played will be chosen. All they know is that whichever game crops up there are likely to be multiple equilibria in the game. One way to make sure that they do not get trapped in a collectively suboptimal equilibrium is to specify one of the players in advance as the "focal player." The idea is that after it becomes evident what the game is that they are playing, it is the focal player who will be selecting and pointing to a specific equilibrium and the players know that that one is the focal point of the game.

This leads us to an interesting realization—an understanding as to why, over and above the law, we may need to specify a leader. A leader is simply a focal player, who directs the group to a certain outcome, by asking people to behave in certain ways, as and when the game they are playing becomes evident. This is the reason why in war and conflict, where one has to encounter sudden and unexpected scenarios, it is important to have a well-specified "leader," where a leader is best understood as a focal player.[30] It will be interesting to study and model how the role of a leader interacts and intertwines with the role of law and conventions.

Though there is need to sharpen these concepts and ideas and give them more formal structure, that is beyond the scope of the present book, which is the economist's jargon for beyond the ability of the author. It is hoped that as more able scholars and practitioners wade into actual, real-life applications of the focal point approach to law and economics, they will make these kinds of modifications and develop these ideas further to suit the context as and when the need arises.

30. In discussing leadership of autonomous village communities and military action needed to defend the village, Myerson (2017, p. 6) points out, "We should understand that a military operation requires a leader who can command people to perform dangerous actions in battle." Myerson was discussing this in the context of Henry Maine's classic work on the need for the state to elevate indigenous chiefs of leading local families to leadership roles (Maine, 1871). While that is not the direction of analysis that Myerson pursues, I believe this discussion does raise the question of why we need a leader and why people obey the leader. Clearly, the act of obedience has to be part of a person's desired behavior. The idea of a leader as a focal player can be usefully developed to enrich our understanding of such situations.

CHAPTER FOUR

The First Mover Advantage

4.1 The Law in the Extensive Form

Up to now, all interaction between players—ordinary civilians and also the functionaries of the state—in the game of life were treated as occurring simultaneously, or what in game theory is called in a normal-form or strategic-form setting. Such games are not strictly a single-point interaction, but they hide the details to appear that way. It is, however, useful to lay out the argument presented in the previous chapter more explicitly in terms of games played out over time, or, to use more formal terminology, in an extensive-form setting. The essential difference between normal-form and extensive-form games is that in the latter the earlier movers often have the advantage of steering the interaction in certain ways—the so-called first-mover advantage. But the analysis is not quite as straightforward as may seem at first sight because the later mover may have the advantage of the final say and also of knowing what has happened before moving. The extensive-form game not only enriches our understanding of how law can shape human interaction but also compels us to confront some philosophical paradoxes.

For an illustration of an extensive-form game, consider a variant of Game 3.2, the Prisoner's Dilemma Game of Life I. This game is played out in two time periods as follows. In period 1, the two ordinary individuals or citizens play the usual Prisoner's Dilemma. Then, in period 2, the police chooses between four actions—punish none (action N), punish player 1 (action 1), punish player 2 (action 2), and punish both players (action 12). Punishing in this case means deducting 2 units of payoff from the player being punished. To describe the game fully we must say what payoff the police, or player 3, gets. The simplest would be to suppose that the payoff of player 3 is unchanged, say stuck at 2 units. A more realistic assumption, and that is the one I will make here, is to assume that to punish each person the police loses one unit of her own payoff (the pain of having to raise the baton and bring it down). This leads to the two-stage extensive-form game described below and henceforth called the Broom, since that is what it looks like (Game 4.1).

The game tree shows that individual 1 makes the first move at a node that is labeled w. She chooses between A and B. Individual 2 does not know what she chooses. This is shown on the game tree by the broken line joining the two nodes that can be reached after 1 makes her choice. Player 2 now has to choose between A and B. The fact that he makes this choice without knowing what 1 has done is meant to make this equivalent to a simultaneous move.[1]

This game has several (Nash) equilibria. One equilibrium consists of the police or player 3 choosing N under all circumstances and individuals 1 and 2 each choosing B. This results in the standard Prisoner's Dilemma outcome. Verify that no one, neither the citizens nor the police officer, can do better by individually deviating to some other strategy.

Interestingly, this game has other equilibria. Here is one: Both players 1 and 2 play A; and player 3 chooses N at node a, she chooses action 2 at node b, action 1 at node c, and action 12 at node d. In other words, player 3 says, if any of players 1 and 2 chooses action B, I will punish that player. This strategy triplet (one for each of the three players), it is easy to see, constitutes a Nash equilibrium. No one can do better by individually deviating to some other strategy.

Suppose a law is enacted that says that whoever plays B will be punished by the police. Note that if both 1 and 2 believe in this,

---

1. There are some philosophically vexing questions about whether two persons making a move each simultaneously and two persons making a move each in a sequence but without the second mover knowing what the first mover has done are equivalent. I have discussed this in Basu (2000, chap. 2). There is no loss however, in the present context, to ignore this conundrum.

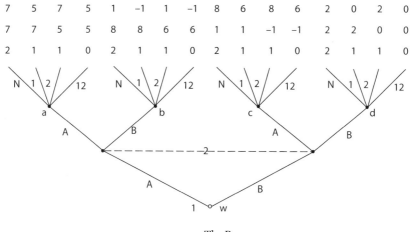

GAME 4.1. The Broom

then they will choose action A. And if the police believes in this, he will have nothing to gain by not doing what the law requires the police to do. In this case, after the citizens choose A, the police does nothing. The new law simply gives salience to the equilibrium just described. The old equilibrium, whereby the citizens choose B and the police does not punish them, is still an equilibrium. The only reason why we may expect the law-abiding equilibrium to occur instead is that everybody believes that everybody will abide by the law. The law creates a new focal point and this, as we saw above, influences behavior.

4.2 Subgame Perfection: A Technical Digression

It may be worth pointing out that the Nash equilibrium described in the above section is not what in extensive-form games is called a "subgame perfect" equilibrium. Since we have decided on the convention of treating the Nash equilibrium as the appropriate equilibrium in this book, this does not matter to us. But in case some reader believes that our analysis is *predicated* on the use of Nash, it is worth dispelling that. Hence, this technical section illustrates that it is possible to extend the analysis in the above section to reach similar results as above even if we use the concept of subgame perfect equilibrium, instead of the coarser concept of

Nash equilibrium. The intuitive idea of subgame perfection is that of a Nash equilibrium in which the strategy that players say they will use in certain future scenarios is actually worthwhile for them to use should such a scenario actually arise. In short, threats that are incredible in the sense that they are not worthwhile carrying out are not believed by anybody and so for all practical purposes cannot be used.

For a quick view of how this works, return to the Prisoner's Dilemma Game of Life I presented in the previous chapter, Game 3.2, and suppose that we make this into an extensive-form game, whereby player 3 or the police first chooses between L and R and then players 1 and 2 simultaneously choose between A and B. This means that by the time players 1 and 2 choose, they know if the game is the left payoff matrix or the right. If it is the left, they will clearly both choose B and if it is the right they will choose A. In other words, 3 knows in advance that if she chooses L the game will end up at (B, B, L), where she earns 2, and if she chooses R it will end up at (A, A, R), where she earns 1. This suggests she will play L and the game will invariably end up at (B, B, L). What I just described is the concept of "subgame perfect equilibrium" for extensive-form games. It is a Nash equilibrium in which what each player says he or she would do for every situation in the game that could potentially arise in the future is something that would actually be in the player's interest to do. In other words, incredible threats are not permitted. If players 1 and 2 said they would always play A, no matter what happened, and that drove player 3 to play R, that would not be subgame perfect. This is because players 1 and 2 are saying that they will play A even if the police chose L. But that is not credible.

In the game just described there is a unique subgame perfect equilibrium that results in the outcome (B, B, L). If this is the game of life and we treat subgame perfection as the right equilibrium concept, the law can do nothing to change this outcome, which is miserable for individuals 1 and 2.

Should we wish to use subgame perfection as the relevant equilibrium concept, there is an easy way to extend the analysis and show the power of law to influence behavior. This entails the addition of a third period to the game, which involves a normal-form game with multiple equilibria (I used this in Basu, 2000). We could, for instance, think of a fourth player, the magistrate being there. After the two stages illustrated in the Broom game is over, the police (player 3) and the magistrate (player 4) have an interaction in which the magistrate has to choose between status quo (action S) and punishment (action P), where he tries to punish the police person. The police, in turn, has to choose between the status quo (S) and taking a defensive position (D) to take cover against the punishment strategy. Suppose this results in the normal-form game, called the Police Magistrate Game, described below.

Now we can think of the full game of life as involving the Broom game, described above, with a third period appended to each terminal node of the Broom. In the third period, players 3 and 4 play the normal-form Police Magistrate Game (Game 4.2). Basically, to describe the full game what we have to do is take the payoffs at the terminal nodes of the Broom game and add to this the payoffs earned in Game 4.2. In other words, the full game of life now is a four-player game involving three periods, with final payoffs as just described.

Note that the game that is played in period 3 has two equilibria, one (the status quo outcome) in which the police earns 4 and, the other (the punishment outcome) in which she earns 1. Depending on how these outcomes are chosen a variety of subgame perfect equilibria can be supported in the full, three-period economy game. The announcement of a new law that declares the use of strategy B as punishable can indeed lead to the police person punishing anybody who chooses action B because, if she does not punish such a person, then there can be a common expectation that player 4 will play P in the last stage, prompting 3 to play D. Hence, the police would get a payoff of 1 instead of 4. It is thus clearly in the interest of the police to enforce the law.

Player 4 (Magistrate)

		S	P
Player 3 (Police)	S	4 , 4	0 , 2
	D	1 , 0	1 , 2

GAME 4.2. The Police Magistrate Game

Of course, the game has other subgame perfect equilibria, so it is not necessary that the outcome suggested by the law will occur. But, as before, the law creates a focal point, and as long as it is an equilibrium it has a chance of being implemented.

If we live in a society in which the law has salience in the sense of everybody expecting everybody to expect a law-abiding outcome to occur, then the law will influence behavior. If the game of life has only one equilibrium, the law will not have any effect because, no matter what it says, society will settle in that only outcome that can be supported in equilibrium. This, in essence, is the focal point approach to law and economics.

4.3 Law as Cheap Talk and Burning Money

Once we view the game of life or the economy game as interaction through time, new avenues open up for using the focal point approach to law to create richer and more complex models. I shall in this section explore two avenues. These are not novel exercises but simple applications of ideas developed by game theorists.

The first entails drawing on the concept of cheap talk in game theory, that is, the ability to talk and make observations, which are costless, in the middle or at the start of a game (Crawford and Sobel, 1982; Blume and Sobel, 1995; Farrell and Rabin, 1996; Ellingsen, Ostling, and Wengstrom, 2013). Being costless, at first sight, this ought to be inconsequential. The act of adopting a law, according to this view, is like a player or a group of players in the middle of a game making a public statement or writing something down on paper. It should be immediately obvious that cheap talk has a natural relation to law and economics.[2]

The second avenue involves what is called "burning money." This is based on the recognition that enacting a law may not be totally costless to the individuals engaged in the process. Minimally, it takes time and effort. If then it does not change the game, as was argued in the focal point approach to law, it is like burning money (a deadweight loss incurred by the person who burns the money).

2. This is used by Mailath, Morris, and Postlewaite (2017) to explain the intriguing idea of authority (see also Zambrano, 1999, and R. Akerlof, 2017).

Fortunately, there is a literature on what burning money can do (Kohlberg and Mertens, 1986; Van Damme, 1989; Ben-Porath and Dekel, 1992; Rubinstein, 1991).

While I am unable to take these approaches to full closure, it will be evident that both of them suggest ways of analyzing the effect of law on society, which are natural extensions of the focal point approach.

Consider first the case of cheap talk. In itself, this is a costless act, and as such some would view it as inconsequential. However, it could be treated as a signal of what the players who do the cheap talking or, in this case, the enacting of the law intend to do in future stages of the game.[3] In other words, the enactment of a new law is a costless announcement of what a player or a group of players intends to do *here onward* in the game.

How consequential this is depends critically on the subgame that lies ahead of the period in which the law is enacted. In case there is only one equilibrium in the subgame ahead, the cheap talk can do nothing. However, if there are several equilibria, the law can, by indicating what the people who announce the law intend to do, influence what others will do. There is a close connection between this and the focal point approach. Here, as before, a focal point is created by the announcement of the law in the subgame that lies ahead. However, in this exercise, the person or persons who enact the law are explicitly treated as players of the game. This makes the focal point even more salient. It is like a case where you and your friend have decided to meet at an airport and forgotten to decide where you will meet and your friend puts up a sign saying "I will wait for you here." This is likely to create an even more salient focal

3. In the present context I am staying with the mainstream assumption that the conversation or words uttered in the middle of a game do not alter payoffs but merely signal future action. There is however a literature that points to the fact that conversation and words can raise expectations on the part of the listeners, which can create pressure on the listener and the speaker by creating expectations, guilt, and guilt aversion (see, for instance, Charness and Dufwenberg, 2006; Ellingsen, Johannesson, Tjotta, and Torsvik, 2010). Likewise, words can create promises, and experiments show that human beings do not like to break their own promises, even if they are relatively indifferent to other people's promise on their behalf (Vanberg, 2008). Hence, the lawmaker's behavior could indeed be affected by the law that he or she makes. In Chapter 7 I discuss how some of these "behavioral elements" ought to be taken account of when doing law and economics.

point than a sign put up by an invisible airport authority saying "Meeting Point."

Complications arise in games in which the two outcomes that the two players are aspiring to get to, from their miserable current predicament, are not equally good for both players. Instead, there may be one outcome better for player 1 (say, the returns are 4 for player 1 and 3 for player 2) and another outcome better for player 2 (the returns are reversed). In such a situation player 1 saying "We will go to the first outcome" may not be quite as effective, since it was a foregone conclusion that player 1 would say so, and so it may be contested whether saying so will have any effect.

But when all players are symmetrically placed in all the superior outcomes, an announcement by one of the players, the lawmaker, can make for a compelling focal point since the announcer is a player who is saying what he or she will do in the periods that lie ahead, with no personal stake in it. In brief, the credibility of the lawmaker is on the line.[4]

What this hints at is a fascinating research agenda, to wit, the need for a model that encompasses not just the effect of a focal point but even the creation of the focal point. In other words, we may eventually wish not just to know what happens after the Meeting Point sign is posted in an airport but to model the person who posts that sign and the decision to post that sign. In brief, the *process* of law creation may matter and, done appropriately, may give the law a legitimacy it may not otherwise have.

The second model, which recognizes that the enactment of a law does have costs and so is like burning cash or money, is in some ways more tractable, though this ends up with a philosophical conundrum. Let me begin by supposing that the enactment of the law is costly for those engaged in this activity. But, after the law is enacted, it is like some ink on paper—it does not make any material difference to the subgame that follows. If, after the enactment,

4. This is closely connected to the idea of credibility of the autocrat or simply the government, on which depends a lot of what actually happens in a collectivity (Myerson, 2008; Schauer, 2015, chap. 7). In Myerson's formulation, it is more than a pointer to a preexisting equilibrium in the subgame ahead, but it is a device used by the autocrat to tie himself or herself down to a certain behavior in the future, because to deviate from a commitment is to lose credibility.

people do what they would have done without the law, they get the same payoffs. In other words, the law does not alter the game. How then can enacting the law, which is similar to burning money, alter the outcome of the game? The answer has to be by signaling something to other players about the future.

This is called forward induction in game theory. The power of forward induction is usually illustrated with the Battle of the Sexes (see Osborne and Rubinstein, 1994, chap. 6; Battigalli and Siniscalchi, 2002; Govindan and Wilson, 2009). Let me instead illustrate this with the Prisoner's Dilemma Game of Life I, as described in Chapter 3.

Suppose that before playing that game, player 1 has the choice of enacting a law that says that the citizens should choose A and the police, that is, player 3, should choose R. Actually, in this approach what the law says is unimportant. All that matters is the fact that enacting the law is costly to player 1, who, it is assumed here, is the lawmaker. Suppose the cost of enacting the law is 1 to player 1. Under this formulation we have a two-period game. In period 1, player 1 chooses to enact the law (burn money) or not do so, and then, in period 2, they play the Prisoner's Dilemma Game of Life I (PDGL).

This full game, in which the person who enacts the law is also a part of the game, will be called the Economy Game with Law Enactment and is illustrated as Game 4.3.

The game starts at the node ω, where player 1 chooses to do "Nothing" or "Enact," the latter inflicting a cost of 1 on player 1. Once this initial choice is made, players 1, 2 and 3 play the PDGL. The only difference between playing the PDGL after enactment and playing after doing nothing is that, after enactment, player 1 earns a payoff of 1 less than what he would have earned otherwise. This is the cost of enactment he has to bear—the burning of money. Hence, the three players playing (A, A, L) leads to the payoff of (7, 7, 0), if no law is enacted. But if the law is enacted, the same action triple leads to the payoff of (6, 7, 0).

How will this game be played? To answer this, note that if player 1 enacts the law, that is, burns money, it must be because he expects that by virtue of doing this the game will end up at (A, A, R) instead of (B, B, L). Burning money was worth it because it signals to the

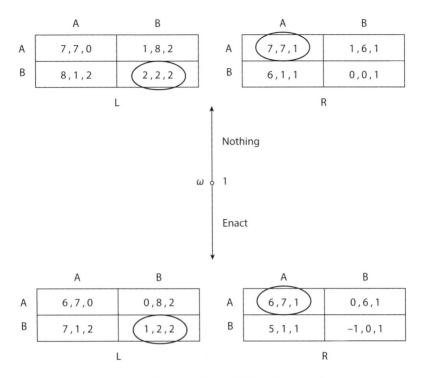

GAME 4.3. Economy Game with Law Enactment

other player that he is now expecting the game to go to (A, A, R). Hence, the law helps to take the economy to the Nash equilibrium outcome that is good for the citizens. The law in this case is very effective. Its role is purely that of signaling what the one who enacts the law will do and expects others to do, and this is a powerful driver of everybody's behavior.

This, in brief, is the signaling story. Practical men, wanting to get on in life and impatient with theorizing, would leave it at this. This is the reason why practical men are disappointing and end up often doing so poorly in life. There are many intriguing philosophical questions that arise with forward induction. And even if we are not able to resolve them, it is worthwhile being aware of them to inject the right dose of skepticism in our practical life and work.

One troubling question that quickly arises with the above kind of reasoning is the following: If burning money can take a player to his or her preferred equilibrium, why is it necessary to burn money? Even if he or she does not burn money, the fact that he or she *could* have done so should be enough to signal to others that that is where he or she is headed and so influence other people's behavior appropriately. In other words, this should automatically take the economy to the equilibrium outcome where the player who could have burned money is better off. It should not be necessary to enact the law. The mere fact that he or she could have enacted the law should be signal enough to influence other people's behavior.

A similar problem arises with rationality. There are games in which rationality being common knowledge is a disadvantage. It enables players to reason in a way that leads to a suboptimal outcome. The Traveler's Dilemma, described in Chapter 2, is an example of this. This gives rise to the following problem. If one of the players, before playing the Traveler's Dilemma, visibly burns a dollar note and then sits down to play the game, this should help with the outcome of the play in the Traveler's Dilemma. This is because such a display, burning money for no reason, is a clear sign of irrationality. And once we know the player is irrational, the logic that takes us to the suboptimal outcome, (2, 2), breaks down. The other player may then be tempted to play a higher number, and that would also be a reason for the first player to play a higher number and both may be better off.[5]

This gives rise to a rather deep problem. If you can do better by displaying irrationality, it is rational to be irrational. But in that case when a person acts irrationally, it should be clear to all that this person is behaving the way he or she does in order to get some advantage. Hence, it is rational to be irrational, which is a rather puzzling observation. This is at the heart of some paradoxes in game theory, and it is arguable that in certain complex situations the assumption of rationality being common knowledge may be meaningless (Basu, 1990; Reny, 1992; Dufwenberg and Essen, 2017).

This is a rather open-ended and troubling way to close the section, but I had warned the reader. The only consolation comes

---

5. There are many examples in industrial organization theory of this kind whereby it pays for someone to be irrational (see Basu, 1993). Likewise, in international relations, it is recognized that, on occasion, it is worthwhile for leaders to appear mad. Regrettably, for some leaders, this is not just a matter of appearance.

from the fact that even in mathematics, as I have already pointed out, there are open-ended issues concerning some of the founding assumptions, and this indeed has given rise to some troubling paradoxes. Despite that, we use mathematics and have had huge benefits from its use. It is in this spirit that we have to proceed with economics, game theory, and the analysis of law. We should continue to use our findings and research, while keeping our antennas on alert for the philosophical conundrums that lurk beneath, and keep up a parallel effort to resolve them. In the end, even the practice of science relies in part on our proclivity for superstition.

4.4 Life and Resurrection

The above discussion allows us to segue to another philosophical problem that arises in all practical applications of game-theoretic economics, and, by implication, in law and economics, and that we deal with, most of the time, by looking the other way. The question pertains to the meaning of "the game of life." This, as we have already seen, refers to a game that includes all the people and in which people can do whatever nature permits them to do. In the words of Mailath, Morris, and Postlewaite (2017, p. 33), "all possible actions he or she can take in every imaginable circumstance."[6] As Binmore (1995, p. 134) points out, the game of life is restricted by "nature's rules, which we have no choice but to obey," unlike "society's rules, which we usually do choose to obey, but could disobey."

When we wish to study the formation of institutions, such as social norms and customs or the law and practice of governance, it seems natural to start from the game of life and then try to understand how what we see has come to be (Binmore, 1995). And that is the approach adopted by Mailath, Morris, and Postlewaite (2017) and is what I have done above.[7]

The troubling question that arises with the game of life is whether it is at all a well-defined game. To be able to do a rigorous analysis and use formal equilibrium concepts, such as Nash or

---

6. I quote from the original working paper version of 2001.

7. By extension, this also applies to Ali and Liu (2017), since they also explicitly recognize that all laws are, in the end, enforced by other players.

subgame perfection, we need to have a well-defined game. Even if the set of players in the game of life is defined properly by including all human beings, there are important questions associated with the assertion that people can choose any action, with no restriction. Trouble stems from the fact that this is not just an ambiguous statement but one that can lead us into paradoxes and impossibilities.

Before turning to the paradoxical matter, there is a simpler point about whether it is right to treat all actions that are viable by the laws of physics or nature as part of an agent's feasible set. When we go to buy groceries, we calculate the aggregate price of what we want to buy, juggle different goods with different prices in our heads, but we (most of us, that is) do not even think about the costs and benefits of running away with another person's purchase or wallet. Our minds are programmed not to even consider this, though it is feasible by the laws of physics. Further, it is not as if it is the case that we do not run with another's wallet because optimization leads us to reject that option, but we simply do not consider it among the options.[8] Moreover, variants of this are true not just for human beings but also for animals. In handling horses, you are told not to stand behind them because they can kick, but it is fine to be near their mouths because they typically do not bite. It is not as if horses cannot bite, but just that they do not, even when they want to attack you. Examples of these kinds, namely, of actions that are physically feasible but are not even considered, create a practical problem in describing feasible sets of actions in the game of life.[9] This is because what is feasible and what is not feasible in this sense have an element of fuzziness and judgment. The only way to solve this problem is to make some assumptions by brute force.

The bigger problem, one that leads us head-on into a paradox, arises from the claim that in the game of life an agent is allowed to choose any conceivable action. This is akin to the problem that afflicted early set theory, which used the idea of a universal set, that is,

8. For further discussions on this, see Basu (1983, 2011a) and Myerson (2004).

9. It also shows that the distinction between behavioral economics models and realistically constructed neoclassical models may not be as sharp as often presumed, since what we describe as a feasible set may have its bounds defined by internalized morals.

the set of every conceivable thing, as the starting point. Operating on the basis of this assumption led to some celebrated paradoxes, such as the Russell paradox. Since the existence of a universal set, that is, a set of all objects, was treated as natural and, hence, beyond the purview of examination, it took logicians a while to realize that the Russell paradox was rooted in the implicit assumption of the existence of a set of everything.[10]

This carries over to the game of life and hence to our conceptualization of law and economics.[11] We cannot just assert that players can do anything because there is no such thing as anything. What we are forced to do therefore is to explicitly define the sets of actions available to each player and not just leave it to a hand-waving assertion that players can do anything. But this also means that we can always think of actions that exist beyond the specified feasible set but are not allowed to be used.

The way to get around this in building game-theoretic models of law and economics is what is done in modern set theory. We have to begin by specifying all the players and all the strategies open to them (and of course the payoff functions) and treat that as the game of life. What this means is that you cannot suddenly, in the middle of a game, resurrect a new player (the police or the judge) who was a dormant presence in the sidelines, or change the rules of the game, and add or subtract strategies, as used to be done in neoclassical law and economics.[12] I call this the "rule of resurrection."

10. The Russell paradox is easy to understand. From among the "set of everything," define a subset, X, consisting of all sets that are not elements of themselves. Now, is X an element of itself? If it is, then it is not an element of itself. If it is not an element of itself, then, by definition, it is an element of itself. What we have in hand is a logical impossibility. It is believed that this is rooted in the assumption that there is a set of everything. The paradox therefore shows that there cannot be a set of everything.

11. There seems to be little writing on these kinds of paradoxes in legal theory. For exceptions, see Hockett (1967) and Jain (1995).

12. What I am suggesting here is close to what Binmore (1995, p. 135) proposes: "Neither our empirical knowledge nor our theoretical apparatus is adequate for us to formulate and analyze the underlying game of life played by the agents we wish to study. If we hope to gain insights into the workings of institutions, we are therefore left with little choice but to invent tractable models of the game of life which we know perfectly well to be drastic simplifications of the real situation." The only possible difference with the line I take is that I believe we should do this not for reasons of feasibility but because the alternative is to run into a philosophical paradox.

In brief, when we describe a game of life we are asserting not that there is nothing conceivable beyond the feasible sets of strategies specified at the start but simply that no new strategies will be wished into existence or made to vanish in the middle of the game; and likewise no dormant player will be resurrected.

In the focal point approach to law and economics, as proposed in this book, this problem does not affect us precisely because we begin by specifying the actual game that is being played, instead of making arbitrary references to the game of life or the economy game. In, for instance, the different versions of the Prisoner's Dilemma Game of Life, described above, the full game is laid out at the outset, and so there is no ambiguity about the game itself, its rules, who the players are, or what they can do. We then *call* this the game of life. *Once this game is specified*, we are committed not to bring in new elements—players or actions—from the outside. In other words, the rule of resurrection is satisfied. This does not *solve* the paradox but allows us to skirt around it.

The consolation is that all formulations of law and economics, and maybe all disciplines, suffer from open questions pertaining to their foundations. Indeed, I believe that the problem of the universal set and, by implication, the game of life is unavoidable not just in building models but also in life.

Suppose your dinner host asks you a day before the dinner if there is anything you do not eat and you say, "Just crabs." Then, at dinner, the next evening, you find two blocks of wood on your plate and you hear your host say, "Enjoy." If you say you do not eat wood, your host could counter by pointing out that you did not then give the right answer the previous day. The problem arises from the unspecified universal set in the background. When asked what it is that you do not eat, there is an implicit set from which you have to choose your answer. Occasionally we run into a problem caused by this ambiguity of universal sets and because different people carry different universal sets in their heads. Contradictions of this kind do not necessarily mean that someone is a sloppy thinker or speaker but simply that our underlying universals are different. I believe that this is an insoluble problem and is the source of some of our cross-cultural conflicts and misunderstandings. The only hope is that this meta realization, to wit, that some of our conflicts have at their base this inevitable philosophical problem, could help mitigate some of their worse fallouts by making us more tolerant of one another.

Returning to law and economics, the above resolution of the problem implies that there will never be a final model. We can always bring more and more dimensions and complexities into the fold. Since I used the analogy of general equilibrium model in economics to describe what this book is trying to do for law and economics, it is worth pointing out that the same problem arises in general equilibrium. There is no such thing as the ultimate general equilibrium. After having constructed the general equilibrium model including all goods and services, we could go a step further and build into our model institutions, politics and sociology, the endogenous formation of social norms, and so on.

In Chapter 3, the focal point approach to law and economics treated all enforcers of the law, those I refer to as functionaries of the state, as part of the game, but it did not treat the act of creating the law as part of the game and left ambiguous who the people are who draft and announce laws. In this chapter, we expanded the scope a bit by bringing in the lawmaker as a player who was signaling what he or she intended do. But it is possible to go further and say that which law will be enacted is also endogenously determined. The scope is endless in general equilibrium economics and in the focal point approach to law and economics. The new approach therefore is best thought of as a starting point for a better understanding of society and the economy and not the final stop.

CHAPTER FIVE

Social Norms and the Law

5.1 Norms, Laws, and Beliefs

This chapter has two objectives. The analysis in the previous chapters brings us to the brink of an important question. Since *any* outcome in society that can be achieved by the use of laws, can be achieved without laws, by agents mimicking the behavior prescribed by the law, because such behavior, once adopted by all, becomes self-enforcing, is there any meaningful way to distinguish between the law and norms? The first aim of this chapter is to answer this in the affirmative. I will show that although behavior enforced by social norms and behavior enforced by the law are, at a fundamental level, the same, there is a sense in which we can distinguish between the two. I shall build up to this conclusion via a set of examples, which serve the second objective of this chapter. Much of the analysis thus far has been conducted in fairly abstract terms. But I want to demonstrate to the reader that the ideas apply to many of our real-life concerns. Multiple equilibria, focal points, and self-enforcing behavior are valuable ingredients for understanding important real-world phenomena. The three examples that I present in the next three sections, en route to an analysis of how we may distinguish between social norms and the law, serve this purpose.

The bulk of the discussion here will be based on the concept of social norms which are often referred to as "equilibrium-selection norms." The use of the adjective should warn readers that there are other kinds of social norms, which entail stepping beyond the conventional rational individual with exogenous preferences. Those other conceptualizations of social norms rely on what is best thought of as behavioral economics, in which we allow for social stigma, morals, envy, and other emotions, which textbook *Homo sapiens* are devoid of. For now all reference to norms will be to equilibrium-selection norms, which fit best in the standard economists' paradigm. We will have occasion to question this paradigm later and especially in Chapter 7.

Equilibrium-selection norms are essentially customs and social norms that are devices for people to coordinate their behaviors, that is to zoom in on a specific equilibrium, knowing that others will do the same, in contexts where there are many equilibria and so it is not evident a priori which one others may choose.[1] The simplest example concerns which side of the road to drive on. Consider a country with no law concerning this. Rural areas and villages in India do make for such a country, since no one enforces any traffic law in these places.

In such a situation there are two equilibria.[2] Everyone drives on the left and everyone drives on the right. Once one of these equilibria settles into place, it is in no one's interest to unilaterally deviate from it. This does not however help in deciding which of the two equilibria will occur. This is where social norms come in. A norm can play the role of creating a focal point. Once the norm is established (wherever it comes from) everybody knows which equilibrium is chosen by society and, by the definition of an equilibrium, it is then in every individual's own interest to adhere to it. In rural

1. The literature is now quite substantial. See, for instance, Akerlof (1976), Granovetter and Soong (1983), Platteau (1994), Schlicht (1998), Basu (2000), Cooter (2000), Posner (2000), Benabou and Tirole (2006), and Fisman and Miguel (2007). For an interesting exercise to understand how norms spill over and get transmitted, see Funcke (2016). An attempt of mine to classify different kinds of norms occurs in Basu (1998). For an early analysis from a legal theory perspective on how norms can trap groups in inefficient outcomes, see Posner (1996). For a recent exercise in *creating* social norms in the laboratory and studying their impact on illegal behavior, in this case bribery, see Abbink, Freidin, Gangadharan, and Moro (2016).

2. I am assuming people use pure strategies. Each person chooses to drive on either the left or the right.

Indian villages, where there is no effective law about which side one drives or plies one's bullock cart on, people do choose the left. This is a common custom that works like a focal point. It is not difficult to see where this rural driving custom comes from. The national law to drive on the left, enforced in cities, spills over as custom in villages. For those planning a first-time trip to India, I may slip in the warning not to take this too literally, and to please look out for the stray vehicle coming straight at you when you diligently drive on the left.

According to the focal point approach to the law introduced in the previous two chapters, the role of the law, in the final analysis, is nothing but the creation of a focal point. Hence, at one level, there seems to be little difference between law and social norm. There are economists and legal theorists who have stressed the role of focal point and related concepts in the enforcement of the law,[3] and so this question will arise in their approach as well. In his recent book McAdams (2015, p. 22) observes, "Because the law is full of requirements, we can easily miss its suggestive influence. . . . Some of the earliest and most informal game theory shows that, if individuals share an interest in *coordinating* their behavior, they tend to engage in the behavior they find mutually salient—the *focal point*. In these circumstances, I claim that law facilitates coordination by making a particular outcome salient." Some of these norms, he points out, echoing an idea first developed by Sunstein (1996b), could be engineered by the "norm entrepreneur," who, like the lawmaker, steers society toward a particular behavior outcome by making it salient.

Eric Posner's (2000) book, which also provides an explicitly game-theoretic approach to law and economics, makes clear the similarities between law and social norms: "In a world with no law and rudimentary government, order of some sort would exist. . . . The order would appear as routine compliance with social norms and the collective infliction of sanctions on those who violate them, including stigmatization of the deviant and the ostracism of the incorrigible" (Posner, 2000, p. 3).

---

3. See Sugden (1995), McAdams (2000), Myerson (2004), Hadfield and Weingast (2014), Hadfield (2016).

I shall however argue that there are some critical differences between the legal theorist's approach and the focal point approach that is being advocated here, even though both are rooted in game theory, in their use of the concept of the focal point. To give the reader a preview of the problem, I may point out that the difference between my approach and that of the legal theorist is captured by the qualifier "In these circumstances" in the quote from McAdams in the paragraph above the previous one. In the view developed in this book, this qualifier is uncalled for; the law does nothing else but enable coordination by creating focal points. This is unconditionally true.

It is useful to begin by elaborating the above idea of social norms, focal points, and multiple equilibria because it is related in an interesting way to ideas on law and focal point discussed in previous chapters and also because it enables me to illustrate how some of the ideas developed in the abstract in the previous chapters can be used to address practical, real-life problems. I consider three examples, pertaining to, respectively, punctuality, discrimination, and labor market practices.

5.2 Social Norms and Multiple Equilibria: Punctuality

Social norms play an important role in determining how societies behave. This received little attention in mainstream economics, at least before the advent of game theory. This is not difficult to understand. In order to facilitate a logically tight and streamlined analysis, economics was built on the assumption of individuals trying to maximize the apples, oranges, guns, and butter they acquire for themselves, and showed how an amazing amount of what happens in our economic lives can be explained by this. This was an exciting project, of immense intellectual force. The mistake that many mainstream economists made was that, having banished other human emotions to the sidelines for ease of analysis, they forgot that those emotions existed in reality.

Illustrations of the power of social norms had cropped up repeatedly in anthropological writings, which marveled at the level of organization some primitive societies had achieved even without the apparatus of any formal law and state machinery to back it up.[4] Fortunately, as game theory became a part of the methodology of economics, it became possible to take on some of the broader questions pertaining to norms without abandoning rigor. For one, the ubiquity of multiple equilibria became apparent (see Hoff and Stiglitz, 2001; Samuelson, 2016) and the natural question arose about how societies navigate through these. Room had to be made for conventions and norms.

Let me illustrate how these models work with the example of punctuality. Successful coordination in time is critical for modern economic life.[5] Yet, when Jorgen Weibull and I undertook our study (Basu and Weibull, 2003) we quickly discovered that the subject, while extensively studied by sociologists and social psychologists, had been rarely analyzed by economists. This social science literature noted with some data and anthropological studies what we would expect, namely, that punctuality norms differ greatly and systematically across societies, nations, and even genders. The residents of Brazil are less punctual than the residents of the United States (Levine, West, and Reis, 1980). A study of student attendance record in Rushville, Indiana, in 1928–29 showed that boys are more often late than girls but girls, when they are late, are more late than boys, and so on. These studies often found that in societies where people are less punctual, watches and clocks are less well coordinated in terms of the times they show.[6] Levine, West, and Reis (1980), for instance, actually examined watches in Brazil and the United States, and conjectured that the reason Brazilians are less punctual than North

4. One of the most celebrated such writings is the book by Gluckman (1955). India's caste system is a good example of a custom working with the tenacity of a well-enforced law (Deshpande, 2011). For a discussion of how lineage structures facilitated the organization of rural life, see He, Pan, and Sarangi (2017). An interesting discussion of such informal laws occurs in Malinowski (1921), in one of his rare publications in an economics journal. Akerlof's (1976) model of India's caste system also belongs to this genre of writing and it was, for me, an important motivation for some of my own work in political economy (Basu, 1986, 2000). See also Zambrano (1999). This does not negate the fact that some seemingly informal social phenomena are made possible by state action and the law, Rothstein's (2017) study of racial segregation being a striking example.

5. For an engaging essay on the creation of global time standards, see Barrett (2007, chap. 6).

6. We are of course not talking of the digital era in which our watches and handheld instruments are often centrally coordinated.

Americans is that "public clocks and personal watches are less accurate in Brazil than in the United States." Some may wish to contest the suggested causal link, but the correlation is indeed quite striking.

When doing this research I was curious about whether watches in India were, like in Brazil, poorly coordinated. I was disappointed that I could not find data. However, while I was doing this research, I traveled to India and on arrival in Delhi, a man strode up to me and asked for the time using a phraseology which, I had forgotten, is common in India: "Excuse me, sir, can you tell me the time by your watch?" At that moment I realized I did not need data because I had just found anthropological evidence. The fact that "by your watch" had seeped into common linguistic practice was evidence that time in India, like in Brazil, was watch-dependent.

While history, climate, and many other factors probably contributed to societal differences in punctuality, we reached the interesting conclusion that it is also in part a matter of an equilibrium-selection norm. Less punctual societies were simply caught in a less punctual equilibrium. There need be no fundamental difference between two societies exhibiting different behaviors. Without going into the full details of the model, the basic argument is easy to see and also a good illustration of how equilibrium-selection norms work by creating focal points.

Punctuality is one behavior where doing it alone is not of much use. If a meeting is to start and needs a quorum, how much effort you will want to put in toward being on time depends on how punctual you expect others to be. In a society known to be tardy, it is not worthwhile for you to unilaterally put in the effort to be punctual since the meeting cannot start with you alone. Likewise, if you are meeting someone for a game of tennis or meeting a school friend to do your homework together. Hence, punctuality and tardiness are, in essence, social norms. Two fundamentally identical societies can exhibit very different kinds of behavior.

This is easy to formalize with a simple model. Suppose two persons plan to meet at 8 AM. For a person to be punctual means showing up at or before 8. By unpunctuality I mean a behavior of showing up at or before 8 with probability p (< 1) and being late, say, showing up at 8:30, with probability $1 - p$. If the meeting starts on time (instead of half an hour late) each player gets a benefit of B

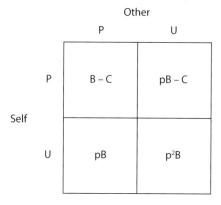

Other

	P	U
P	B – C	pB – C
U	pB	p²B

Self

GAME 5.1. The Game of Punctuality

units. Being punctual is, however, costly to the person involved. You may have to take the earlier train or you may have to stop reading the crime thriller to make sure that you are there by 8 AM. Simply put, being punctual entails a cost C (> 0) to the person.

It is now obvious that the two individuals are locked in a game that is described below. Think of yourself as choosing between rows and the other person as choosing between columns. Each of you has to choose to be punctual (P) or unpunctual (U). Since this is a symmetric game, I just display your payoffs (Game 5.1).

If both players choose P clearly the meeting will start on time. You will get B for that but lose C for the effort you have to put into being punctual. This explains the payoff of (B – C) in the top left-hand corner. If one of you two is punctual, the probability of the meeting starting on time is p. If you are unpunctual you do not expend the cost of being punctual, but if you are punctual you entail a cost of C. This explains the payoffs of pB and pB – C in the payoff matrix. I leave it to the reader to verify that if both are unpunctual, each earns a payoff of p^2B.

Since, p is less than 1, it is entirely possible for the following to be true:

$$B(1 - p) > C > pB(1 - p). \tag{1}$$

Suppose that is the case. Then, clearly,

$$B - C > pB \qquad (2)$$

and

$$p^2B > pB - C. \qquad (3)$$

Now, (2) implies if the other person is punctual, you are better off being punctual; and (3) says, if the other person is tardy, you are better off tardy. In other words, this game has two Nash equilibria: both players being punctual and both being tardy or unpunctual.

This is where the norm comes in. If you are in a society where it is the norm to be punctual, you have reason to expect that your meeting partner will show up on time. And for that reason, you will choose P. Likewise in a society where the norm is tardiness. The social norm is nothing but a convention that helps you to guess what the other is likely to do. Punctuality does not have to be a hardwired human trait or a genetic proclivity. It is a response to the social environment.[7]

One of the most striking examples of the relevance of the above model comes from recent history. Here is a report on a European visitor's description of the atrocious punctuality norm in the country he was visiting in early twentieth century (I present the quote deliberately, for the moment, blocking the name of the country):

---

7. I recall making an appointment to meet with the eminent economist and Nobel laureate Arthur Lewis in Princeton in the late 1980s. Not wanting to keep him waiting, I made sure I was there outside his office well in time. He was not well, and his wife, who had kept him company, opened the door and let me in. I vividly remember his first sentence: "You Indians are so punctual." It threw me off for a moment, coming from a country notoriously easygoing about time. I wondered, was he, in his old age, confusing Indians with Japanese? I soon realized his reference point was Indians in the United States, working in Silicon Valley, in hospitals, and in universities. They had, indeed, shed their old custom and responded to their surroundings and had become punctual, as the above game would predict. Even in India, during my nearly three years' work in government, 2009–12, I felt, at least in New Delhi, that punctuality norms were rapidly improving. It is difficult to say quite what was causing this, but in government offices punctuality had clearly improved compared to what one was familiar with even a decade or two earlier. Some of this happens because of "norm entrepreneurs" in the sense of Sunstein (1996b); a few top leaders can initiate such a change often by setting an example through their own behavior.

In his published memoir, Kattendyke (a Dutchman visiting the country) cited a series of events to illustrate the frustrating slowness of the nation. For example, the supplies necessary to make repairs, which he had specifically ordered to be delivered at high tide, did not arrive on time; one worker showed up just once and never returned. . . . Kattendyke's frustrations were in fact shared by most of the foreign engineers in the country. . . . They often found themselves vexed by the work habits of the locals, and the main reason for their vexation was the apparent lack of any sense of time. To these foreigners, the locals worked with an apparent indifference to the clock. (Hashimoto, 2008, p. 124)

The unpunctual country being described above is Japan, arguably the world's most punctual society today—some would argue over-punctual—with individuals incurring excessive personal cost to avoid the shame of tardiness. It therefore comes as a surprise to learn that this was not the case in 1857-8 when Kattendyke visited Nagasaki. The above description of Japan makes it clear that there is little difference between Japan of a century and a half ago and the most tardy nations of today; and it also suggests that punctuality is not something written in the DNA of the Japanese but a socially acquired norm, which is now rational for individuals to adhere to.[8]

5.3 Discrimination as Focal Point

Group discrimination is an ancient phenomenon and, likewise, its analysis by economists also has a long history. An important role was played by Becker's (1971) analysis, which gave a salient role to people's innate preference for one group over another. With the rise of information economics, there were new explanations that relied not on innate preferences but on signaling and statistical discrimination (Becker, 1957; Phelps, 1972; Arrow, 1973, 1998; Stiglitz, 1973, 1974). Statistical discrimination is a powerful concept that can explain a lot of reality but can, at the same time, be morally

---

8. In his essay "Punctuality Pays," James Surowiecki (2004) writes about Ecuador's attempt to make the switch from "Ecuador time" to a nation that is punctual, overnight on October 1, 2003. The idea was exactly as in our model, to wit, that punctuality is a collective trait that is worthwhile if everybody effects the switch together. Such a gestalt switch however is not easy. More than a decade later, Ecuador remains largely on Ecuador time.

troublesome. It entails developing opinions about individuals based on the statistical qualities of the group that the person belongs to. This is a subject in which legal scholars have also taken considerable interest (Cooter, 1994; McAdams, 1995).[9]

A fascinating new way of understanding group discrimination can be developed by using the idea of focal points and norms. The model that I am about to sketch, based on Basu (2017), illustrates some of the diverse manifestations of equilibrium-selection social norms. Some of these happen in such subtle ways, as in this model, that we are often not aware of them. This particular topic, group discrimination, is enormously important in understanding today's world and some of our strife and troubles.[10]

Discrimination against certain groups of people has occurred in different societies and throughout history.[11] India's caste system, with its attendant practice of intolerance and effort to marginalize large groups of people, is a pernicious example, as is the history of apartheid in South Africa and of racial discrimination and slavery in the United States.[12] From an analyst's point of view, they are troubling because norms and the law merge into each other. Some of these heinous practices were explicitly backed by the law, as in

9. For an excellent summary of issues that arise in law and economics pertaining to group discrimination, see Posner (2000, chap. 8).

10. This is part of a literature dealing with the larger subject of group identity in which economists have recently taken interest (Kuran, 1998; Varshney, 2002; Genicot and Ray, 2003; Basu, 2005; Sen, 2006; Esteban and Ray, 2008; Akerlof and Kranton, 2010; Morita and Servatka, 2013; Mukherjee, 2015; Landa, 2016; Ray and Esteban, 2017). Identity can be remarkably sticky, allowing generations that may be dead and gone to influence the identity of new members (Tirole, 1996).

11. The extent of group discrimination in a society depends on how we measure. This raises questions that straddle statistics and ethics, as discussed comprehensively by Subramanian (2011). What is interesting about this paper is that it recognizes that discrimination can have some redeeming features as well, which have to do with externalities. This does not mean that we have to tolerate discrimination, but it does mean that we have to be aware of some critical trade-offs.

12. It is important to recognize that social history shapes the character of individuals. As Durlauf (2001) points out, one can see the influence of the plague on the subsequent Athenian "character." In traditional economics, individual choice is shaped by market-based interaction. But for a broader understanding of human behavior, including the formation of group identity, it is important to understand the influence of social interaction on individual choice. Social-interaction-based models can, in principle, be used to model the behavior of groups rather than the single individual (Blume and Durlauf, 2003).

the case of South African apartheid and US slavery. At other times, such as with India's caste system, while it is not backed by the law, its social code is so well structured and so well enforced that it calls into question whether we can draw a meaningful distinction between the law and custom.

As a mirror image of this, we often see certain groups benefiting from discrimination in their favor. This has been true of males through long stretches of history and even now in most societies. Similarly, in the United States or in India during colonial times, if you could choose your skin color, I would strongly recommend white. Where do these discriminatory preferences come from? While in reality they can have many sources, I want to present to the reader a rather vexing explanation whereby discrimination has no innate origins,[13] but is a pure product of the free market and the compulsions of economics. It immediately alerts us to the fact that even if this discrimination is not caused by the law, we may need the law and intervention in the market to negate it.

To understand this consider the important research by Bertrand and Mullainathan (2004), which demonstrates the presence of racial bias in labor markets.[14] When we see discrimination, the question always arises as to whether it is innate bias or something else that correlates with race or gender or caste, and so creates the chimera of bias. Thus if an employer hires more whites than blacks, is it really a preference for whites, or is it merely a reflection of the fact that the employer needs PhDs and white job applicants are more likely to have PhDs? Bertrand and Mullainathan tried to set up controls for this by sending out job applications with fictitious

13. The possible lack of innate origin is captured beautifully in Tom Stoppard's *The Real Thing* (1982, pp. 57–58):
Billy: You approve of the class system?
Annie: You mean on trains or in general?
Billy: In general....
Annie: There's no system. People group together when they've got something in common. Sometimes its religion, and sometimes it's... being at Eton.... There's nothing really *there*—it's just the way you see it. Your perception.
Billy: Bloody brilliant. There's people who've spent their lives trying to get rid of the class system, and you've done it without leaving your seat.
14. See also Thorat and Newman (2007), Reuben, Sapienza, and Zingales (2014), Thorat, Banerjee, Mishra, and Rizvi (2015).

resumes to help-wanted advertisements that had appeared in Chicago and Boston newspapers.

Their experiment revealed that, controlling for all other things, candidates with white names were far more likely to get callbacks for interviews than those with black names. There were striking results such as having a typical white name being equivalent to 8 years of work experience with a typically black name. In brief, they had engineered the celebrated "ceteris paribus" condition that traditional economists so often talked about but were seldom able to demonstrate. And the findings were striking.

What I do in Basu (2017) is to cast doubt on this necessarily demonstrating racial bias. It may, but it also may not. When the latter happens, it is disturbing in a different way; it shows that discrimination can arise naturally, out of the free market, and then take roots in our beliefs. It is a focal point. Let me explain.

For most tasks in life, to conduct them effectively you need to successfully do other tasks. If you work for a firm's sales department to promote sales, you need to be able to successfully interact with buyers' groups and delivery services units. If the buyers' groups and delivery services units shun you, you will not be able to properly do your sales work. And of course the problem is similar for the buyers' group. When they reach out to you they know they will get better services from you if you are trusted and used by the sales department and the delivery services unit. Likewise for the delivery services unit. They have to gauge how successful you will be with the sales department and the buyers' group. This is where the name acquires significance beyond pure racial preference. If you feel Emily—a common white name—is more likely to do your task more effectively, you will prefer to hire Emily over Lakisha. If all three units do that, this becomes self-fulfilling. The white name provides a focal point in a labor market for tasks that exhibit "strategic complementarity"—economists' term for work in which being involved in one task raises your productivity in another.

The basic idea, which shows the relation between discrimination and focal point, can be illustrated with a simple example. Suppose there are two entrepreneurs, 1 and 2, who have the need for certain tasks to be done, and there are n (> 2) service operators or laborers who can do these tasks. Suppose, for instance, entrepreneur 1 needs a person to look after his lawn—buy and apply fertilizer, sow seeds, mow the lawn, and so on—and entrepreneur 2 wants to lend money to someone. The person who is able to borrow the money can buy fertilizers and seeds easily and so do the lawn work better. If entrepreneur 2 manages to lend to a person who gets the lawn work contract, he or she will be more likely to pay back the loan with the agreed interest. What the entrepreneurs may not know is the underlying causation of what makes a laborer more productive, namely, that if both reach out to the same laborer they get better value. This is not unlikely in a real setting where thousands of entrepreneurs reach out to hundreds of thousands of laborers. They realize some are more productive than others and may search for markers of that without quite knowing the fundamental model that drives this.

The above paragraph may be summed up as follows. Each entrepreneur picks one citizen for the task he needs to get done. If he picks a citizen who is not picked by the other entrepreneur, he gets a benefit of x and if he picks someone the other entrepreneur also picks he gets y. Given what we said about strategic complementarity,

$$y > x. \tag{4}$$

The entrepreneurs are not aware of this strategic complementarity. All they know is that they may get x or y, without being aware of what drives the difference. The only critical assumption in this exercise is (4). All other structures of the model can be varied and we will still get the same essential result. I should clarify that I am not claiming that strategic complementarity is always the case but simply that it is realistic in many situations and, when that happens, a kind of discrimination occurs that requires no innate bias and no differences in ability or skill across groups and arises entirely through natural market processes.

To convert this to a game that can help us understand discrimination, we need to put in a little more structure to the model. Assume that the n laborers are of two races: w (> 1) of them are whites and b (> 1) are blacks. Hence w + b = n.

Each entrepreneur, in selecting a laborer to get his or her task done, uses one of the following rules: no discrimination (strategy N), discrimination in favor of whites (strategy W), and discrimination in favor of blacks (strategy B). If they choose N, it means they randomly pick one of the n citizens, with 1/n probability of each citizen being chosen. If they choose W, it means each white person faces a probability 1/w of being selected.

It is easy to work out the payoffs of the two entrepreneurs depending on the choice each of them makes. This is displayed in the payoff matrix described below, in the Discrimination Game (Game 5.2a). Since it is completely symmetric, there is no need to show the payoffs of both entrepreneurs. I show the payoff earned by entrepreneur 1.

To understand the payoff, let us check the top left-hand box. Both entrepreneurs choose N, that is, pick a laborer with no attention to race. After you have chosen, the probability that the other person will choose the same laborer is 1/n. When that happens, you get a payoff of y. The probability that the other entrepreneur will choose someone else is $(n - 1)/n$. When that happens you get x. So your expected payoff is $y/n + x(n - 1)/n$. It is easy to work out the payoffs in the other boxes by similar reasoning.

It is simple to check that this game has three equilibria: (N, N), (B, B), (W, W), that is, no one discriminates, everybody discriminates in favor of blacks, and everybody discriminates in favor of whites. To see this, note that if the other person chooses N, no matter what you do you will get the same payoff. So you cannot do better by unilaterally deviating from N. Next check that, as long as y exceeds x, as we have already assumed, and given that, by definition, $n > w$:

$$y/w + x(w - 1)/w > y/n + x(n - 1)/n,$$

and

$$y/w + x(w - 1)/w > x.$$

In other words, if others discriminate in favor or whites, whites will be on average more productive and so it is in your interest to choose a white to do your task. In other words, (W, W) is an equilibrium. It is easy to check that (B, B) is an equilibrium as well.

(a)

	N	W	B
N	$\dfrac{y}{n}+\dfrac{x(n-1)}{n}$	$\dfrac{y}{n}+\dfrac{x(n-1)}{n}$	$\dfrac{y}{n}+\dfrac{x(n-1)}{n}$
W	$\dfrac{y}{n}+\dfrac{x(n-1)}{n}$	$\dfrac{y}{w}+\dfrac{x(w-1)}{w}$	x
B	$\dfrac{y}{n}+\dfrac{x(n-1)}{n}$	x	$\dfrac{y}{b}+\dfrac{x(b-1)}{b}$

(b)

	N	W	B
N	5/4 , 5/4	5/4 , 5/4	5/4 , 5/4
W	5/4 , 5/4	3/2 , 3/2	1 , 1
B	5/4 , 5/4	1 , 1	3/2 , 3/2

GAME 5.2. (a) The Discrimination Game
(b) The Discrimination Game: A Special Case

For those with an aversion to symbols, let me convert Game 5.2a to a society in which there are 4 citizens, 2 whites and 2 blacks. And suppose $y = 2$ and $x = 1$. By inserting these values, the discrimination game collapses into the special case illustrated in Game 5.2b.

The three equilibria are now obvious. If others discriminate, you had better do the same. As always in games with many equilibria, there is need for a focal point for players to coordinate their behavior. What I am claiming is that in markets with strategic complementarity, race or gender or caste can be the focal point.[15] It is important only because others think it is important. You prefer Emily to Lakisha not because you have a preference for a white over a black but because all entrepreneurs need to zero in on some group.

One important implication of this is that the popular view that if you leave it all to the market, with no government regulations and intervention, discrimination will go away, is not valid. Discrimination arises from the free market. If you want to stop discrimination, you may, in fact, need regulation, and conscious affirmative action. And when we go for affirmative action we must not indulge in the politically correct banter, so often heard, that by doing affirmative action you do not hurt your returns. The truth is that your returns may indeed be diminished by such action. The appeal has to be that, even if your return drops, there are certain actions in life that ought to be indulged in for their innate moral goodness. Affirmative action is one of those.

The model opens up some fascinating policy questions. It should be evident in the above model that GDP or the aggregate payoff earned by all is higher when there is group discrimination.[16] Since a certain amount of multitasking enhances productivity, it is better to have a subset of population multitask rather than spread work thinly across all individuals. With this in mind, note that there are two ways of achieving an equitable distribution of incomes or payoffs. The first is straightforward affirmative action. Compel employers to choose a diverse workforce so that the total work is spread equitably across individuals. The second is to let a limited number of people do all the work and then tax them and give subsidies to those who did not get work. The latter will give a higher per capita income since the workforce (that is the people who find work) will be more productive. Some may rule out the latter on the ground

15. I am calling this "focal point," while aware that to develop this idea formally we may have to use some kind of a set-valued concept of the focal as discussed in Chapter 4.

16. This is admittedly a static analysis of discrimination and efficiency. Recent research involving dynamics shows there can be unexpected links between the size of the cake and its division. In a recent model involving macrodynamics, Giraud and Grasselli (2017) develop a model in which greater inequality can lead to a larger pie, but this gives rise to a dynamic whereby the economy invariably reaches a critical point where there is a collapse resulting in a radical shrinking of the pie.

that work gives people dignity, and one getting the same ultimate income but without having to work causes a diminished sense of self.

I have never been persuaded by this argument. Through history there have been the leisure classes—the British landed aristocracy, the Indian *Zamindars*—who did precious little work and lived lives of luxury, and there is no evidence of them feeling diminished by the experience. What people need is a sense of legitimacy for what they do and earn. In a world where either one group or the other gets to work and there is no essential a priori difference between the two groups, for one group to work and the other to be subsidized seems like a legitimate strategy.

There is no need to resolve the policy dilemma here, but I want to point out that regular, relatively unskilled work is steadily shrinking in the world. The share of GDP that accrues to workers as aggregate wage bill in society has been falling steadily in all high- and middle-income countries from 1975 onward (Karabarbounis and Neiman, 2014; Basu, 2016b). Hence, we have to face up to the challenge of whether we forcefully distribute the limited work thinly across the entire labor force (thereby impairing productivity) or let a few people work (and be productive) and then tax their earnings to subsidize the others.

This focal point model of discrimination can be put to other uses as well. Consider the idea of deliberately promoting the belief that a certain group is in some sense better and more productive than others in order to promote that group's self-interest. Indeed, people have done so. In everyday life we look for signals of one group being better than another. Alumni associations and fraternities often promote the college or frat label. Berkeley students are better than others, Cornell graduates are more productive than some other group (this one happens to be true), and so on. People do pick up these kinds of ideas, and once the ideas become a norm, they can be self-fulfilling because they serve as a focal point.

Most of us, human beings, have multiple identities, race, nationality, language group, ethnicity, gender, and so on (see Sen, 2006, for discussion). Now, if you want to deliberately nurture the view that one of these identities is a mark of greater productivity, this model suggests it may be worthwhile to pick on a group that is less populous than a large group.

To see this, consider the payoff an entrepreneur gets from the equilibrium in favor of whites. This is given by $[y + (w - 1)x]/w$. And the equilibrium in which blacks are favored is given by $[y + (b - 1)x]/b$. Let us call the former whincome, and the latter blincome. Recall $b = n - w$. Now, it is easy to see, as w becomes smaller, whincome rises and blincome falls. Both (W, W) and (B, B) are still Nash equilibria, but the former becomes more and more dominant as the white population becomes smaller. In brief, if you want to promote the idea that a particular group you belong to is more productive, you will be better off if you choose a small group. Among other things, this explains why raising the profile of women is such a hard task. They constitute roughly half the population.

Considering the case of nationalities, if you promote the idea that the British are more productive or the idea that Chinese are more productive and people buy into this belief, the British will turn out to be even more productive. There is surprise expressed in the fact that Britain, a small nation, once virtually ruled the world. What is being argued here is that this is not surprising.[17]

In closing the section, I want to remind the reader that while this focal point model of discrimination is important, as with all theory, to take it to the real world and to put it to use, we must enrich it with our common sense and reasoned intuition.[18] Hence, the above theory must be combined with other ideas and our own experience before it is put to use. It is, for instance, worth reminding ourselves that productivity and even intelligence are dependent on how a person is treated, the view that society takes on this person's group identity. Even if the discrimination is purely a focal point at work, it can leave scars on people, making the ones believed to be less intelligent actually so.[19] Unlike in a strategic game where a

17. Taking the analysis to the limit may suggest that each person should form a one-person group. A fuller model would recognize that most observers are not able to carry such granular information. Hence there will be limits to how small the groups can be.

18. It is not a matter to go into here, but this reference to common sense and "reasoned intuition" is not a casual side remark. I have argued at length elsewhere that for science to be useful we must combine it with these skills. Pure analysis of data or pure theory cannot help us help the world till we combine them with reasoned intuition (Basu, 2014).

19. Among the most notable findings on this are studies by Shih, Pittinsky, and Ambady (1999), and Hoff and Pande (2006). See also Hoff and Stiglitz (2015) and World Bank (2015).

switch from one equilibrium to another can be effected in the twin-kling of an eye, in reality these changes are likely to take time and entail interventions that involve economics and social psychology.

The above exercise also raises some important questions con-cerning the meaning of statistical information and the morality of using it to form judgments about individuals. These are interesting matters but not central to the thesis of this monograph. I shall re-turn to address them briefly in the last chapter.

5.4 Child Labor and the Law

There are many other areas of economics where multiple equilibria crop up in natural ways (Hoff and Stiglitz, 2001; Bowles, Durlauf, and Hoff, 2006; Barrett, Garg, and McBride, 2016). In all these cases people's beliefs play a critical role in determining what out-come we will see in society, which raises a slew of important ques-tions about the possibly unusual role of law.

India's age-old caste norms and their powerful grip on society is a topic on which anthropologists and sociologists have writ-ten extensively. Economists have written less on it,[20] but with the profession's artillery of equilibrium analysis, economists are able to take on an important question. Is the caste system, for what-ever reason, hardwired into the Indian mind, or the outcome of rational individual response, seemingly rocklike, but at the same time actually founded on nothing but beliefs, rather like the hand of the law? Akerlof (1976) pointed out that caste practices could be a self-fulfilling equilibrium. Consider, for instance, the dreadful practice of untouchability. Why did upper caste people ostracize the untouchables? Is it possible that they did so for fear that, if they did not, they would in turn be ostracized by others in society?

But why would others ostracize the upper caste person who did not ostracize the untouchables? The answer is that they in turn believe that if someone does not ostracize someone who does not ostracize someone who hobnobs with untouchables, they would in turn be ostracized. With a little bit of modeling it can be shown that

---

20. See Deshpande (2011) for a comprehensive review of caste and economics in con-temporary India.

such behavior constitutes an equilibrium in a society with multiple equilibria.[21] In other words, we do not need anything hardwired into our genes or even the psyche for such social practices to occur. Of course, any practice that has existed for a long time does influence habits of thought and can result in mechanical behavior instead of a rational response. But the origins of such practices lie in human beliefs and equilibrium response. These explanations of unseemly social practices are, at one level, more benign but, at another, more disturbing because they show how they can occur in any society and, once they get a hold, they can be as oppressive as a structure set in bricks and mortar.

The argument is powerful because it applies widely, from bullying in school yards, caused by peer pressure, through political oppression, such as in totalitarian states, and during the McCarthy period in the United States, and to understand free speech in society, all subjects of the next chapter.

Let me here illustrate the plausibility of multiple equilibria with an example, that is, in analytical terms, simpler but with huge practical implications. This pertains to child labor. The persistence of child labor has been a source of much contention, with calls for legal intervention and state action. While writing on this subject in a popular vein (in the *New York Times*, October 29, 1994), it occurred to me that, in some societies, child labor could be a manifestation of multiple equilibria. The argument is surprisingly simple. It is based on one critical assumption that in Basu and Van (1998) was called the "luxury axiom." It asserts that parents send children to work only when they are driven to it by poverty. More formally, child leisure or child schooling is a "luxury good"; parents cannot indulge in it until the household is above a certain minimal level of income. The assumption was made in response to the popular belief that child labor was an outcome of (1) employer greed (they wanted the cheapest possible labor to get their unskilled work done) and (2) parental sloth (they would merrily send their children to work

---

21. I do this, in the context of political economy, in Basu (2000) and go further and show that it can be a subgame perfect equilibrium. In the next chapter I sketch a model of political power that uses the same logic. This is part of a larger literature on triadic interactions. See also Hatlebakk (2002), Villanger (2005), Yang (2014), and Han (2016).

for a little extra income). In the *New York Times* article, I agreed with the first and contested the second, and in the formal analytical work done with Pham Hoang Van, codified the objection to (2) in the form of the "luxury axiom."

The luxury axiom implies that if adult wages are very low, as often happens in developing countries, parents are forced to send their children to work to ensure that the household has survival income. But the children supplying work in the labor market can in turn be a cause of adult wages being low, since child labor is a substitute for adult labor for unskilled work; and so with many children out looking for work, adult wages get bid down. This has an interesting implication. If child labor is legally banned, then with children withdrawing their labor, adult wages could rise since the employers have to compete for the more limited aggregate labor available on the market. It is then possible, again by the luxury axiom, that if adult wages were that high to start with, parents would not have sent the children out to work in the first place.

This argument shows that labor markets in some countries could have at least two equilibria—one in which wages are low and children work and that in turn keeps the wages low, and one in which wages are high and so children do not work, and that, in turn, keeps the wages high.[22]

Now we are in a similar situation as in the case of punctuality and discrimination. In a class of developing economies, if the social norm develops of sending children to work, wages will be low and that will reinforce the decision to send the children work. If on the other hand the norm develops of not sending children to work, wages will be high and it will be in the interest of the parents (remember the luxury axiom) not to send their children to work.

Let me formalize this argument[23] with a model, which, for those interested, is easy to modify and use in different ways.

22. The parametric conditions under which multiple equilibria occur can be worked out by constructing formal theoretical models (see, for instance, Basu and Van, 1998; Basu, 2005; Doepke and Zilibotti, 2005). The theory, as originally construed, was not of a game model but a competitive equilibrium model; but it should be possible to create a related game-theoretic model that exhibits multiple equilibria.

23. This argument, unlike in the past two sections, is not based solely on a game since it uses one feature of competitive equilibrium analysis, namely, that firms and individuals are subject to price-taking behavior.

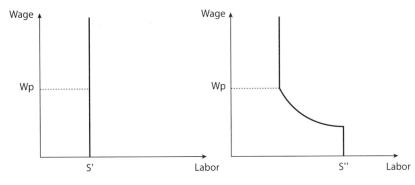

FIGURE 5.1. Child Labor: Demand

Suppose, for ease of analysis, adults always work, no matter what the wage. This will mean the household's adult labor supply curve will look like the vertical line in the left panel of Figure 5.1. No matter what the wage, the adults in the household supply S' units. Let an income of Y_p denote extreme poverty for the household. Define w_p such that $Y_p = S' \times w_p$. The left panel in Figure 5.1 shows w_p. Hence, w_p denotes an adult wage such that once wages go below this, the household faces extreme poverty and would prefer to send their children to work. This is what the luxury axiom says. This means that the household's supply curve of labor will look as shown in the right-hand panel of Figure 5.1, where S" denotes the total labor available in the household, that is, adults plus children.

The exact nature of the supply curve will of course vary from one economy to another, but what is interesting is that an enormous amount of empirical research confirmed that the luxury axiom is valid and so the broad feature of the supply curve, whereby for sufficiently low wages we have a backward-bending segment, as in the right-hand panel of Figure 5.1, is valid.[24]

If all households have such a supply curve, the aggregate supply curve of labor in the economy will be similarly shaped. This is depicted as line S in Figure 5.2. What is now obvious is that, if we

24. The empirical literature on child labor is enormous. See, for instance, Ray (2000), Emerson and Souza (2003), Cigno and Rosati (2005), Edmonds and Schady (2012), Bhardwaj, Lakdawala, and Li (2013), Humphries (2013), Del Carpio, Loayza, and Wada (2016), and Menon and Rogers (2017).

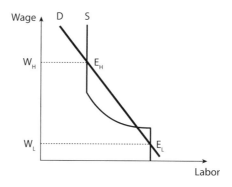

FIGURE 5.2. Child Labor: Equilibria

have a regular, downward-sloping demand curve for labor, there can be multiple equilibria, that is, wage rates where the demand for labor equals supply. In Figure 5.2, we show the two stable equilibria, depicted by E_H and E_L. At the former, the wage rate is high and is denoted by w_H. And in the other equilibrium the wage rate is low and is denoted by w_L.

The reader ought to be warned that just because the luxury axiom is valid does not mean that there will be multiple equilibria. However, we can get strange paradoxical results even in the absence of multiple equilibria.[25] But what I am focusing on is the case of multiple equilibria. This means that two societies that look very different in terms of the incidence of child labor may be at a fundamental level identical and simply be trapped in different equilibria, which no person or household is in a position to shake off by its own actions.

What is interesting in the context of the present book is the fact that when in a society with ordinary citizens taking decisions and without the need for law enforcers to take any action, there are multiple equilibria, as in the above case, the nature of state intervention needed to change the outcome is unusual. In such a case, as depicted in Figure 5.2, if the economy is settled at the equilibrium point E_L, with low wages and children working, what we need is a

---

25. See Basu and Zarghamee (2009) and an article in *Forbes* by Tim Worstall (2016) on how certain kinds of bans can actually exacerbate the problem of child labor. See also Baradaran and Barclay (2011) and Bagenstos (2013).

one-time intervention, such as a law declaring child labor as illegal that deflects the economy to the other stable equilibrium, E_H. Once this equilibrium is established, we will not need the law banning child labor or any state intervention to hold the economy there. We can call this a "nudge intervention"—a one-time intervention that can thereafter be removed without the economy reverting to the bad equilibrium.[26]

This is in contrast to contexts where we are trying to shift the economy to an outcome that is not self-enforced by ordinary citizens. A good example is a severe speeding restriction. Just because others adhere to this does not in itself create an incentive for you to adhere to it. This is a critical difference between requiring individuals to drive on the left and drive at less than 70 mph. In the latter case we need "sustained intervention," such as a permanent speed limit law, enforced by the police and the traffic warden.[27]

This may be a good occasion to point out, as already mentioned above, that equilibrium-selection norms are not the only ones we encounter in our social lives. There are other kinds, to model which we have to step out of the comfort zones of economists and abandon some of our neoclassical precepts. It may be worthwhile to think of two other approaches. The first entails the idea of "stigma," which has a long literature outside of economics, from Émile Durkheim and Erving Goffman to more contemporary scholars. The idea of stigma is the recognition that people have attitudes toward other people's attributes and behaviors, and can speak adversely or just show their disdain for them; and this, in turn, can cause pain to

26. This model may be viewed as part of a larger problem, namely, how to use the formal law to change the customary law. Aldashev, Chaara, Platteau, and Wahhaj (2011, 2012) develop formal models of how the state can use formal legal instruments to dislodge society from a customary equilibrium in which large groups are disadvantaged and the elites benefit disproportionately. It has to be kept in mind of course that formal legal rules are not always the fair ones. Formal legal rules have often been the instrument of attack for colonial rulers. And in many countries, formal laws have been used to disenfranchise the local population of their rights to, for instance, land and mineral resources.

27. The difference between nudge interventions and sustained interventions becomes very significant in long-run models and intergenerational systems, where a one-time intervention can yield benefits in the long run without the need for future interventions. From a fiscal policy point of view, this often means that nudge interventions are hugely more socially profitable than politicians realize.

the targeted individuals, causing them to have a diminished sense of self. In brief, to be stigmatized is painful, and we, as individuals, often take actions to avoid stigmatization. It is this idea that has in recent times been picked up by economists to model and explain different kinds of economic outcomes, from unemployment and child labor to labor discipline and truancy at work.[28]

We can go further and think of social norms as internal processes in our own heads that make us desist from certain kinds of behavior. I believe that most people do not steal other people's wallets in crowded public places not because of the conclusion reached via cost-benefit analysis that the expected amount in the wallet is less than the expected cost of punishment, nor because such behavior is stigmatized by others, but simply because that is a norm that we have internalized. We treat that action as either not available or one that will give us a strong negative utility or psychological payoff (Basu, 1995).[29] I shall return to some of these matters when discussing human rationality and behavioral economics in Chapter 7.

5.5 *Citizens, Functionaries, and the Game of Sovereign*

Social norms, as we just saw, can take society to exactly where the law can, to outcomes that are self-enforcing. In all societies, cultural norms and their accompanying rules of how one should behave and norms of how one should be punished if one violates those rules are examples of what kind of control over individual behavior can be achieved by such means. The same is true of punctuality norms, certain kinds of group discrimination, and even phenomena like child labor. But this raises the question: in what sense, if any, can we think of laws as being distinct from social norms?

28. See Lindbeck, Nyberg, and Weibull (1989), Besley and Coate (1992), Fehr and Falk (2002), and Lopez-Calva (2003).

29. There are many other such norms that we have, in greater or lesser measure, internalized, such as fairness norms, revenge norms, and even norms of kindness and altruism (Fehr and Gachter, 2000; Platteau, 2000). For a discussion of some of these in the context of law and behavioral economics, see Jolls, Sunstein, and Thaler (1998) and Cameron, Chaudhuri, Erkal, and Gangadharan (2009).

A hint of the answer is already evident in the three examples discussed in the three previous sections. To answer this more explicitly we have to think of the economy game more elaborately than we have done thus far. In particular, we need think of the set of players as partitioned into the set of (ordinary) "citizens" and the set of "functionaries." By a "functionary," also referred to as a bureaucrat, civil servant, or official, I mean an agent of the state— the police, the magistrate, the traffic warden, the judge, the president or the prime minister—who of course has his or her personal life but is, in addition, expected to play the role of enforcer. The functionary has the ability to punish others and typically earns an income that comes from the tax revenue of the state. By a "citizen" I mean all ordinary individuals in society, who may or may not be passport-holding citizens, but whose main distinguishing mark is that they are not *expected* to be enforcers of the state's dictums and, typically, their salaries do not come from the state. Thus the set of citizens will consist of workers, entrepreneurs, the unemployed, students, professors, illegal immigrants, shopkeepers, and the list goes on.

In writing up a game we have to formally specify who are the functionaries and who are the citizens. A functionary is someone who has certain available actions that have significant effects on other people's payoffs, since it is the functionary who imposes fines and taxes and also gives out rewards. In the above three-person Prisoner's Dilemma, it seems reasonable to think of players 1 and 2 as citizens, and player 3, who chooses between L and R, and so effects punishment on 1 and 2, as a functionary.

Once we have designated some people as ordinary citizens or civilians and some as functionaries, we can distinguish between social norms and the law. Social norms are patterns of behavior that can be self-enforcing *without need for functionaries to enforce the law*. Legally enforced patterns of behavior, on the other hand, rely on the functionaries taking certain actions.[30]

---

30. This is close to the idea of third-party enforcement discussed by many economists. For an engaging discussion of this, along with the pitfalls, see Ferguson (2013, chap. 10). What is germane to the analysis here is the insistence that the third party also must be thought of as part of the game and that its actions, which may be viewed as exogenous by

Thus, at an intuitive level, driving on the left can easily be a social norm. You do not, typically, need police officers to enforce this on drivers (the civilians). Once the norm is in place, it is in the interest of citizens to abide by it. "Do not drive above 50 km per hour" is, on the other hand, unlikely to be a (equilibrium-selection) social norm for the drivers. You need functionaries to enforce it by threatening to punish those who violate the rule.

If the speed limit law is to be successfully adhered to, you will want the law-abiding outcome to be self-enforcing, but in a game that involves the citizens *and the functionaries*. The focal point approach, developed in this book, entails all law-abiding behavior to be self-enforcing. But if the self-enforcement occurs without needing state functionaries, simply because it is worthwhile for citizens to adhere to it when other citizens adhere to it, then it can be thought of as a social norm. The social norm can of course also be the law (which side of the road you drive on is typically a law). But over and above the kinds of behavior that can be implemented by social norms, there are others that can be implemented by using the law where the state functionaries have a critical role to play.

It may be worthwhile resorting to some formal modeling to illustrate this and also to elaborate on how it differs from the cases discussed in the previous three sections. Further, modeling this can give us insight into why some nations are more successful in implementing laws compared to others and to develop a notion of the limits of enforcement. It shows how in this new law and economics approach, we can model and understand compliance and obedience, on the one hand, and dissent and insubordination, on the other. This relates to a large literature on "state capacity," or institutions that play a supporting role in enabling ordinary people to lead orderly lives, for markets to function, for financial transactions to be possible (see Besley and Persson, 2009; Acemoglu and Wolitzky, 2015).

One way to give a formal structure for such an analysis is to consider a polar case where the distinction between a functionary and a citizen is stark. For this, it is useful to define a special kind of

---

the first and second parties, must however be treated as endogenous and integral to the game of life in its entirety.

game that I will refer to as a "partitioned game." Consider a game in which M = {1, . . . , m} is the set of all players. This is a partitioned game if M can be partitioned into two sets, B and C, such that actions chosen by players in C cannot influence the payoffs earned by players in B. In other words, if the players choose a vector of actions, and then the players in set C change their actions, this will leave the payoffs earned by players in B unchanged. That is, all externalities go (at most) one way. Given such a partitioned game, we shall refer to C (that is, the set of people who cannot affect those in the other set by their actions) as the set of (ordinary) civilians and B as the set of bureaucrats or civil servants. Without loss of generality I shall treat B = {1, . . . , n} and C = {n + 1, . . . , m}, where n < m.

Given a partitioned game, we can think of the bureaucrats as playing a game among themselves, which is carved out of the partitioned game as follows. For any vector of actions, v, chosen by the players in set B, define the payoff earned by each player in B as what he or she would have earned in the partitioned game if all the players chose a vector of actions (v, w), where w is any vector of actions chosen by players in C. By the definition of a partitioned game each bureaucrat's payoff is independent of how w is selected. I shall refer to this game that is carved out of the partitioned game and is played by the bureaucrats as the Game of Sovereign, where the word "sovereign" is used in the sense of a *group* of rulers or bureaucrats with authority. Each partitioned game clearly gives rise to a well-defined Game of Sovereign.

It is now easy to see that if a vector of actions (v, w), where v pertains to choices made by the n bureaucrats and w to choices made by the m – n civilians is a Nash equilibrium of the partitioned game, then v must be a Nash equilibrium of the Game of Sovereign. It is the game that the bureaucrats play and the set of equilibria within this game that give the bureaucrats their power. It is like having the first-mover advantage. By varying how they play the Game of Sovereign, they can coerce the civilians to behave in certain ways. This allows us to understand state capacity and the power of the sovereign much more clearly. The power is not given exogenously but arises out of the nature of the game. In this sense, it shows that conceptions of the state à la Hume and à la Hobbes can be brought under one overarching description, namely, the Humean one. The sovereign can exercise power, but the sovereign's power comes from the nature of interaction among the rulers or bureaucrats, creating a self-enforcing mechanism for coercing others. There will however be limits to how far the bureaucrats can push the civilians, defined by the set of Nash equilibria in the Game of Sovereign.

To give greater transparency to this abstract description, I shall now present a specific example of a model in which the state's power comes from a self-enforcing mechanism, with some natural limits to what the state can deliver.

Consider a society in which there are n + m individuals, named 1, 2, . . . , n, n + 1, n + 2, . . . , m. The first n of these we will refer to as (ordinary) civilians and the last m as civil servants or functionaries of the state.[31]

Assume each civilian has his or her own regular (socially harmless) activities, but also an activity that can have negative externality on other civilians, such as driving fast or burning coal in order to run a side business and make some extra profit. Let me go with the burning coal story. Burning coal enables a civilian to earn some extra income but generates enough pollutants so as to be not worthwhile for society as a whole. If we impose a tax on burning coal, people cut down on this activity. The tax rate, t (in percentage), can go from 0 to 100. As t increases, total coal burning goes down, and at t = 100, it stops altogether. Assume that from society's point of view, as t rises from 0, aggregate welfare increases and reaches a maximum when t = 100.

The problem is, how do we implement the tax? Just announcing a new law that asks people to pay a tax of t for burning coal will not mean people will pay. This is where enforcement comes in. Societies that are successful in implementing the law have bureaucrats or functionaries for whom it is in their interest to enforce whatever the law is, *at least within a range of possible laws*. What this means is that, once the law is announced, it is in the interest of the functionaries of the state to enforce the law, maybe because if they do not enforce it, other functionaries will punish them. Societies that

31. For another game-theoretic model of law that distinguishes explicitly between civilians and state functionaries, see Davis (2016). His model goes further in recognizing that the enforcement agency is not one homogenous group but multijurisdictional authority.

manage to create such a structure end up being known for having state capacity and for their good implementation of the law. The qualifier stated in italics above is important for it is always possible to think of laws that the bureaucrats will refuse to enforce. This is what explains "non-cooperation," a tactic that Gandhi used so effectively in fighting for India's independence. This is also what explains mutinies.

To capture all this in a model we need think of an informal game structure in which initially the civilians decide how to behave and the bureaucrats decide whether or not to punish them. Then in the second period the bureaucrats have to decide how to behave with one another. The judge can punish the police person who does not do her job, and the police can hurt the judge by not providing protection, and so on. All I want here is the simplest structure to capture these ideas. So suppose now that the civil servants have a structure of interaction among themselves, in the second period, which I shall refer to as the "Bureaucratic Game," whereby they can play cooperate (C) or punish (P). If all m civil servants play C, they all get a payoff of 8. If all play P, they all get 2. For any other play (that is, some choose P and some C), they all get 1. It should be evident that in this game if all but one civil servants choose P, the last civil servant is better off choosing P; and if all but one choose C, that last person is better off choosing C. Thus the Bureaucratic Game has two equilibria: everybody plays C and everybody plays P.

Now, the full model, which will call the Zone of Compliance Game (admittedly, I am taking some liberty with the term 'game' here) is played as follows. In period 1, each civilian decides how much coal to burn and each bureaucrat decides whether or not to enforce the tax. The higher the tax t that civilians are forced to pay, the less coal they burn, and if $t = 100$, they give up burning coal. The only people who can enforce the tax are the bureaucrats. Let us suppose each civil servant is put in charge of n/m civilians. To collect taxes however is costly for the civil servant or bureaucrat. He risks confrontation and violence. Let us say that for each civil servant the cost of enforcing and collecting the tax from all the persons he or she is responsible for is $t/10$. That is, the higher the tax rate, the costlier it is to enforce the law.

In period 2, the m civil servants play the Bureaucratic Game.

Since enforcing the tax entails incurring a cost by the bureaucrat and seems to have no immediate benefit, why would anyone enforce the law? Interestingly, they may do so for fear of being punished by other civil servants in the Bureaucratic Game played in period 2.

Now we can see how the Zone of Compliance Game will play out. Suppose a law is declared that each citizen is to pay a tax of t for burning coal; and all civil servants are told to enforce the law.

Assume now that this is a society in which it is commonly believed that if any civil servant does not enforce the law, then in the Bureaucratic Game others will punish him by playing P. But if all civil servants enforce the law, they will play C in the Bureaucratic Game. Once these expectations become focal it is easy to see how the game will play out.

In period 1, each civil servant has to decide whether or not to enforce the law. Suppose she expects others to enforce the law. If she also does so, she expects a total return of $8 - t/10$. The 8 is from the outcome in the Bureaucratic Game, and the $-t/10$ is from the cost of enforcing the law. If she does not enforce the law, she expects a return of 2. This is because she is punished in the Bureaucratic Game and so gets a return of 2.

Clearly, she will enforce the law if the tax rate is anywhere less than or equal to 60 percent.[32] But, if the rate is above 60 percent, the law enforcement will break down. The cost of enforcement is so great that civil servants would prefer not to do their work and suffer the punishment in the Bureaucratic Game, instead. That is, people opt out of abiding by the law and even enforcing the law.[33] In brief, any law that sets the tax rate t in the range [0, 60] will be within the "zone of compliance." Such a law will get properly enforced in this society. Enforcing the law is a focal equilibrium. Setting t above 60, will, on the other hand, result in a bureaucratic mutiny and insubordination. The civil servants will refuse to carry out their job.

32. I am making the harmless tie-breaking assumption that when indifferent between enforcing the law and not enforcing, the civil servant chooses to enforce.

33. There is a large literature, empirical and theoretical, that explains different forms of opting out (Bernstein, 1992; Acemoglu and Jackson, 2015).

The Zone of Compliance Game is a kind of partitioned game, and the Bureaucratic Game can be thought of as the Game of Sovereign in my abstract description. This example sheds light on why societies that are law-abiding are so. They have reasonable laws, that is, laws that are within a zone that is *enforceable*, but, over and above that, these societies have a culture of civil servants punishing one another for not doing their job. This is a focal point in such a society. Once this focal point is established, there is a whole set of potential laws that, as soon as they are enacted, will get enforced. The key is building up and nurturing this bureaucratic culture. Of course, to do so in real life will require an understanding of incentives and individual motivation, but the principle is the same as in the game of life just described.

In this society, the optimal state, where $t = 100$ and no coal is burned, is not achievable, but we can achieve any state where the tax rate t is less than or equal to 60 and is fully enforced. Since burning coal is an unmitigated bad in this model, presumably, what we will see in this society in equilibrium is a law that sets $t = 60$ and is fully enforced.

Unlike in the models of punctuality, group discrimination, and child labor, we cannot sustain this good equilibrium, where people burn less coal and pay a tax of 60, by the ordinary civilians changing their behavior with no outside enforcement. But we can get to the equilibrium with enforcement by functionaries of the state, but what is important to understand is that their enforcement is also part of an equilibrium behavior.

This is the subtle but critical difference and also differentiates the approach taken here from that by legal scholars, though both rely heavily on the beliefs of ordinary people and on creating good focal points. What is being asserted is not that laws that get successfully implemented often constitute a focal point but that they always do so. At times, they can be focal without requiring the police and the judge to act, as happens in cases where social norms uphold the law; at other times, they require the police and the judge to get into the act, as we saw in the model just described; but they are always focal for the game of life, that is, a fully described game that includes not just the citizenry but also the functionaries of the state.

In his book on how laws work, often touching on law and economics, McAdams (2015, pp. 7, 9, *my italics*) gives many illustrations of the power of beliefs and how they lead to coordination. But there is a difference between the line he and several other legal theorists take and the approach in this book that I have alluded to before but can make more explicit now. He notes, for instance, "Using rational choice assumptions, I hope to convince economic thinkers that we must amend the conventional wisdom of legal jurisprudence. Law deters and incapacitates, but it *also coordinates and informs*." Again, "In sum, most of this book explicates law's function in providing coordinating focal points and information, *functions I aim to place alongside deterrence, incapacitation and legitimacy.*"

The difference shows up in the use of the words "also" and "alongside." In a rational choice setting, I argue that the law works by doing nothing else but coordinating and informing. So it is not that it *also* does so; it *invariably* does so. The law deters and incapacitates because, in the end, it is in the self-interest of the police, the magistrate, and other functionaries of the state to deter and incapacitate, for fear that they will, in turn, be deterred and incapacitated.[34]

The approach to law and economics made by legal scholars and philosophers makes an *existential* claim. They point to the fact that there are situations where the law does not need enforcers. Once others follow it, it is in your interest to follow it. This is true and important, as the examples of punctuality, discrimination, and persistence of child labor illustrate, but I am arguing for a more fundamental methodological shift. It makes not an existential claim but a universal one. What the above analysis shows is that the creation and shifting of the focal point is the *only way* that the law

34. And here, once again, is W. H. Auden's description, both more lyrical and more inchoate, of the law (from his poem "Law, Like Love"):
Law is neither wrong nor right,
Law is only crimes
Punished by places and by times,
Law is the clothes men wear
Anytime, anywhere,
Law is Good morning and Good night.

works. At times this can be achieved without requiring any action on the part of the functionaries of the state, at times it is necessary to have them act to enforce and punish. But in all situations the law works by influencing human beliefs and creating new focal points. In brief, we are condemned to the republic of beliefs.

CHAPTER SIX

Law, Politics, and Corruption

6.1 Law, Governance, and Development

January 9 was an important day in Adam Smith's life. That day in 1751 he was elected to the Chair of Logic at Glasgow University and from that year he began his serious teaching career. He was asked to teach the Logic class. From all accounts, he left the title of the class unchanged and taught what he found most interesting, thereby giving a display of individual rationality. As a student in the class, John Millar, respectfully noted, "Mr. Smith . . . soon saw the necessity of departing widely from the plan that had been followed by his predecessors, and of directing the attention of his pupils to studies of a more interesting and useful nature than the logic and metaphysics of the schools" (Smith, 1762 [1978], p. 1). What he taught instead was moral philosophy, jurisprudence, and the law. The influence of these lectures was so big on John Millar, who had joined Glasgow University at the age of 11 and began attending Smith's lectures by the time he was 16, that he became a "follower" of Smith, and would later hold the Chair of Civil Law at Glasgow University.

In November 1751, Thomas Craigie, who was professor of moral philosophy at the same university, died, and in April 1752, Adam Smith was appointed to the Chair of Moral Philosophy. He could now teach what he wished without having to take liberties with the course title, thereby giving in to moral sentiments. Again, in John Millar's words, he ranged over natural theology and the progress of jurisprudence and, most importantly, "he examined those political regulations which are founded, not upon the principle of *justice*, but that of *expediency*, and which are calculated to increase the riches, the power, and the prosperity of a State. . . . He considered the political institutions relating to commerce, to finances" (Smith, 1762 [1978], p. 3). A lot of this would make its way into his classic, *An Inquiry into the Nature and Causes of the Wealth of Nations*, published in 1776.

I stress this early interest of Smith in the interface between law and economic development and growth because this is so often overlooked in the popular imagination. There is no surprise in this because, as Heilbroner (1986, p. 1) points out, in opening his book evaluating and reproducing some of Smith's more important essays, "No economist's name is more frequently invoked than that of Adam Smith, and no economist's works are less frequently read."

In the popular view, Adam Smith's central contribution was the concept of the "invisible hand," which coordinated and directed the selfish drives of a multitude of individuals, each striving to do well for himself or herself, to achieve the collective good. As I pointed out elsewhere (Basu, 2011a), Smith clearly did not see this as his central message because in the first edition of *Wealth of Nations* "invisible hand" did not even make it into the index. It did so only in posthumous editions of his classic.

What Smith stressed was that nations rise and fall by their power to coordinate, govern, and create appropriate laws. He stressed the duty of the sovereign to protect members of society from oppression and injustice from other members of society and the importance of establishing an "administration of justice." He was acutely aware of the importance of law and justice for a society's economic progress.[1]

---

1. As Besley and Persson (2009, p. 1239) observe, in building a model to illustrate this, "The historical experience of today's rich nations indicates that creation of state capacity to collect taxes and enforce contracts is a key aspect of development." Acemoglu and Wolitzky (2015) distinguish between community-based enforcement, often made possible merely by the threat of ostracism, and enforcement by a special force. It is also arguable

How does one square this with individual drive to consume and accumulate more, which we also know is important for economic efficiency and growth? It is arguable that there are three critical inputs for economic progress: (1) the individual drive for material betterment, (2) integrity and altruism, and (3) good governance and law. Because the social good seems so far removed from individual self-interest, (1) captured human interest and curiosity in a way that (2) and (3) did not. Smith's invisible hand, which relates to (1), was indeed a stunning discovery. It had surprise value. But that is no reason to dismiss (2) and (3) as unimportant as many ideologues went on to do. It is impossible to have every transaction, exchange, and trade be enforced by contracts and the third party. Further, for some rather intriguing reasons, contracts are often deliberately left incomplete (Rasmussen, 2001). Hence, personal integrity and altruism are important ingredients for the smooth functioning of markets, exchange, and trade. If (1) constitutes the fuel that drives the economic machine, (2) can be thought of as the nuts and bolts that hold this complex machine together.

There are however limits to individual honesty and altruism, and there are some collective action problems that are beyond any individual's reach. And that is where governance and law come in. There is an important reason why (3) may be the more important explanation of the success and failure of nations. It is arguable that in smaller or greater measure (1) and (2) are present in all societies, or, at any rate, the variance in these is not as great as the variance in different nations' ability to govern and create and implement good laws. In such a situation it is right to focus on the critical role of governance and the law. This is so in the same sense in which, when investigating the cause of a building's collapse, we do not list gravity as a major factor. Gravity is indeed a cause, but since it is there behind every building that has collapsed, it is not an interesting cause to investigate.

It is in this broad spirit that I take some of the methods of analysis developed in the previous chapters to analyze governance, politics, oppression, and corruption.

---

that special forces are empowered by the attitude and behavior of the community in which they function.

6.2 Power and Oppression: Dictatorship, McCarthyism, and Witch Hunts

One of the most important ideas that come to light with the focal point approach to law is the thin line that divides social outcomes that are achieved by the law and the ones achieved by seemingly more endogenous processes such as social and political norms, people's culture, and customs. To be aware of this is to get a much deeper insight and understanding of political phenomena, from tolerance to totalitarianism and witch hunts.

To social scientists, one of the most troubling concepts is power. We can all see its ubiquity and importance but find it very difficult to lay our hands on quite what it means. The big mistake is to expect political power to be grounded in something visible and big. That it can be a manifestation of thousands and millions of ordinary people going about their daily chores with their beliefs about what others may do and what others expect them to do escapes our grasp. But in truth lots of gigantic forces and movements have roots in what is seemingly small and trivial. There is something chilling in such a scenario since the politically grotesque can emerge from almost innocuous actions and beliefs of a large number of ordinary people. As I argued in my book (Basu, 2011a), Franz Kafka grasped this, as did his fellow countryman, Václav Havel, when he was a dissident moving in and out of jail.

I will explain the central idea for the sake of completeness, but briefly, since some of these ideas were dealt with more fully in my other works (Basu, 1986, 2000). I owe my interest in the subject of political power to an elegant little book by Steven Lukes (1974), titled *Power: A Radical View*, and a chance meeting with him in Oxford in the early 1980s, when he was writing an introduction to Havel's seminal essay, "The Power of the Powerless," which had been smuggled out of a Czechoslovakian prison where Havel was incarcerated. He gave me a freshly typed copy of an English translation of that essay. Initially banned and available only as a samizdat document, this essay would eventually become a manifesto for dissent in Czechoslovakia in the early 1980s. While it became a rallying call for revolutionary groups like Charter 77, what is not adequately appreciated is that it is also a deep, intellectually powerful essay, virtually laying out a game-theoretic concept of power and political oppression.[2]

It is also, I believe, widely misunderstood. It is often treated as an argument against communist dictatorship. But a careful reading of it shows that it is much more than that. It is about the human predicament; it is as applicable to communist dictatorship as to right-wing totalitarianism and to anticommunist vilification and persecution as during the period of McCarthyism in the United States. Havel shows how each individual going about his or her quotidian tasks can unwittingly unleash vicious forces, persecute groups, and prop up leaders who are tyrants. In short, he drew our attention to not just the nature of oppression that was prevalent in Germany in the 1930s, in Russia and Czechoslovakia in the 1970s and 1980s, in North Korea in recent decades, but also to the incipient risk that is there in all countries, including the United States.

I do not know if Havel knew of the existence of Nash, the person or the equilibrium. But the argument he constructed, rooted in individual beliefs about how other individuals may behave, comes remarkably close to the idea of Nash equilibrium.[3]

Havel named the system he was describing "post-totalitarianism." This runs on "auto-totality," in which the oppression is perpetuated by not just the rulers but also ordinary people, from the greengrocer who proclaims "loyalty" to the system by putting up sycophantic posters to the party official who displays her "loyalty" by harassing any greengrocer who does not display his loyalty. Let me quote Havel (1986, p. 36, my italics),[4] whose literary flair is hard to paraphrase:

> If an entire district town is plastered with slogans that no one reads, it is on the one hand a message from the district secretary to the regional secretary, but it is also something more: a small example of the principle of social auto-totality at work. Part of the essence of the

2. Among recent works that have begun developing ideas along similar lines, see Hatlebakk (2002), Villanger (2005), Yang (2014), Acemoglu and Wolitzky (2015), Oleinik (2015), Ledyaev (2016), Joshi and Mahmud (2016), and Han (2016).

3. In my analysis in Basu (1986) I suggested this but was not able to formally demonstrate Havel's argument as a Nash or subgame perfect equilibrium.

4. He wrote this essay originally in 1978.

post-totalitarian system is that it draws everyone into its sphere of power, not so they may realize themselves as human beings, but so they may surrender their human identity in favor of the identity of the system, that is, so they may become agents of the system's general automatism and servants of its self-determined goals, so they may participate in the common responsibility for it, so they may be pulled into and ensnared by it . . . ; so they may create through their involvement a general norm and, thus, bring pressure to bear on their fellow citizens. And further: so they may learn to be comfortable with their involvement, to identify with it as though it were something natural and inevitable and, ultimately, so they may—with no external urging—come to treat any non-involvement as an abnormality, as arrogance, as an attack on themselves, as a form of dropping out of society. By pulling everyone into its power structure, the post-totalitarian system makes everyone an instrument of a mutual totality, the auto-totality of society.

Everyone, however, is in fact involved and enslaved, *not only the greengrocers but also the prime ministers*. Differing positions in the hierarchy merely establish differing degrees of involvement: the greengrocer is involved only to a minor extent, but he also has very little power. The prime minister, naturally, has greater power, but in return he is far more deeply involved. Both, however, are unfree, each merely in a somewhat different way. *The real accomplice in this involvement, therefore, is not another person, but the system itself.*

Havel wrote this famous essay in Hradecek, his country cottage in North Bohemia, in 1978, in a surreal setting. Across the field from his home, the police made a watchtower on stilts, which Havel referred to as the Lunokhod, since it resembled the Soviet moonwalker device with that name. The police ran shifts on that tower and kept continuous watch on him. Reflecting his belief that the perpetrators of a post-totalitarian system are also victims of the system, Havel felt instinctive sympathy for the police who kept watch on him. As his biographer Zantovsky (2014, p. 208) noted, "Havel bore no grudge against his watchers, most of them local policemen. . . . Often, Havel would empathize with the policemen's ordeal and go out of his way to make them feel at ease by engaging them in small talk. . . . He sometimes offered them tea or coffee." It was this remarkable ability of his to view the world from others' shoes that enabled him to develop such a deep, Humean understanding of how political power is sustained.

What is surprising about this essay is that it stands up to game-theoretic scrutiny. I shall now demonstrate this by developing a formalization of Havel's ideas that will put it in the structure of a game and so facilitate a formal analysis of its equilibria.

Consider a society with a large population, with individuals named 1, 2, 3, and so on. For every positive integer there is a person with that name. So this is a picture of the people in this society:[5]

1   2   3   4   5   6   7   . . .

Having them stand in a line, as I have done, makes it easier for me to refer to them and their neighbors. I shall thus speak of person n − 1 as being on the "left" of n, and n + 1 as being on the "right." In brief, it is best to think of these people standing in a line looking at the direction of the top of the page.

In this society, trade could occur between person 1 and person 2 and, for all persons n, where n > 1, there can be trade between this person and n − 1 and n + 1. In brief, using the pictorial depiction above, each person can trade with his or her immediate neighbors. For any two persons, n and n + 1, trade occurs if n + 1 wants to trade with n. In other words, each person is always willing to trade with the person on her right; and so trade actually takes place if the person on the right is willing to trade with the one on her left.

When trade occurs between persons n and n + 1, person n gets a payoff of $3 and person n + 1 gets $1. Consider a case where all persons trade with their neighbors on both sides (person 1 of course has only one neighbor and so I am assuming he trades with just that person, namely 2). Then 1 gets a payoff of $3 and every other person gets a payoff of $4.

---

5. Technically, what is being assumed here is that there is a countably infinite number of individuals. This is similar to what I assumed, in a different setting, in Basu (1994a), and what is assumed in Voorneveld (2010). In addition, Voorneveld discusses at length how such an assumption may be reasonable (see also Rubinstein, 1991, p. 918). In the present exercise I make this assumption to be able to establish subgame perfection in a relatively simple setting. It should be emphasized that it is possible to create similar arguments with finite individuals but the games are typically more complex (see Basu, 2000).

Now suppose a dictator shows up in this society and insists that each person has to give him $1. This is pure extortion, since this dictator gives nothing to the people in return. Will citizens comply with this demand, especially if the dictator has no ability to hurt or punish anybody, like David Hume's tyrant with limited ability to inflict direct physical hurt? At first sight it seems the answer has to be no. But in case this is a society where not listening to the dictator results in punishment and ostracism from other citizens, people may comply with the dictator's diktat. It is this mutual fear across the citizenry that enables the dictator to extort from them all, and that is what I will model presently.

Consider the following definition. A citizen n is "disloyal" if she does not give the dictator the $1 that he demands or if she trades with person n − 1 who is "disloyal." It follows that if person t does not give the dictator $1 and t + 1 trades with t, then t + 1 is also treated as disloyal. And, if after that happens, t + 2 trades with t + 1, then t + 2 is also disloyal, and so on.

The game proceeds as follows. First citizen 1 decides whether or not to give the dictator $1. Then in period 2, citizen 2 decides whether or not to give the dictator $1 and whether or not to trade with citizen 1. Then in period 3, citizen 3 decides whether or not to give the dictator $1 and whether or not to trade with citizen 2. And so on.

Now consider the case where no citizen n acts in a way to be disloyal; and when n − 1 is loyal, she trades with her. It is easy to see that this strategy on the part of everyone is an equilibrium. If you believe others do not want to be disloyal, you will not want to be disloyal; and this behavior is a Nash equilibrium and also subgame perfect. That is, what you expect people to do in the future, they would indeed do, if the situation arose.

To prove this, consider citizen 1. If she believes everybody wants to be loyal, she will give the dictator $1. This results in an expected net payoff of $2 for her. This is because person 2 will trade with 1, which will give her $3. She gives 1 to the dictator and so has a net payoff of $2. If, on the other hand, she decides not to give the dictator the unfair tax he is imposing, she will be labeled disloyal and expect player 2 not to trade with her and so her payoff will be 0. This is illustrated in Figure 6.1. Citizen 1 can choose G or N (give

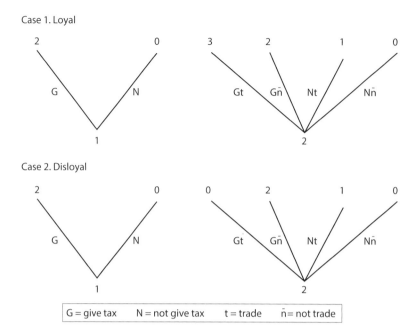

Case 1. Loyal

Case 2. Disloyal

G = give tax   N = not give tax   t = trade   n̄ = not trade

FIGURE 6.1. The Loyalty Dividend

tax or not give) and the payoffs she expects in each of these cases are displayed.

Next consider citizen n, where n > 1. If n − 1 is loyal, her best option is to trade with n − 1 and give the dictator $1. That way she is labeled loyal and expects n + 1 to trade with her. Hence, her payoff is $3. No other action gives her as much. This is illustrated in the top panel of Figure 6.1 for the case where n = 2. There it is assumed citizen 1 acts loyal, that is, chooses G. Citizen 2 now has to choose whether to give the dictator the tax and trade with 1 (option Gt) or to give the dictator the tax and not trade with 1 (option Gn̄) and so on. All her expected payoffs are then displayed. She is clearly best off choosing Gt.

In case citizen n − 1 is disloyal, the best action for n is to refuse to trade with n − 1 and give the dictator $1. That way she is labeled loyal and expects n + 1 to trade with her. The payoff she gets by this is 2. It is easy to see that by any other action she will do worse because she would be labeled disloyal and so not get to trade with n + 1. This is illustrated in the lower panel of Figure 6.1 in the case where n = 2. Here it is assumed that when 2 has to move, she knows that 1 has chosen action N and so is labeled disloyal. Citizen 2's expected payoffs are displayed in the figure. Clearly, she will choose Gn, that is, she will ostracize citizen 1. This completes the proof.

The dictator is propped up and allowed to tyrannize entirely because of mutual fear of ostracism among citizens.[6] The dictator need not have the capacity to hurt anyone directly. And here is David Hume's (1742 [1987], p. 11) amazingly perspicacious observation in his celebrated essay "Of the First Principles of Government," published in 1742:

> Nothing appears more surprising to those who consider human affairs with a philosophical eye, than the easiness with which the many are governed by the few; and the implicit submission, with which men resign their own sentiments and passions to those of their rulers. When we enquire by what means this wonder is effected, we shall find that, as Force is always on the side of the governed, the governors have nothing to support them but opinion. It is, therefore, on opinion only that government is founded; and this maxim extends to the most despotic and most military governments, as well as to the most free and most popular. The soldan of Egypt, or the emperor of Rome, might drive his harmless subjects, like brute beasts, against their sentiments and inclination. But he must at least have led his *mamalukes* or *praetorian bands*, like men, by their opinion.

Once this argument is understood, it becomes clear that there is nothing specific to oppression under a communist regime in this argument, even though that was the context that prompted Havel to write. In essence, one can see the same argument play out in the case of fascism and also when Senator Joseph McCarthy triggered a process of red-baiting in the United States in the early 1950s.

---

6. As Carothers (2003, p. 8) notes, while talking about the efficacy of the law, it is a system that "resides in the minds of the citizens of a society." The model just constructed formalizes in what sense that can be the case. In this sense this can be viewed as an alternative form of corruption. Corruption usually requires a façade of good behavior. As Moene and Soreide (2015, p. 47) observe, "In their purest form, facades are used for the personal enrichment of government representatives." While that is often the case, what this model shows is that enrichment can be a more blatant activity once the beliefs of ordinary people are suitably aligned.

It all began with a fear-mongering speech by McCarthy to the Women's Republican Club in Wheeling, West Virginia, on February 9, 1950, where he claimed, "In my opinion the State Department, which is one of the most important government departments, is thoroughly infested with Communists. I have in my hand 57 cases of individuals who would appear to be either card carrying members or certainly loyal to the Communist Party" (Schrecker, 1994, p. 212). This became a period of vitriol and witch hunt because once a person was charged as being a communist or "un-American," anyone who tried to challenge this was promptly labeled a communist or un-American.

The way in which, in the game depicted in Figure 6.1, the definition of a "disloyal person" can spread almost by infection—a person who trades with a person who is labeled disloyal gets labeled disloyal—the label communist or un-American could travel from one person to another merely by a person trying to contest the label being put on someone else. It is not surprising that by June 22 of the same year the blacklist had become very long, including celebrities such as Larry Adler, Leonard Bernstein, Walter Bernstein, Aaron Copland, Pete Seeger, Margaret Webster, and Orson Welles.

As Supreme Court Justice William Douglas, who played a major role in bringing an end to McCarthyism, wrote in the *New York Times* (pp. 37–38) on January 13, 1952, "Once we had confidence in each other. Now we have suspicion. Innocent acts become telltale marks of disloyalty. . . . Suspicion grows until only the orthodox idea is the safe one. Those who are unorthodox are suspect."

To close the story, luckily, opposition to McCarthyism built up, led by prominent senators, both Democrats and Republicans, some prominent business leaders, and judges. By early 1954 there was a groundswell of opposition behind what came to be called the "Jo Must Go" movement. On December 2, 1954, the Senate voted to condemn McCarthy, and that was pretty much the end of the McCarthy period. As President Dwight Eisenhower observed with an obvious sense of relief, "McCarthyism" was now "McCarthywasm" (Fried, 1990, p. 141).

What is interesting from the perspective of this book is that no law had to be changed to trigger McCarthyism. Yes, there was a shift in the focal point of society, of what we expected of one another.

Senator McCarthy probably played a role in triggering this change, but once it got going, he did not need to wield a whip. It was interpersonal fear that made the movement gather strength, leaving individuals powerless against it. His role was merely that of shifting the focal point.

Fascinating recent research in semiotics illustrates the same idea. This concerns the practice of *pai ma pi* in China (Yang, 2014). *Pai ma pi* literally means "patting the horse's ass" and owes its origins, in all likelihood, to Mongolia, where the horse symbolized status. In contemporary China, it refers to flattery or sycophancy in the workplace and in hierarchical organizations.

The analysis here is entirely in the mold of the focal point approach. All agents are part of the model. No one had to be specially resurrected by virtue of a new law or a proclamation. It is the equivalent of general equilibrium analysis. We described a game of life and showed how it can settle on a vile equilibrium conferring huge powers on some. It is critically important for ordinary citizens to understand this logic in order to devise ways to nip despotism in the bud, and end hate mongering that can get out of hand once it is allowed to brew for a while. Yang (2014, p. 2) argues that the widespread use of the seeming deference toward one's seniors associated with *pai ma pi* in contemporary China "serves as both survival strategy and a mode of semiotic control." This is made possible by the associated rule of *dang'an*, the maintenance of a dossier or record of the behavior of employees or members of an organization. This allows information of one's behavior to be transmitted across people and compels individuals to behave in ways they otherwise may not for fear of how other people will treat them. The process is similar to what happens in Havel's totalitarian state and in the model of power described above and in Basu (1986). As Yang puts it (p. 9), "Once *pai ma pi* becomes an equilibrium-selection norm in the bureaucratic system, it compels people to conform."

6.3 Freedom of Speech, With or Without Law

An excellent example of how the law and nonlegal social pressures and sanctions can be substitutes can be found in the practice of freedom of speech. We usually compare freedom of speech across countries by looking at their laws and constitutions and, depending on the context, actual state action. These methods give some interesting results and insights, and in our ranking-obsessed world, there are websites and groups that have ranked nations. Thus according to a popular website,[7] the country with the greatest freedom of speech is New Zealand, followed by Australia, the United Kingdom, Japan, and United States. The bottom end of this league table is also interesting. The country with the least freedom of speech turns out to be Eritrea. In reading this the reader may suppose that North Korea was not a part of the study. But that is not so. The study assures us that North Koreans have a little more freedom, and so they rank as the country with the second least freedom of expression. Relatedly, when it comes to a press freedom index, Finland tops the chart, with New Zealand in the fifth spot. The tail end looks much the same: North Korea retains its unvarnished record of beating Eritrea.[8]

What all these studies share is that they are focused on what the law and rules made by government allow, in terms of the freedom that people and the press have in speech and writings.[9] The state is an important actor and it deserves attention, but what I want to draw the reader's attention to is the fact that the freedoms and the lack of freedoms that are made possible or not possible by the law can be replicated without the law, by social pressures, norms, the use of ostracism, and punitive action across ordinary individuals. This is an important fact that gets highlighted by the focal point approach to law and economics. After all, any outcome in society (recall this includes not just ordinary citizens but the police, the magistrate, and the head of the state) that can be achieved by the use of law can be achieved without the use of law. This is because the outcomes that can be achieved by the law are ones that are anyway equilibrium points of the game of life. The law merely helps

7. See http://www.therichest.com/rich-list/10-countries-with-the-most-freedom-of-speech/.

8. This refers to the 2016 World Press Freedom Index, prepared by Reporters without Borders.

9. It is important to realize that freedom of speech also includes the right not to speak. Interestingly, tobacco companies tried to resist publicizing the damage that can be done by tobacco by arguing that being forced to talk about this is a violation of the Free Speech Clause of the US Constitution (Jolls, 2013).

give salience to the outcome that may have been chosen by society without that nudge.

One can see this by actually constructing situations where social monitoring is enough to restrict freedom of speech. This task becomes easy in the light of the previous section. Suppose a nation either has no laws or has laws and a constitution that protects freedom of expression. In this society an atheist wants to publicly proclaim his belief. He wants to say: "I don't believe God exists." Suppose by being able to speak out openly on this he gets a satisfaction equal to a dollar. In other words, if he cannot say this, it is like giving up a dollar.

Now consider a societal set up exactly as in Section 6.2. Person 1 may trade with 2, 2 may trade with 1 and 3, 3 may trade with 2 and 4, and so on. In this society, exactly by the construction illustrated in the previous section, you can trigger sanction or ostracism on anyone who says "I don't believe God exists," or trades with someone who says "I don't believe God exists," or trades with someone who trades with someone who says, "I don't believe God exists," and so on. This will support an equilibrium in which all atheists will be silenced. The state does not have to be involved in any way. As long as people have the freedom to trade or not trade with whomever they wish, we can have punitive sanctions that obstruct free speech. Further, it does not have to be trade. Not to have people speaking to you can be painful. So the punishment can take the form of 2 refusing to talk to 1 or 3 refusing to talk to 2 and so on.[10]

It should be transparent now that we can use this construct in a variety of contexts. Suppose in North Korea the state does not place any restrictions on speech and you, a North Korean citizen, want to say, "I don't think Kim Jong-un is the best dressed man in Democratic People's Republic of Korea." For those not familiar with the background, in 2016, a North Korean agency allegedly declared (I cannot testify to its authenticity) Kim Jong-un to be the best dressed man in the country for the seventh consecutive year. As we just saw, it is possible to make it so costly for you to utter the

10. By this same argument, the freedom of speech can be used by big businesses and large organized groups to deliberately distort information and opinion. As we all know, protecting the press from censorship does not guarantee that all truths will be presented to the public in a fair and open manner if the press is controlled by a handful of tycoons and corporations (Lebovic, 2016).

above words in public in terms of having to face ostracism that you would refrain from it. And the functionaries of the state need not play any role in this. Wherever you live, no matter how much legislative freedom the law of the land grants, your freedom to speak can be curtailed through pure social sanctions. It is like the workings of *pai ma pi* discussed in the previous section. In many countries, especially (but not only) in times of war, if you wanted to say that you think (as I indeed do) that lives lost are a tragedy whether they belong to your nation or that of the enemy, you would not need the state machinery to stop you; people pressure and harassment and, in many cases, the threat of violence would do the job. Likewise, in many countries you can be restrained from criticizing your prime minister's policy or from saying that you do not want the current president to be president.

Before moving away from the topic of freedom of speech, it may be worthwhile to point out, though this is not germane to the discussion being conducted here, that it is not obvious that our freedom of speech should be unequivocal. As I argued in Basu (2000, chap. 5), if you believe that people should have the freedom to say or write whatever they wish, you must defend Salman Rushdie's right to publish *The Satanic Verses*. But, by the same argument, you should then defend Ayatollah Khomeini's right to declare *fatwa* against Rushdie, as long as he himself does not carry out the *fatwa*. This is not as abstract a matter as may seem at first sight. In the context of America's free speech, in the early twentieth century, it was debated if the trade union's right to criticize the employers should mean that employers also have the right to express anti-union views or whether we should treat the latter as inherently coercive (Weinrib, 2016). In 1937, when there was dispute between Henry Ford and his employees, several members of the board of the American Civil Liberties Union did take such a view (Cole, 2017a).

Moreover, there are statements that can be as painful as or even more painful than a slap or a kick or a whiplash. On pure consequentialist grounds, it would seem, if you object to these physical assaults, you should object as much to speech that hurts.[11] What

---

11. Since the United States is often upheld as among the finest examples of nations that legally guarantee freedom of speech by virtue of its First Amendment, it is worth noting

I mean is this. Suppose every time you utter a certain sentence, a person feels bad hearing it. Now change the world so that every time you utter that sentence, the person does not feel bad hearing it but that sentence acts like a digital command that makes an arm appear from a gadget and slaps the person inflicting a pain that is of the same intensity as the emotional hurt in the previous world. On consequentialist and in particular welfarist grounds, if in this second world you do not allow people to command a slap to be administered to the other people, you should not allow the same sentence to be *spoken* in the first world. So by this argument there should be restrictions on freedom of speech.

There are however two important differences here that need to be kept in mind. The first is that while a physical assault is a well-defined act, hurtful speech is not. Hence, purely for reasons of definitional problems and the risk of perpetual litigation, we may decide not to place restrictions on hurtful speech. Further, we may have some control over how much another person's speech hurts us. Some of this is socially conditioned. We could learn to ignore such remarks or not read the offensive passages. For these reasons, I do believe that while freedom of speech cannot be total, it should by and large be extensive and be cherished and protected. We must be very cautious in stopping it on grounds that it hurts. That should be rare and in extreme cases (see Fish, 1994, for an excellent discussion).

The discussion in this section reveals both the dangers and advantages of informal social controls. They can be used to unleash and encourage dreadful forms of behavior—severe restrictions on what people say or write, on what religion a person chooses to

---

that exceptions of this kind are allowed under US law. Much of this began with the celebrated 1942 case *Chaplinsky v. New Hampshire,* and the emergence of the "fighting words" doctrine, whereby words that directly prompt violence may be prohibited. This led to additional clauses such as the state's right to stop "such words that are akin to verbal assaults and inflict emotional distress upon their recipient" (Gard, 1980, p. 524). The trouble is, as soon as one opens this window of exceptions, it is prone to be misused, usually by the government to guard the interests of civil servants and political leaders by silencing dissent. At the same time, it is impossible not to recognize that there will be exceptions. This shows that the efficacy and fairness of the written law depend on how society reads those words. Our innate senses of fairness and integrity are essential to create a fair, law-abiding society, because ambiguity is inevitable.

practice, and a person's freedom not to practice any religion. They can be used to bully individuals and groups and suppress different kinds of freedoms. To quote Mailath, Morris, and Postlewaite (2017, p. 33–4), "In the United States the law is clear that an individual may tell any other individual his opinion of him, and that murder in retaliation for doing so is against the law. For a large part of the previous century in a substantial part of this country, however, a black man who told a white man his views might well have been hanged for doing so. The hanging clearly constitutes murder, yet any policeman foolish enough to arrest the murderers would (in the unlikely event that he could find a prosecutor willing to consider this a crime) likely confront a jury that did not find it a crime."

On the other hand, social pressures can be used to reject adherence to unjust laws, to create pressures to boycott political leaders who are blatantly unjust or unfair. The key almost always is to use a system of boycott or ostracism that is infectious. If A interacts with the unwanted political leader, others plan not to interact with A. If B, nevertheless, interacts with A, others plan not to interact with B. And so on. The same method that was used in India's caste system, for instance, to propagate untouchability can be put to good use as well.

I talked earlier in the book about how some laws are totally overlooked by all and so are effectively of no use.[12] The same reasoning can be used to deliberately bypass laws that are obviously unjust or immoral. In India's freedom struggle, Gandhi often used this method, appealing to the citizenry and also the enforcers of the law to collectively violate the law. There are, after all, limits to what a leader can individually do using his or her own muscle power. Power, as we have seen earlier in this chapter, comes from ordinary people behaving in certain ways and holding certain beliefs. By the same argument, disempowering a leader can be done by ordinary people behaving in certain ways and giving rise to a collective force that no one can resist.

---

12. I quoted Mailath, Morris, and Postlewaite (2017) above; they discuss many other examples of laws that gather dust in the books with no consequence on behavior, even in advanced industrialized nations.

6.4 The Scourge of Corruption

It is time now to return to where we began in Chapter 2, to crime and punishment, as analyzed by the early thinkers of law and economics. Crime and punishment are closely connected to corruption. Corruption typically refers to the violation of the law with the connivance of the enforcers of the law, to wit, the police, the bureaucrat, or the politician. For an ordinary citizen to steal is a crime, but it would not be described as an act of corruption. Corruption usually involves a functionary of the state being complicit. Shleifer and Vishny (1993, p. 599) are explicit on this, defining corruption "as the sale by government officials of government property for personal gain." If licenses and permits have value and are sold for a bribe, this is effectively a sale of government property and thus constitutes corruption.

The existence of corruption is smoking-gun evidence of the flaw underlying traditional law and economics. Most of the standard approach to corruption takes a very partial equilibrium approach, treating the enforcers of the law as somehow beyond the frame of analysis. They are to be resurrected as and when the need arises. This has greatly handicapped our analysis of corruption and fails to explain its pervasiveness in some societies and rarity in others. For that we have to view the problem at a societal level in the same way that we analyzed power and politics, above. We have to treat the functionaries of the state as human, with their own motivations and interests. This was the motivating model I used in Chapter 2. I want to pick up the thread here once more, now using the hindsight of the discussion in the previous chapters and sections.

What I want to show is that, following the development of the original neoclassical model of crime and punishment in the 1960s, there were steps taken recognizing that the functionaries of the state were also human beings. In other words, the problem that led to the focal point approach had been subliminally recognized for quite some time; and there were interesting efforts to model the state and its agents. Yet the agenda remained incomplete.

What was understood early is that the assumption, unwittingly made by Becker (1968), of the enforcers of the law being robots, doing their work mechanically, was wrong. This assumption needed to be relaxed to understand corruption. There is an enormous literature on corruption that in different ways tries to do so[13]; and this literature is in some sense the precursor to the focal point approach.

To see what happens to the analysis of crime and corruption once we allow the police arresting the criminal to have features of *Homo sapiens*, return to the crime and punishment model of Becker introduced in Chapter 2. To quickly recapitulate, in that analysis, a person was contemplating a crime that gives him a booty of B dollars. But there is a probability p of being caught by the police, and if caught, he has to pay a fine of F. In that model, no crime will be committed if:

$$B \leq pF.$$

This model changes if the police is a utility maximizer, like other ordinary citizens, and is willing to take a bribe. In such a setting, after the criminal is caught, the police and the criminal will get into a bargaining situation. If they fail to reach an agreement, he has to pay F dollars to the government and she, namely, the police, gets nothing. But if they agree on a bribe of b, he loses b and she gains b. Clearly the bribe will never be more than F because then he is better off paying the fine. In brief, between the criminal and the police they have F dollars to split. Given such a symmetric situation, it is natural to expect they will split it in half. That is, the bribe will be F/2.[14]

This little modification begins to give us some interesting results. The fine will of course never again be paid. Each time a person is caught doing something illegal, he will strike a bargain with the officer who catches him, pay a bribe, and get away. Interestingly, even though the fine is never paid, it plays a role in curbing corruption. Since the booty from the crime is B, the probability of

---

13. See, for instance, Rose-Ackerman (1975), Klitgaard (1988), Mauro (1995), Mookherjee and Png (1995), Bardhan (1997), Mishra (2002), Kugler, Verdier, and Zenou (2005), Bose and Echazu (2007), Treisman (2007), Wihardja (2009), Yoo (2008), Gautier and Goyette (2014), Suthankar and Vaishnav (2014), Banuri and Eckel (2015), Dixit (2015), Popov (2015), and Gamba, Immordino, and Piccolo (2016).

14. This solution is exactly what we would get if we wrote this up as a Nash bargaining problem and solved it. In other words, the reader can have the comfort of knowing that this solution is backed up by all the axioms of the Nash bargaining solution (Nash, 1953).

getting caught is p and, if caught, he pays a bribe of F/2, but he will not commit the crime if:

$$B \leq pF/2.$$

Clearly, the fine that is never paid can still be used to control crime because the fine determines the size of the bribe. It is evident, by comparing this with the above condition, that now the fine has to be twice as high or the probability of detecting a crime twice as high to deter crime.

This is an important insight. Once we recognize that the police officer is also rational and, given the social context, will be willing to take bribes (and so you can get away without having to ever pay the penalty), it does not mean that the penalty does not play a role. It does but it is less effective now. You have to double the penalty to get the same result. Clearly with rational functionaries of the state, the analysis and the prescription change.

There is, however, one immediate question that arises above and is left unanswered. In most societies taking a bribe is a crime, just as stealing is a crime. In some societies, giving a bribe is a crime as well, but let us, for the moment, leave this aside and assume that only taking a bribe is a crime. In that case, the police person who takes the bribe will surely be nervous that she may be caught by a super cop and asked to pay a fine for taking a bribe. And of course if that happens then the police and the super cop can try to work out a bribe, this time from the police to the super cop to avoid paying the fine to the state.

This clearly opens up a chain of possible acts of corruption and bribes to escape being fined. This turns out a fascinating problem both because it describes what is quite realistic in many countries, namely, the high incidence of bribery, and also because it is theoretically challenging to solve such a chain of bargaining problems. This was the core concern of Basu, Bhattacharya, and Mishra (1992). It is such a natural concern that there is a large literature that investigates these kinds of problem and their many manifestations.[15] In

---

15. See, for instance, Bac and Bag (2001), Polinsky and Shavell (2001), Rahman (2012), Acconcia, Immordino, Piccolo, and Rey (2014), Makowsky and Wang (2015), Sanyal (2015), Rose-Ackerman and Palifka (1999 [2015]), and Burlando and Motta (2016).

some sense, this literature is a precursor to the focal point approach to law and economics. It dismantles the assumption of robot cops, one cop at a time, creating and analyzing a chain of problems. The focal point approach goes all the way at one go.

It opens up new ways of thinking about the law. Once we think of the law enforcer as a player, new avenues and new ways of intervention open up. For a lot of matters of corruption, punishment is meted out to all those involved without thought given to the strategic response of the people. In India, for instance, under the Prevention of Corruption Act, 1988, whenever there is a case of bribery all those involved are deemed guilty and punished. On a little reflection it is evident that this may exacerbate rather than curtail corruption.

If you will hold the person giving the bribe and the person taking the bribe equally guilty, as is the case under Section 12 of the Prevention of Corruption Act, 1988,[16] then, after the act of bribery has taken place, the bribe giver and the bribe taker have a common interest in colluding and hiding the fact of bribery. Such collusion makes it very difficult to detect bribery; and the assurance of not being detected makes the government official more brazen in taking bribes. Hence, such a law is likely to cause bribery to increase. It is noteworthy that Gambetta (2009), in his far-reaching study of corruption, finds the level of trust among the partners in crime to be the key to understanding corruption.[17]

Once we think through this game-theoretic aspect of the interaction, it becomes clear that one way to cut down bribery is to introduce asymmetric punishment, by declaring the giving of a bribe legal while maintaining that taking a bribe is a crime. This can in fact be accompanied by an increase in the punishment meted out

16. I quote from Section 12: "Whoever abets any offence [pertaining to bribery], whether or not that offence is committed in consequence of the abetment, shall be punishable with imprisonment for a term which shall be not less than 6 months but which may extend up to five years and shall also be liable to fine."

17. In a later study, using Treisman's (2000) comprehensive cross-country study of corruption as the context, Gambetta (2017) uses the same idea, to wit, honor among the corrupt, to explain Italy's high corruption. As he notes, elevated corruption is usually a hurdle preventing countries from reaching high levels of socioeconomic development. Italy presents a puzzle because it seems to have overcome that hurdle.

to the bribe taker (Basu, 2011b). Once the punishment is made asymmetric, the bribe taker knows that, after the bribery has taken place, the bribe giver will not have any qualms talking about having paid a bribe, thereby increasing the chance of the bribe taker getting caught. Knowing this, the bribe taker will be more hesitant to take the bribe in the first place, thereby lowering the incidence of bribery. What we just went through was a two-period backward-induction argument, used in locating subgame perfect equilibrium that was introduced in Chapter 4 and used a few times above.

Reality, as always, is more complicated than a model, and the above argument has many caveats and provisos that we need to be aware of, but the point remains that building more complete models and allowing for the gaming elements to be taken account of more explicitly enable us to enact better and more effective laws. There are real historical examples where a change in the law did take place in asymmetric ways. In a recent paper, Berlin, Qin, and Spagnolo (2018) look at some changes in the Criminal Law of the People's Republic of China that were made during the Eighth National People's Congress on October 1, 1997, and then they use a remarkable data set to analyze the incidence of corruption. They find a reduction in corruption detection and deterrence, possibly linked to poor design. The reasons are complex and cannot be viewed as an endorsement or rejection of the above theory, but their analysis shows the significant impact on judicial behavior that a law of this kind can have. There have also been laboratory tests and other more descriptive empirical investigations, with mixed results.[18] My interest here is however not in this specific legal change but in the shift in the method of law and economics it marks by trying to endogenize the behavior of the agents of the state.

These analytical steps are moves in the right direction, but they do not take us all the way to the focal point approach because in these models, when you alter a fine, exempt someone from having to pay it and double the punishment on some, all the agents responsible for executing these orders are not modeled explicitly.

18. See Li (2012), Wu and Abbink (2013), Abbink, Dasgupta, Gangadharan, and Jain (2014), Dufwenberg and Spagnolo (2015), Oak (2015), Popov (2015), Suthankar and Vaishnav (2015), Angelucci and Russo (2016) and Basu, Basu, and Cordella (2016).

Indeed, when it comes to taking law and economics all the way to the real world and devising policy, it will not always be easy to use the full-fledged focal point approach. It will take us a while to develop all the analytical wherewithal to get there.

In the interim, the aim should be to use fuller descriptions of the agents involved, taking account of their strategic proclivities as explicitly as possible and then designing measures for corruption control.[19] It is important to recognize that corruption has a systemic side to it, and while we should work on the fine tuning of punishments and strategies for detection, a failure to recognize the systemic aspect can cause the best of plans to unravel. We also need to recognize the pervasiveness of multiple equilibria. The same society can get caught in an equilibrium in which virtually everybody is corrupt and also in an equilibrium in which virtually no one is corrupt. Bringing in an element of behavioral economics—done more explicitly in the next chapter—demonstrates this very well.

In reality, and unlike in the neoclassical model, people, including those indulging in corruption, are aware of the moral dimensions of corruption. However, when corruption is widespread, it may seem a more tolerable form of behavior. It can then be like an equilibrium-selection norm of the kind described in Chapter 5. As is pointed out in the "World Development Report 2015: Mind, Society, and Behavior" (World Bank, 2015, p. 60), through much of history and in many contemporary societies, corruption happens to be "a shared belief that using public office to benefit oneself and one's family and friends is widespread, expected and tolerated. In other words, corruption can be a social norm."

An interesting recent study (Abbink, Freidin, Gangadharan, and Moro, 2016) tests this by artificially *creating* the social norm in a laboratory setting, and checking out on people's behavioral response (see also Bicchieri and Xiao, 2009; Banerjee, 2016). The study sorts people according to their corruption proclivity and then

19. In Basu and Dixit (2016) we try to show how some of the task of regulation can be divested from the government to private firms and corporations. Further, Dixit (2015) has outlined how private firms could think in terms of designing collective action among themselves, without the need for government intervention, to control corruption. These blurrings of lines between the private person and functionary of the state are steps in the right direction.

pairs participants, some with the more corrupt and some with the more honest, and lets the participants know what kind of people they are paired with. It is found that the probability of offering a bribe doubles when paired with a likely corrupt partner rather than a likely honest partner. The social setting influences individual behavior.

These arguments explain multiple equilibria and why corruption is either widespread or rare.[20] They have big implications for corruption control and explain why so many genuine efforts go haywire. We have seen this happen, time and again, in different countries—China, India, Brazil—where a leader is serious about corruption control but fails to do much, and often ends up in a worse situation. The trajectory is uncannily similar. The leader announces draconian measures to punish corruption. It then soon becomes clear that corruption is so widespread that he or she (and this is not a politically correct usage of pronouns; I can give examples of both him and her) can dip into the pool and pick any fish and the fish will turn out to be corrupt.

Suppose now you have the capacity to catch and prosecute n corrupt persons. Which n corrupt persons will you pick? In the divisive world of politics, if you pick your friends and those in your party and begin to punish them, you will soon be alone and isolated. Your friends and party will desert you, and it is not the case that the opposition will be so appreciative as to become your supporter. Politics does not work that way.

---

20. There is also a lot to be learned from history. There are many examples of countries switching from one kind of equilibrium to another. Glaeser and Goldin (2006) document the steady decline of corruption in the United States from the late nineteenth century to the early twentieth centuries. Sundell (2014) and Rothstein (2011) provide interesting insight into how Sweden moved from a patrimonial and corrupt system of public administration in the nineteenth century to one of the most corruption-free nations. In the early nineteenth century government employees held multiple jobs and were often absent from their main government job for months at a time, and it was common for them to collect informal payments in the form of "sportler." There can be dispute about whether it was a big bang change or gradual reform, but the nature of the change was dramatic. Importantly for the discussion here, the Sweden case suggests that the same society can be caught in strikingly different equilibria. In recent times there are also examples of societies, such as Singapore and Hong Kong, in which corruption declined relatively rapidly. These cases give hope to countries with dismayingly high levels of corruption and deserve further study.

So it will be natural for you to go after the corrupt in other parties and the opposition camp. This means that what began as a genuine campaign to end corruption ends up as a witch hunt against opposition parties and individuals who criticize the leader.

The world is replete with leaders who are not serious about ending corruption because they gain so much by it. But the world also has examples of genuine initiatives going wrong because the leader discovers that in controlling corruption in a society where corruption is pervasive, to be even-handed is political suicide for him or her.

It is a common belief that all one needs to end corruption is grit and determination. In reality, corruption is a complex phenomenon, in which economic incentives intertwine with social norms, customs, and strategic considerations and explains why many genuine efforts end up in failure.[21]

Economists and lawyers, unlike most political leaders, recognize the intellectual and scientific component of corruption control but have not been too successful in producing practical policies and plans. One reason for that is the flaw in the way we conceptualize law and economics. This is not to deny that a discipline with fault lines beneath it can serve a useful role in many ways, but the fault lines show up in some specific areas. This happens for law and economics most severely when it comes to the area of corruption control. This is not surprising since corruption control is an area where the need for modeling the functionaries of the state well is critical, and that is the weakness of traditional law and economics. It is hoped that one practical area where the focal point approach will make an important difference in the not-too-distant future is in controlling and curbing corruption.

21. See World Bank (2017). This report talks at length on the role and rule of law in taking on these challenges. For an attempt to empirically investigate the connection between the rule of law, norms, and socially desirable outcomes, see Pistor, Haldar, and Amirapu (2010).

CHAPTER SEVEN

Rationality, Law, and Legitimacy

7.1 Beyond Rationality

Barring an occasional foray into broader human motivations, I have all this time stayed with the assumption of rational individuals with exogenously given utility or payoff functions, which is standard in mainstream economics and the assumption under which modern thought on law and economics originated. In the previous two chapters, I did touch on matters of stigma and social sanctions, matters not commonly addressed in mainstream economics textbooks. The chapters drew on some recent literature to enrich the framework of analysis by recognizing that human beings do not get utility only from what they consume but also from how others treat them and think about them. Social approval gives joy and social stigma hurts. But barring these brief digressions, we remained within fairly standard confines.

There are three reasons for this. First, I wanted to highlight a critical fault line underlying mainstream law and economics and to demonstrate that the fault line can be corrected without abandoning the founding assumption of the discipline, namely, individual rationality.

Second, I wanted to emphasize that, while we should make every effort to correct the flaws in our scientific discipline, we may have to be reconciled to the fact that a full correction and a completely consistent science may not be possible and that must not be used as reason to abandon science. A scientific description of a phenomenon invariably omits some parts of reality (Sen, 1980). Without that, a description would be a meaningless verbatim recapitulation of what happened and contribute little to understanding. Omission is an essential counterpart to understanding.

Even as I go about critiquing it, this may well be an occasion to point to some of the strengths of traditional, neoclassical economics. To do any science it is necessary to use some simplifying assumptions. Exogenous rationality was one such assumption. The fact that that is not always true is not in itself reason to jettison it. We may be unable to replace it with anything and be left unable to comment on any policy. There are two kinds of neoclassical economists. There are, first, those who, having made the assumption of totally rational and selfish individuals, delude themselves into believing that this assumption is always valid.[1] Second, there are those who realize that this is not always true but believe that it is an assumption that can nevertheless be put to good use in many situations to get some broad predictions right. I could name several progressive economists who fall in this second category but will refrain from doing so in order not to make enemies of the unnamed.

Third, and this is closely related to the point just made, we are not yet in a position to replace the assumption of rationality with a comprehensive alternative and build a full, usable model. The critique of rationality and the building blocks we can put up in its place are just that—building blocks. Hence, this chapter is best viewed not as closure but as a prelude to a law and economics that is based on the focal point approach and, in addition, recognizes the diversity of human motivation and the fact that these can change in response to experience, social context, and even well-written books.

When economists say research shows that not all human beings are always rational, it may seem embarrassing because economics

---

1. As Rodrik (2015, p. 29) notes, in discussing the role of axioms and assumptions in economics, "Ultimately, we cannot avoid unrealism in assumptions." A mistake happens when we forget that we made an assumption. This mistake is, unfortunately, not as rare as one might expect.

is the only profession that seems to need research in order to make such an assertion. Others know this by their lived experience. And, as I will argue later, lived experience and intuition as sources of knowledge are not to be chaffed at. On the other hand, the cussedness of economics did result in something very useful—the discovery of "systematic irrationality" and the role it plays in determining what happens in society and the market. The mapping of systematic irrationality relied on drawing on preexisting research by psychologists and supplementing it with our own studies in laboratories and in the field. This is what created behavioral economics, but what can give it extra reach and intellectual depth is the blending of these findings with the idea of equilibrium, which is so central to economics and game theory.[2]

My aim in this and the next section is to present an admittedly idiosyncratic critique of the rationality assumption, idiosyncratic because no attempt is made to be comprehensive. Instead I pick and choose from behavioral economics and use pure reason to illustrate how some of our systematic irrationalities have important implications for social policy, law, and market interventions.

I begin with two examples of the value of understanding systematic irrationalities. The first one is drawn from my own experience and informal (and unpublishable) experimentation. Suppose you are planning a meeting with friends at a certain time; an interesting way to get them to show up more punctually than they normally would is to give them a later time for it, in the following way.

Let us suppose you want to meet at 5:00 PM. What I am asserting is the following. If you tell them, "Let us meet at 5:05 PM," they will be more likely to show up on time than if you tell them, "Let us meet at 5:00 PM." In fact, they will probably arrive earlier when asked to come at 5:05 than when asked to come at 5:00. My casual experiment shows that this works very well. When you plan on a 5:05 meeting people show up almost on the dot, whereas when you plan on a 5:00 meeting people show up late by 5, 10, or 15 minutes, depending on the country, the region, and the cultural background

---

2. This is rightly stressed in Akerlof and Shiller (2015). Indeed, my one critique of behavioral economics is that it has not exploited this link enough to blend the findings of behavioral economics with economic theory to extend our understanding of economic and social phenomena. Without this, behavioral economics runs the risk of being a lanudry list of experimental results (Basu, 2018).

of the people. You may be able to get even more punctual behavior by asking them to come at 5:02 PM, but at the expense of them speculating about your sanity.

This shows that there is more to life than the literal. People read cues into speech. The time 5:05 sounds precise and sets off psychological triggers in the head of the listener and affects his or her behavior. It could be that 5:05 puts us in a more precise frame of mind. It could also be that when someone invites you at 5:05 you feel that this person manages her time very precisely and you do not want to disappoint her or jeopardize her evening. After all, contrary to what many textbooks say, altruism and other-regarding preference are as innate to human beings as selfishness.

The second example is actually a business proposal. Roller coasters give joy and people are willing to spend money to get rides on them. Not surprisingly, amusement park entrepreneurs have made a lot of money. But they can do better. Most people underestimate the fear they feel once the ride begins. So here is my proposed pricing strategy. Charge a small fee to get on the ride. Then, midway through, stop the roller coaster and give the riders the option to pay a large fee to get off, that is, to forgo the rest of the "joy" ride.

The confluence of psychology and behavior is what behavioral economics is all about. Luckily, we no longer have to rely on casual experiments, like the above. The coming together of economics and psychology and the collection of data from laboratories and the field have played a major role in enriching our understanding of human behavior. That is the big contribution of behavioral economics.

Turning to matters of relevance to this book's project, consider once again the Prisoner's Dilemma discussed in Chapter 2. At one level, it is an abstract game-theory exercise with two players and two strategies or actions each. Its enormous reach is because it appeals to our psychology and troubles us. Interestingly, the game's rise to prominence owes a lot to the fact that its most popular form, involving the fable of the two prisoners, arose out of a mathematician's attempt to hold the attention of psychologists.[3] The

---

3. Princeton mathematician A. W. Tucker created the story of the Prisoner's Dilemma to explain his work to the students and professors in Stanford University's psychology department. This happened because, thanks to a lack of office space in the mathematics

Prisoner's Dilemma is troubling to the trained economist because it warns us about the dangers of unmitigated selfishness and how the invisible hand can fail disastrously, as happens in the context of various commons problems, including the most pressing one of our time—climate change. It also raises the question of whether or not, in reality, people are totally selfish. Early experiments showed that people played the Prisoner's Dilemma differently from what theory would predict, and this may reflect how we think of ourselves, our attitude to others, team affiliation, and altruism.[4] It is, for instance, arguable that when we play the Prisoner's Dilemma by choosing the non-cooperative action, that is, action B, in Game 2.1, we feel remorse. If the remorse is like an exogenously imposed fine, then the game, in effect, becomes like the Prisoner's Dilemma with Fine, illustrated in Game 2.2. Hence, human psychology can do what we often try to achieve through law, punishment, and rational calculus.

New research shows such altruistic proclivities may have a stronger analytical foundation than we had earlier thought. A study by Alger and Weibull (2013) shows that evolution may not favor people who are totally selfish. Individuals who have an innate tendency to do the right thing may have greater survival value, thereby explaining the prevalence of prosocial behavior in society and why Immanuel Kant's categorical imperative may have evolutionary roots (Alger and Weibull, 2018).[5] Bowles (2014) points out how this distinction between the presumption of self-seeking individuals and that of civic-minded ones goes back into history, to Machiavelli and Aristotle, and to the need to cultivate good citizens. Calabresi (2016) also points to the importance of prosocial

department, Tucker, as visiting professor, was provided an office in the psychology department of Stanford; and his office neighbors, curious about his endless scribblings on paper, invited him to talk to them and explain what he was working on. As I mentioned in Basu (1993), I learned this from a conversation with Harold Kuhn, Princeton professor and Tucker's coauthor in creating the celebrated "Kuhn-Tucker condition." I do believe that the Prisoner's Dilemma would not have had the kind of impact it has had on economics if it were not for the story or the fable created by Tucker. That is what drew our attention to how this dry numerical exercise relates to markets, neoclassical rationality, and the invisible hand.

4. See Michael Bacharach's (2006) posthumously published book.

5. A different but theoretically well-grounded explanation of Kantian behavior on the part of individuals is modeled by Roemer (2015).

preferences in human beings and cites its absence in the traditional economist's approach to law as the source of his disappointment with the mainstream (see also Sunstein, 2016).

What the Prisoner's Dilemma, despite the use of the word "dilemma," does not do, however, is question the *meaning* of rationality and selfishness. The game that brings in some of the features of the Prisoner's Dilemma and also raises questions about the meaning of rational behavior, and hence relates more directly to some of the questions raised by modern behavioral economics, is the Traveler's Dilemma, which was briefly presented in Chapter 2. The Traveler's Dilemma illustrates how, in sufficiently complex situations, we may be logically compelled to go beyond neoclassical rationality. This *logical* compulsion, being the traditional concern of analytical philosophers, has not received much attention from economists and legal scholars.

7.2 Traveler's Dilemma and the Meaning of Rationality

In the Traveler's Dilemma both players could have earned $100 each, but each player being selfish and trying to get minor gains results in both of them doing poorly and ending up with $2 each. Is this what actually happens in reality? Is this valid even in terms of pure reasoning? These questions are critical because the level and nature of legislative intervention needed depend on how we answer them.

In traditional law and economics, we would quickly jump to the conclusion that we need third-party intervention to change the incentives and therefore the behavior of the two players. But in case we find that individuals can and do solve some of their own problems, we have to think very differently about legal interventions and punishments. There is a large literature, experimental and theoretical, showing how the formal game-theoretic prediction is contestable.[6] The backward-induction argument or the iterated deletion of dominated strategies or rationalizability, for instance, uses

---

6. See, for instance, Goeree and Holt (2001), Gintis (2009), Velu, Iyer, and Gair (2010), Arad and Rubinstein (2012), Manapat, Rand, Pawlowitsch, and Nowak (2012), Capraro (2013), Morone, Morone, and Germani (2014), and Bavly (2017).

the assumption of rationality being common knowledge between the two players. That is, A knows B is rational; B knows A is rational; A knows B knows A is rational; B knows A knows B is rational; and so on, endlessly. We can try to contest this assumption.

The empirical and experimental literature is quite unequivocal in its criticism. It shows that few individuals in laboratories playing the Traveler's Dilemma or in answering hypothetical survey questions of how they would play, pick 2. Choices tend to cluster around the top end, generally in the range of 95 to 100, given the strategy sets described in Chapter 2.[7]

Without going into this large empirical or theoretical debate, I want to focus here on a couple of matters of significance, which go beyond the game, to issues pertaining to the economy and society. First, the Traveler's Dilemma, like the Prisoner's Dilemma, is a sharp reminder that the claim that the invisible hand of the market leads individually selfish behavior to socially optimal outcomes is not always true. If the economy game changes from a perfectly competitive one with no externalities to some other structure, individual rationality may fail us miserably as happens in this game. Indeed, it is arguable that, thanks to the march of technology, the market structures are changing in ways that need smart, collective interventions to make sure we do not sink the boat by each trying to enhance our own self-interest. As technological advance changes our world and the marketplace, we may need to think of different kinds of legal and governmental interventions to enable the economy to function effectively.

Second, in light of the large empirical evidence cited above, whereby individuals do seem to behave differently from our textbook assumption, we are fortunately urged to recognize that individuals are motivated by more than self-interest. There are two

7. See Capra, Goeree, Gomez, and Holt (1999), Becker, Carter, and Naeve (2005), and Rubinstein (2006). In several formulations of the game, the number to be chosen is between $180 and $300, with a penalty and a reward of $5. Rubinstein put the problem to his lecture audiences at several universities, Ben-Gurion, Tel Aviv, Technion, Tilburg, LSE, British Columbia, York (Canada), Georgetown, and Sabanci. The average number chosen was just short of 280, with the average choice being highest at LSE (281) and lowest at Sabanci (263). There were a few who made the Nash equilibrium choice of 180, described by Rubinstein (2006, p. 875) as "victims of game theory."

separate routes that we can take. One is to assume that each player is interested in only his or her own payoff but nevertheless does not simply try to maximize it. Let me call this the "payoff-focused critique." The other is to recognize that players are interested in more than their own payoffs. Other people's payoffs, the names of the strategies, the name of the game, and maybe who the other player is matter. Let me call this the "generalized critique." These critiques show that if the players were left to themselves the outcome would be different from what the standard model suggests, and so the intervention may also have to be different.

There has been some interesting research on payoff-focused critiques. To take one example, it is recognized that, even when people are interested in their own payoffs, they are interested not simply in *maximizing them* but also in *mitigating the regret* they may feel in the end (Savage, 1951). This approach, in particular, that of regret-minimizing behavior, has been elegantly formalized in a paper by Halpern and Pass (2012). The idea is the following. Consider each of your options. Start with, for instance, 2. Then think of each of the actions that the other player may take and the maximum regret you would feel for having chosen 2, that is, the amount you would lose out by having chosen 2. Thus if the other person chooses 90, you will get a payoff of 4, but if you had chosen 89, you could have earned 91. So the regret associated with 2, if the other person chose 90, would be $91 - 4 = 87$. If the other person chose 2, your regret would be 0, since you could not do better by deviating from 2. If the other person chose 100, it is easy to see, your regret would be 97. And so on.

In other words, for the choice of 2, you get a vector of regrets associated with each choice made by the other player. The "maximum regret" associated with option 2 is the largest number in that vector. "Regret-minimizing" behavior entails choosing the option that minimizes the maximum regret.

What is interesting is that, in the Traveler's Dilemma, regret minimization by all players yields a clear outcome. Each player will choose any of 96, 97, 98, 99, 100. Hence, the equilibrium, when players are regret minimizers, is a pair of actions, chosen from the set {96, 97, 98, 99, 100}. What adds to the interest in this outcome is the paper by Becker, Carter, and Naeve (2005) in which members of the Game Theory Society were asked how they would play the Traveler's Dilemma and the most popular answers were 2, 96, 97, 98, 99, and 100. If we dismiss 2 as the answer given by members proving their credentials as game theorists who can spot a Nash equilibrium, the coincidence of regret-minimizing behavior and this empirical finding is noteworthy.

Regret minimization is certainly not the final word in this, since, as Halpern and Pass (2012) are well aware, it can lead to some unrealistic answers in certain other games.[8] Other approaches, such as those based on evolutionary dynamics, or getting genetic algorithms to repeatedly play the game without knowing the structure of the game but committed to maximizing each player's own payoff, have been tried and have given us insights into why rational agents may end up playing in ways that deviate from the Nash outcome.[9]

One route that has not been explored but would seem to me to be worth exploring is the following. One big conceptual difference between the Prisoner's Dilemma and the Traveler's Dilemma is this. Place yourself in the shoes of one of the players and assume the other player is a person who can reason perfectly well. Say you both agree to be perfectly selfish and this is common knowledge. Now ask yourself, how would you play the game? In the Prisoner's Dilemma you will clearly play the dominant strategy, B, and will therefore get to the Nash equilibrium.

My hunch is, in the Traveler's Dilemma, you (and, by the same reasoning, the other player) will not opt for 2, the Nash equilibrium strategy, but will go for a large number—maybe in the 90s. In other words, even if we assume away altruism, fairness, and other human traits, and ask you to be ruthlessly selfish, in the Traveler's Dilemma, you would be unlikely to play the Nash equilibrium strategy. This is because, in this game, it is arguable that it is rational to reject rationality. Both players can see this and will do so and gain by that. The scientific problem lies in the fact that "rational

---

8. Moreover, some recent research in behavioral economics and psychology shows that there are other ways in which people deal with the problem of regret. One of them is "deliberate ignorance," or the preference to not know. As Gigerenzer and Garcia-Retamero (2017) show, faced with a negative event in the future, 85 to 90 percent of people prefer deliberate ignorance, and they explain this as a way of dealing with regret.

9. See Pace (2009), Manapat, Rand, Pawlowitsch, and Nowak (2012).

rejection of rationality" is a philosophically difficult idea, as we already saw in the context of forward induction in Chapter 4.

There is clearly something in this idea. To me the secret lies in recognizing that both players choosing a "large number" is a sort of Nash equilibrium. You will not want to spoil the outcome by individually deviating to a "small number." However, the essence of this lies in the fact that large and small numbers are ill-defined sets and the ill-definedness is critical for this line of analysis. If you are given well-defined sets, each player will try to go one below the other and both would end up choosing 2. But ill-defined sets and rational rejection of rationality are difficult concepts. I do not have an answer on how to formalize them but I believe that many paradoxes of rationality are rooted in this and will leave this as an open problem for the reader.[10]

The Traveler's Dilemma illustrates how even before individuals play this game it may be in their interest to signal their irrationality to the other player, since rationality is the source of grief in this game. This is the burning money problem that we discussed in Chapter 4. The focal point approach equates the enactment of a law with some ink on paper, but since the enactment of a law is not a costless process, there is a burning money aspect to the legislative process, which can act as a signal about how individuals, in this case, the lawmakers, will behave once the law has been enacted. In

10. The closest exercise to this in the literature is the recent paper by Arad and Rubinstein (2017). They begin from the empirical observation that when individuals have to choose from a large and complex set of strategies, they do not deliberate over this entire set but partition the set in meaningful ways and then examine the join of all the partitions. I am skipping over the details, but the upshot is that this analysis leads to a set-valued equilibrium concept, the MD-equilibrium. In the Traveler's Dilemma, if individuals think in terms of whether to play a single-digit, double-digit, or triple-digit strategy, they will be looking at the sets $S = \{2, 3, \ldots, 9\}$, $D = \{10, 11, \ldots, 99\}$, and $T = \{100\}$. It can be shown that this game has two MD-equilibria, S and D. In other words, the two individuals deciding to play any strategy from the set $\{10, 11, \ldots, 99\}$ constitutes an equilibrium. The one problem with this is, if you allow the individuals to do a second round of thinking, namely, after they have chosen the MD-equilibrium, if they try to dissect which particular strategy they will choose from within the MD-equilibrium set, you could, under some formulations, get an unravelling to the lowest integer. This suggests that the way to proceed is to combine some idea similar to the one developed by Arad and Rubinstein but with ill-defined sets or characteristics. Thus we may decide to choose a "fairly large number." Since there is no common, precise understanding of what is "fairly large," there is no largest number in this set from which to begin the backward-induction unraveling. How to formalize this idea, however, remains an open question.

the Traveler's Dilemma your burning money can signal to the other individual that using the assumption of traditional rationality on your part will be an error, and this could in turn lead to a better outcome. Hence the making of the law is more than just costless ink on paper.

This opens up a big vista of research expanding the focal point approach to law and economics. The meaning of rationality in these contexts is a philosophically troubling question that deserves further analysis, as an end in itself, but also to provide us a richer view of what law does to societal outcomes.

7.3 Focal Point Approach with Behavioral Features

Once we move beyond payoff-focused critiques to generalized ones, many other challenges open up. Human beings are guided not just by their own payoffs but also by habit, fairness, altruism, empathy, envy, and many other emotional and psychological proclivities. When contemplating playing 100, many will consider it wrong to even think of deviating to 99 and letting down the other player to pick up an extra dollar.[11] It is arguable that a society's success depends as much on this sense of fairness and altruism as on individual drive, as clearly happens in the Traveler's Dilemma. Conservative economists, who condone selfishness by believing that Adam Smith's concept of the invisible hand will invariably lead such a society to optimal results, end up creating failed societies and also promoting an erroneous view of Adam Smith's own idea of a successful economy.[12]

The rise of behavioral economics helped bring some of these critiques into the mainstream. Modern behavioral economics and experiments done in laboratories and fields provide strong evidence of such varied motivations.[13] But we also know this from our lived

---

11. Capra, Goeree, Gomez, and Holt's (1999) finding that the outcome moves toward the Nash equilibrium as one raises the size of the punishment and reward (what in the current game is $2) indicates people do think along these lines, being prepared to undercut others only if the reward is sufficiently big.

12. See Gintis, Bowles, Boyd, and Fehr (2005, esp. chap. 1).

13. Gintis (2003) talks persuasively about human prosociality that gets transmitted vertically from generation to generation and also obliquely across society through socialization institutions. And this permits human beings to adopt group-beneficial but personally costly behavior.

experience and by introspection. It is worth asking oneself: How would I play the Traveler's Dilemma? Since we know from empirical studies that a vast majority would choose a number greater than 90, a vast majority of people would reach the conclusion that they would choose a number larger than 90.

Experiments have in fact shed light on how and how much people think in making a decision. Rubinstein (2016) has studied how much time people take in making decisions and the kinds of answers they give in games like the Dictator game, Ultimatum game, and Traveler's Dilemma. There is evidence that some decisions are cognitive and thought-through, while some are instinctive. This has a background in psychology and, in particular, in the work of Kahneman and Tversky (1979), which challenged the "economic man" paradigm and provided the foundations of behavioral economics (see also Kahneman, 2011). They showed that while some decisions are indeed made through deliberation, a lot of human choice is automatic, almost preprogrammed, depending on the context. This has enormous implications for policymaking and promoting development, as illustrated in the World Bank's "World Development Report" titled "Mind, Society, and Behavior" (World Bank, 2015).[14]

There are also purely deductive ways to reach this conclusion. The first route is to recognize that cognition and deliberative decision making entail costs. One has to collect information and think. So when choosing between A and B, one faces a prior choice, whether to evaluate A and B, incur the thinking cost, and then choose the one that gives greater utility (call this option A') or to snap up an option without thought, automatically or randomly (call this B'). But then we face the same dilemma in choosing between A' and B', which is whether to cogitate and then choose the better of these two or pick one thoughtlessly. It is evident that there is an infinite regress problem here, making it logically impossible to be the conventional rational person (Basu, 1980).

---

14. Further, there is research to show not only that humans are not guided by exogenously set self-interest but that cognitive behavioral therapy can be used to alter their sense of identity, such as enhancing their noncriminal identity and thereby deterring crime (see Blattman, Jamison, and Sheridan, 2017).

The second route is to recognize that there are more choices we have to make in life than we have the time available to make deliberative choices. After all, choices go from whether to study mathematics or literature when you finish school, to whether to part your hair on the left or the right every morning. Hence, by virtue of the way the world is, some choices have to be made without cogitation, automatically. The actions chosen under the latter method may not always maximize utility, and moreover it is not clear that what we cast into the basket of automatic choosing is itself done deliberatively.[15] The assumption of the forever maximizing agent is not just a myth but may well be a logical impossibility.

We therefore have to go beyond this to allow for the kinds of consideration behavioral economics has brought to economics. This, in the present context, means opening the door to human beings who may follow the law because they are supposed to follow the law, human beings who enforce the law because they are supposed to enforce the law, human beings who, when they violate the law, worry not only about the fine they may have to pay but also the guilt they will have to nurse.[16]

All this can have a large social element. In some societies, laws are meant to be followed, and to not do so is to face social stigma. In some societies, laws—at least some laws—are meant to be violated, and it may even be seen as a kind of weakness to be law-abiding. If you are wondering about this, try waiting for the pedestrian signal to come on before crossing a busy street in India; and check out the amusement you cause among other pedestrians. In brief, once we go beyond neoclassical economics' *Homo sapiens*, in doing law and economics, a research agenda opens up, which uses the focal point approach but allows for a broader characterization of human

15. Some of this would be optimal or quasi-optimal for evolutionary reasons. People who systematically leave the more momentous decisions to automatic or random choice will do so poorly in life that they and those with their genetic disposition will tend to disappear over time. Such evolutionary arguments are now a part of mainstream game theory (Weibull, 1995).

16. This is often described as an internalization of the norm. People feel an internal sense of impropriety for violating the norm (see Young, 2008). This can be part of the reason why informal institutions so often run so well. For an excellent discussion of informal institutions and the typology of such institutions, see Ferguson (2013, chap. 8).

behavior, making room for morals and psychological hindrances.[17] The remainder of this chapter and the next one venture into these possibilities.

Behavioral economics beckons us to question the assumption of exogenous individual rationality but it does more; it has unearthed *patterns* of irrationality that are common and can be used to predict human choice and ultimately design better policy. There is now an array of research showing that how a choice is framed, what the default option is when a person refuses to make a choice, how far away in the future the choice becomes effective, and what people believe constitutes normal behavior, all influence the choices people make (see O'Donoghue and Rabin, 2001; Thaler and Sunstein, 2008; Kahneman, 2011; World Bank, 2015). Whether we call the Prisoner's Dilemma by that name or some kindlier one like "cooperation with the fellow prisoner" can make a difference to how one plays the game.[18] The words spoken before a person is made to do a task can affect how the task is performed (Hoff and Pande, 2006; Field and Nolen, 2010). In some early papers, Sen (1973, 1997) showed how the mere presence of certain options, which may never be chosen, can cause a reversal in preferences between two other options. A particularly delightful example is when a person you meet for the first time asks you whether you want to (A) "come to my place and have some tea" or (B) "go home". It is entirely possible you would choose A. But if the person threw in a third option, (C) "come to my place and snort some cocaine with me", it is possible that you would switch to B.[19]

There is research to show how people's selfish rationality is tempered by altruism, other-regarding considerations, envy, and impatience, and a lot of this happens in systematic, predictable ways.[20]

17. The importance of this in the context of law is empirically demonstrated in Tyler (2006).

18. For analyses of how naming games and strategies matter, see Dreber, Ellingsen, Johannesson, and Rand (2013) and Georg, Rand, and Walkowitz (2017).

19. Sen (1993) used this to argue that consistencies of certain kinds, such as the weak axiom of revealed preference, may be violated by reasonable players.

20. The literature now is enormous. See, for instance, Loewenstein (1987), Frank (1988), Akerlof (1991), Sunstein (1996b), O'Donoghue and Rabin (2001), Ariely (2008),

Given the rise of behavioral economics, it is natural to ask if words uttered in parliament and written down as statutes, that is, some "ink on paper," can, under some circumstances, influence people's preferences, and, through that, behavior. If so, then are we not back to the traditional approach to law and economics, which was earlier rejected in this monograph? The answer to the first question is yes, and to the second, no. The words and the utterances in a legal statute can affect preferences and behavior. The literature on the expressive function of the law alludes to this (Lessig, 1996; Sunstein, 1996a; Cooter, 1998). However, there is no reason to believe that the effect of the law is for people and enforcers to do literally what the law commands. It is one thing to agree that the law can affect behavior and quite another to assume that the effect will be of the kind that is literally specified by the law. In other words, it does not follow that if the law requires the police to catch speeding drivers, the police will do so.

In getting into this matter, let me begin with an example. For this, let me return to the subject of food subsidies discussed in Chapter 2. Consider the case of a nation adopting a new law that requires the government to give food vouchers or stamps to the poor. Some may argue that the reason this works in many societies is because if after the legislature passes this law the functionaries of the government do not give out the vouchers and food shops do not give food in exchange for the vouchers, ordinary people will be angry with the government functionaries and stigmatize them. It is this fear of stigma and ostracization that makes the bureaucrats perform their designated task; and that in turn is what makes the law effective.[21]

This argument is correct in the sense that governments do often perform their task well because of this kind of citizen monitoring. What is however important to realize is that this argument takes us beyond the standard model of law and economics. That model, as propounded by Becker and Coase, was so effective because of

---

Karna Basu (2011), Ifcher and Zarghamee (2011), Mullainathan and Shafir (2013), Rabin (2013). A lot of this work, especially in the context of development, is summarized in World Bank (2015). In celebrating this new literature, we must not fail to recognize some early pioneering works, such as Veblen (1899) and Leibenstein (1950).

21. This is an argument that came up following my D. Gale Johnson Lecture at the University of Chicago.

its sparse characterization of human preferences. Human beings had no innate attitude toward the law. A punishment for driving fast was like a higher price for oranges. Laws made people desist from driving fast the same way that the higher price reduces the demand for oranges. It had nothing to do with people's moral attitude toward the law. Indeed, that is what made traditional law and economics distinct from the argument that legal philosophers had propounded for a long time.[22] I am not here deciding whether traditional law and economics is right or wrong in making this assumption regarding human preference, but simply pointing out that the above argument, based on citizen sanctioning of bureaucrats, takes us beyond traditional law and economics.

Further, once one takes this route, it is not clear why we need bureaucrats and the police. Citizens could sanction one another for failing to respect the law, and that could lead to conformity with the law, obviating the need for law enforcers. And finally we could assume that there will be no need for sanctioning either because people will simply do what the law asks them to do.

In sum, in the light of the new research in behavioral economics, we have to recognize the possibility that laws can change the economy game. However, even if that were the case, the game is not necessarily altered in the way in which it is assumed to in the standard law and economics literature. In other words, findings from behavioral economics egg us on, not to return to traditional law and economics but to an even newer course, which I shall refer to as the "focal point approach with behavioral features."

This approach acknowledges that a new law can affect human preferences and values. It can in some situations prompt conformity with the law, as just discussed in the case of food vouchers, but it can also have arbitrary effects, and in some cases the orthogonal effect of causing perverse behavior that deliberately contradicts the law. During India's independence movement, Indians marched to make salt from the sea, in response to a colonial law that prohibited this kind of salt manufacturing. It is doubtful if Indians would have made salt from seawater on a large scale if not for the fact that this was not allowed under colonial law.

22. It is interesting to read Calabresi's (2016) retrospective reflections on this.

Until now I have stayed largely with the neoclassical assumption of rational individuals with exogenously given preferences. I could have called the approach thus far, more accurately, the focal point approach with neoclassical features. What I am moving on to now is a recognition that human preferences are malleable and can change, which is the behavioral part.

It is worth pointing out that one kind of non-neoclassical feature, namely, the possibility that human preferences evolve through time and experience, can be modeled well using extensive-form games that we have already encountered in Chapter 4. It is of course true that human preferences change through life. But this kind of preference endogeneity can be captured by using the idea of multiple selves through time. In other words, think of person i in time t to be a different person not only from person j in time t or k but from person i in time k, where k is different from t. This is in fact a method that can be used in models of addiction to allow for preference change over time, or models of procrastination, whereby the person regrets after procrastinating and so on (Akerlof, 1991).

The recognition that the law can affect human preferences opens up new avenues of research and also the quest for new ways to influence behavior and outcomes in society. An ultimate objective, often attempted by societies, is to have all individuals in the game of life be so programmed as to carry out the dictates of the law (as long as that is consistent and feasible), simply because they are the dictates of the law. This is not without a downside for it can make society too dormant and lacking in creativity. All societies can do with a shot of anarchy. But leaving aside such objections, it is interesting to see that this may not be as impossible as may appear to mainstream economists. After all, in limited measure, we already do so. People widely respect the law not to smoke in public gatherings not out of fear of the police and functionaries of the state but simply out of regard for a law that they consider is in some sense legitimate. If this attitude can be taken to all laws, we can do away with the enforcement machinery altogether.

This is however not likely to happen in the near future. An important intermediate step is to persuade at least the functionaries of the state to obey the law and do as the law suggests simply because that is the law, without regard to their self-interest. In some societies this has been at least partially achieved. For instance, one reason why the law is implemented better in developed countries is that this value is reasonably inculcated in the police and the judges. These agents of the state may do utility maximization the same way everybody else does when they go shopping, choose a college for education, and play the market but, at least in some societies, they do not do so when managing traffic or passing judgments (for contrasting views on this, see Meade, 1974, and R. Posner, 1993). One of the problems of developing countries is that all individuals, including the functionaries of the state, fit the neoclassical assumption of rational individuals rather better than in developed countries. The direction of causality here is not clear, however. It is entirely possible that societies that manage to inculcate these values in the functionaries of state (and, in some measure, even in the citizenry) are ones that become developed. Nevertheless, it is worthwhile to try to instill these values in bureaucrats, police, and the courts. Minimally, this will help create a fairer society. In Chapter 6 we saw how, to get the bureaucrats to enforce the law, we needed to lock them in a game that makes them monitor one another to ensure that they monitor the citizens. What I am suggesting here is that, once we recognize the malleability of human preferences, this may not be the only approach.

For fuller clarity of the two approaches involving the law affecting human behavior, it may be useful to explain the idea with an example. Let me modify the Prisoner's Dilemma Game of Life described in Chapter 3 to yet another version, displayed in Game 7.1. As before, this is a three-player game. Player 1 chooses between rows, player 2 between columns, and player 3 between the left matrix (L) and right matrix (R). In this game, if player 3, the police, chooses L, it means she just sits back and does nothing. As we can see from the payoff matrices, she gets a payoff of 2 in that case, no matter what players 1 and 2 do. If she chooses R, she is vigilant—in regulatory mode. She now goes out and punishes whoever chooses action B. But this vigilance is costly to her, and so when she chooses R, she gets a payoff of only 1.

Now we can see how the two different levels of moral compliance work. Suppose that only the functionaries of the state, in this

	A	B
A	7,7,2	1,8,2
B	8,1,2	2,2,2

L

	A	B
A	7,7,1	1,6,1
B	6,1,1	0,0,1

R

GAME 7.1. Prisoner's Dilemma Game of Life II

case player 3, internalize the law. Then as soon as the law says that players 1 and 2 should not play B, and that, if they do, player 3 should punish them (that is, choose R), player 3 feels bad not to play R, since that is what is required of her by the law. This may be captured by saying that if she moves L, that is, does nothing, she feels pangs of guilt and the payoff of 2 that she earlier got from L now becomes 0. Hence, as soon as the law is announced, she will "prefer" to play R. Knowing this, players 1 and 2 will choose A and get a payoff of 7 each.

In this case, the players are assumed to be of mixed types. Players 1 and 2 are standard neoclassical players with exogenously given payoff functions, while player 3 is a moral person whose preference is shaped by the law.

But if this is possible, it is also possible to think of societies where the citizens themselves are moral. As soon as the new law is announced, players 1 and 2 feel pangs of conscience to play B. If they do, each gets lower utility, by 2. In other words, enforcement occurs without the need for enforcers. Both these approaches require us to break away from the neoclassical view of individuals. This shows that the idea of a state where the law is enforced without enforcers may not be quite as utopian as it sounds in today's world. Behavioral economics is a reminder that such constructions are not as impossible as it seems today and as neoclassical economics made us believe would be the case in all times to come.

7.4 Interest, Resentment, and Legitimacy

The legitimacy of the law has been a subject of much discussion and debate among legal scholars and philosophers. Given the possible connection between legitimacy and compliance, the topic is of moral and practical significance.[23] In the light of the above discussion, it is now within our reach to show how the focal point approach combined with behavioral economics can be used to give clarity to this debate.

It is often suggested that legitimacy of the law is necessary for people to comply with it. But that is not true. As we have seen, compliance, both by ordinary citizens and by state functionaries, occurs in the end because it is in their interest to comply. Ordinary citizens comply because they know that not to comply is to risk punishment; and the state functionaries punish the ones who do not comply with the law because they know that they will be punished if they do not do so. This was the central idea behind the focal point approach. But, once we bring behavioral economics into this, we can formally separate the concepts of interest and resentment, and allow for the possibility that we may comply with the law because it is in our interest but still resent the law.

Let me explain this with an example. Consider the Interest Resentment Game, Game 7.2, described below. This is a three-player game. Player 1 chooses between the rows X and Y, player 2 chooses between the columns X and Y, and player 3 chooses between L and R. If he chooses L the relevant payoff matrix is the one on the left, labeled L, and if he chooses R the relevant payoff matrix is the one on the right, labeled R.

The payoffs are read off as before. If 1 chooses X, 2 chooses Y, and 3 chooses R, which is often written as (X, Y, R), then they get payoffs of, respectively, 0, 1, and 4, which may be written as (0, 1, 4).

It is easy to see that this game has two equilibria: (X, X, L) and (Y, Y, R). Suppose this was a lawless society, which happened to be settled at (X, X, L). We have an egalitarian outcome with all players earning 5. Now, suppose we have a new law, and I will leave it to the reader to speculate about who engineers this, which declares

23. This goes back to Max Weber and H.L.A. Hart and has been a persistent theme (see Cotterell, 1997). For more recent contributions to this debate, see, for instance, Macey (1997), Singer (2006), Huq, Tyler, and Schulhofer (2011), and Tyler and Jackson (2014). For formalizations of the concept of legitimacy, not necessarily in the context of the state but in organizations, which raises issues similar to ones raised here, see Kornhauser (1984) and R. Akerlof (2017). For an interesting study, based on a large survey, of why people actually obey the law, see Tyler (2006).

	X	Y			X	Y
X	5,5,5	0,1,5		X	0,0,4	0,1,4
Y	1,0,5	1,1,5		Y	1,0,4	1,1,6
	L				R	

GAME 7.2. The Interest Resentment Game

X as an illegal action. Hence, the only two law-abiding outcomes are (Y, Y, L) and (Y, Y, R). If everybody believes that everybody will abide by the law, then (Y, Y, R) becomes the focal outcome, that is, an outcome that is an equilibrium and salient, and we will soon find 1 playing Y, 2 playing Y, and 3 playing R. Of course, 1 and 2 will now be miserable, earning only 1 each. To the question of why they abide by the law, the answer is however simple. They do so because it is in each of their interest to do so. They are better off by compliance.

Standard neoclassical economics would leave it at this, but we now know that people have more layered preferences. Something may be in their self-interest, but they may nevertheless feel morally resentful about the overall outcome. This seems eminently reasonable in the outcome just described, inspired by the law. The first two individuals, 1 and 2, could very reasonably feel "resentment" about the new law because an outcome with payoff of (1, 1, 6) may seem morally wrong when an outcome with payoff of (5, 5, 5) is available in the game of life. Resentment and compliance are two different matters. You can comply with the law because it is in your "interest" to do so, but at the same time feel "resentful" about the law. And when many people feel resentful about the law it robs the law of legitimacy.

The above example shows that it is not impossible for an illegitimate government to be effective and get its way. Going beyond the formal model, we can think of a government that splits the interests of the players, letting a small minority (player 3, above) gain, inflict a large loss on the majority (players 1 and 2), and siphon off the difference. The key is to make it in the interest of each individual to abide by what this government desires. In a fully told story, the government cannot be exogenous. One way of doing this is to think of government as individual 3. This person creates a law that deflects society to the outcome (Y, Y, R), where person 3 does very well leaving 1 and 2 miserable. But the interests are so well constructed that it is worthwhile for 1 and 2 to comply.

Colonialism is a good example of this. Unlike the ancient conquering kings, who came with their own soldiers to dominate and exploit the people of other lands, colonialism's distinguishing mark was its fine innovation in management, whereby you use a handful of the local, indigenous people to exploit a mass of the local, indigenous population. The amazing feature of European colonization in Africa, Asia, and Latin America, and especially the former two, is how few of the colonizers were actually needed to run and exploit these large economies. In either case, those conquered or those who came under colonial control did not like the outcome but because of the foreign armies in the former case and local bureaucrats and officers in the case of colonialism, they cooperated. It was in each person's individual interest to comply. In the end that is always the case. Hence, compliance and noncompliance cannot be treated as an indicator of legitimacy of a regime and its rules and laws.

Let me now take this analysis a little further, into uncharted territories that cannot as yet be rigorously expressed. I do this to place some important topics on the table for future (or contemporary but more able) researchers to formalize.

Consider first the complications that arise from the fact that there are situations where people are prepared to act against their own interest. Human beings do not like to feel wronged and resentful and need to deal with that in one way or the other. This takes us into matters of multiple preferences and meta preferences.

Different human beings deal with these feelings of resentment in very different ways. One way is to explain (often to themselves) their predicament as natural, inevitable punishment for their own past misdeeds and sins, and so on. More minimally, people who are exploited for a long stretch of time get used to it and cease to complain, and even acquiesce to their situation. At one level, this is a pure survival strategy. It is difficult to live with anger and resentment. That is the reason why colonialism, racial exploitation, oppression of women, and discrimination against some groups have persisted for long stretches of time. Those at the receiving end of these unfair arrangements have reconciled to their plight being just deserts. Often the exploiters have perpetuated such feelings by say-ing that slavery and the oppression of women are God's will.[24]

The other way to deal with the feeling of resentment is the op-posite, to be prepared to hurt one's own interest simply to make a point. This is what revolts, freedom movements, and mutinies are all about. In Game 7.2, it is possible to visualize either of player 1 and player 2 or both of them deciding that they will choose X even though the law does not allow this and even though to choose X is to hurt themselves. They do this to hurt player 3, the oppressor or the government whose legitimacy they wish to challenge.

In the above example a law that seems to unfairly hurt the in-terest of the people is the source of resentment and the view that the law is illegitimate. But behavioral economics enables us to recognize that the reverse could also happen. We may *want* the law to overrule our immediate interest. What conservative econo-mists learned from the laboratory studies of behavioral research and other human beings know from their experience of life is that human beings are often endowed with a multiplicity of preferences. This can happen in many different ways:

1. A child-bearing mother in the first trimester may prefer to give birth naturally, without painkillers, and in the third trimester prefer the idea of taking painkillers at the time of delivery.
2. Given a choice between a small apple 100 days later and a larger apple 101 days later, Pepi may prefer the second op-tion. But when the 100th day arrives, Pepi may take the small apple that day, forgoing the larger one the following day.
3. Ory likes to smoke and wishes she did not.

In some of these cases, we may view a third party's use of force, such as a potential fine to alter our choice, as legitimate. If a big fine is imposed for buying an apple on the 100th day in order to help Pepi make a "better" choice, that entails force but it is force to

24. In the third century BCE classic, Kautilya's *Arthashastra*, which is Sanskrit for "laws of wealth," and a treatise celebrated for its early Machiavellian insights, the king's adviser is quite explicit in reminding the king how easy it is to exploit people by creating the impression that their plight is God's will.

help Pepi make the choice her better self would. In game-theoretic contexts, the way we deal with case 2 above is to think of the same person at different points of time as being different persons. This enables us to predict how people will actually choose and how the welfare of the many selves will be affected.[25] But it leaves us with tricky questions about the primacy of these persons and on whose behalf we should intervene.

All the above examples create room for interventions being described as legitimate on the ground that individuals have multiple selves and so it is not an outsider's interference but a mere creation of primacy from among the same person's many selves.

There are, however, cases where government intervenes because the government feels it knows better what is good for the individual. This may have nothing to do with multiple preferences on the part of the individuals. Thus, the state may impose a tax on smoking or a law requiring seat belts to be worn by drivers, even when individuals may have a clear preference for smoking or not wearing seat belts.

Some of these cases involve intricate issues concerning individual liberty and paternalism. I myself am ambivalent about the law concerning seat belts when no one else is in the car. It is not clear to me why it should be fine for governments to insist on this and, at the same time, to allow mountaineering. What if I enjoy risk taking and like the challenge of trying to get to my destination without wearing a seat belt? It is like me trying to get to Mount Everest, and in fact much safer. Minimally, for consistency, if we have laws saying you have to wear a seat belt when driving, we should have laws banning mountaineering.

What I am concerned with here is when people have multiple selves. There may indeed be a case for using the force of law to give salience to one self over another. There can be some questions asked about which self gets to override which, but that is unavoidable when we have multiple selves. At times, the problem is made easier by the fact that people often have meta preferences, that is,

25. This feature of hyperbolic discounting was one of the founding ideas for behavioral economics and has a large literature. See Akerlof (1991), Laibson (1997), O'Donoghue and Rabin (2001), and Karna Basu (2011).

preferences over preferences. This allows for a hierarchy of choice where there is no paternalism involved. We are using the person's own higher self to deter the person's base self. In the three examples, 3 actually is not so much a case of conflicting multiple preferences as that of having meta preferences. It is not as though Ory has two preferences: Ory likes to smoke and Ory does not like to smoke. Ory's preference is quite unequivocal. She prefers to smoke; but between preferring to smoke and not preferring to smoke she prefers the latter.

It is fortunate that human beings have not only multiple and conflicting preferences but also meta preferences. Especially in such cases, interference, even with some force, can be justified as legitimate. In behavioral economics, it is commonly believed that this is true of hyperbolic discounters, who give up a lot just for the immediacy of the pleasure of consumption. In many of these cases the person knows this and wishes her preferences were different. The use of the law to create the right incentives seems justified in such cases.

Once we move to the domain beyond neoclassical economics to the focal point approach with behavioral features, we have to allow for not just multiple preferences carried by the same person but also a distinction between a person's "selfish" preference and moral preference. This creates interesting circularities. For instance, people are more likely to adhere to the rule of abiding by the law *purely because it is the law and even when it goes against their narrow self-interest*, if they treat the law as legitimate and feel that the state has legitimacy (see Bilz and Nadler, 2009; Feldman and Teichman, 2009; McAdams, 2015).

Interestingly, we can distinguish between two notions of legitimacy, which I shall refer to as first- and second-order legitimacy. First-order legitimacy is a kind of minimal legitimacy whereby the functionaries of the state, that is, those who have taken up jobs where they are supposed to uphold the laws of the state, abide by the law. That is, they enforce the law as they are expected to, but the citizens are driven by self-interest and conventional utility maximization.

Second-order legitimacy, on the other hand, is defined as something more all-embracing. This is the case where all players—citizens and functionaries alike—are imbued with the internalized norm of following the law because it is the law.

In cases where the law has first-order legitimacy we are in the world of traditional law and economics, where a new law changes the game citizens play since the functionaries robotically follow the law. On the other hand, as we already saw above, if the state and the edicts of the state have second-order legitimacy, the law will not only be effective but will also be so without the need to have anybody enforcing it.

It is arguable that some high-income countries do approach something like first-order legitimacy and that is the reason why the laws are generally effective in these countries. How such legitimacy is achieved is not always clear but evidently this is something nations should aspire to, since it can make the laws more effective and thereby help growth and development. In brief, legitimacy of the state is not just good for democracy but may also facilitate economic efficiency and development.

I end this chapter with two digressive comments arising out of the above discussion on psychology and behavioral economics. They do not influence any of my immediate argument but have important spin-offs that can be used in future work and research.

The first concerns "created targets." Once we recognize the frailty of the neoclassical assumption of human beings having exogenous preferences, other opportunities and challenges open up. What we do not recognize in economics but is pervasive in life is the phenomenon of what is best called "created targets." The stark examples come from sports. Think of soccer. You construct two rectangular bar arrangements at two ends of a field and give a ball to a group of people and tell them that those wearing red shirts should kick the ball through one set of bars and the ones wearing blue should kick it through the other set. Moreover, you will keep count of which side manages to do this more frequently. Soon you will have people falling over one another, willing to take injuries, to get the ball into or to stop the ball from going into those rectangles. You do not need to give the players money or apples or oranges or clothes. For them, the joy of getting the ball into the rectangle and to watch the score is enough motivation.

Indeed, you can, over time, get onlookers identifying with team A or team B and cheering to see them score, so much so that many will try to get away from work and leisure to watch this "game" and even be willing to pay to boost the chances of the team they identify with, not to mention drinking beer and then beating up supporters of the other group.

So much for exogeneity of preferences; life is full of such created targets, and this has implications for how society or the economy functions. Worryingly, electoral politics is often like that. Once people begin to back the Democrats or Republicans, or Tory or Labor, after some time it becomes like ordinary people supporting Liverpool or Chelsea. It is not the manifesto or ideology of the party that prompts the support (even if that was the original impetus). One backs Republicans only because the joy of seeing Republicans win is the same as the joy of seeing Liverpool score.

For politicians, corporations, and powerful organizations, this human faculty of created targets is an opportunity. Once a target gets into people's heads, that can become an end in itself, and shifting that goal post around can result in huge shifts in societal outcomes. When I worked at the World Bank, the division that produced the Ease of Doing Business rankings across countries was my charge. It soon became evident that for many countries moving up this ranking ladder had become an end in itself. Some wanted to move up the ranking ladder not to get greater growth or higher standards of living or less poverty or more jobs but to move up the ranking ladder. That was the game, like scoring a goal in soccer. This made me acutely aware that these rankings can be misused. If we changed the criterion of ranking slowly so that, if a country allowed investment banks more space to exploit customers, the country would move up in the ranking, we could have nations creating this extra space for exploitation.

Another example pertains to patriotism. To some orthodox, neoclassical economists, patriotic preference is a hardwired part of utility maximization.[26] But once we are aware of behavioral

---

26. Some people manage this art of fitting everything into the textbook model by falling into a tautological trap. I know mainstream economists who, when they see a businessman working around the clock, think of this as a manifestation of selfish utility maximization. Then when they see a saintly person give up all belongings for the poor, they think of this as a manifestation of selfish utility maximization. They are unmindful of the fact that they have to contort the notion of selfishness and utility maximization into a tautology to be able to hold on to their beliefs.

economics and created targets, we know that patriotism can be fueled and whipped up, at times unwittingly but often deliberately, by elites and political leaders, and for a reason. Patriotism is good fiscal policy. It allows political leaders to recruit soldiers without having to pay them the breakeven wage that they would demand if they joined the forces purely as another job. By whipping up the emotion that your country is more important than others, and that the lives of those who live in your country are more important than the lives of people in other nations, patriotism can be a useful emotion. For one, it allows us to underpay soldiers and garner huge fiscal savings.

As must be evident by now, these created targets, impossible according to mainstream economics but prevalent all around us, can be a major force for good and for bad. Societies can be steered in different ways. And along with that will arise questions of legitimacy and illegitimacy of such shifts. Once again, one will have to use criteria of the kind used above, that is, to check if it is being done in the interests of the people themselves, that is, higher order preference of people *by their own judgment*. These grounds of legitimacy will never be free of controversy, but if we can have some consensus about its basic idea, at least the most egregious violations of legitimacy will be obvious to all and hopefully will create forces to thwart them.

The second digression concerns the fact that the law is usually supposed to be backed up by force and punishment. What this means in the context of a game is evident in the many cases discussed above. But going beyond these models, the very meaning of force and coercion is widely misunderstood by economists and other social scientists.

This has a bearing on legitimacy. Traditionally, the idea of legitimacy has been contrasted with force. As Singer (2006, p. 229) puts it, "Thus, legitimate government is distinguished from, and seen conceptually as opposed to, mere control by force. It seems universally accepted that such a distinction is to be drawn, so that the idea of legitimacy, with its concomitant notions of authority and right to govern, is universally recognized." However, on close scrutiny, even this seemingly obvious contrast between "control by force" and "legitimate government" runs into difficulty. The source of the problem is ambiguity in the meaning of force and coercion and, by their obverse, voluntariness.

Following Friedman (1962) there is a widely held view that if a person chooses voluntarily from a set of options then he or she cannot be said to be coerced. This "neoclassical criterion" is misleading, at best. The reason why this problem has persisted is that coercion is not easy to define. It does seem that if we cannot define coercion, we cannot show if something is or is not coercion. Luckily, there is another approach that we can take. In the absence of a commonly accepted definition, the other way is to think of stories where we all agree that coercion has occurred, even though we cannot define coercion (in the same way that children can identify elephants without being able to define them),[27] and then see how the neoclassical criterion holds up.

In that spirit, consider a person, P, who gives up his watch to a robber, R, who in a dark alley, with a gun in his hand, asks for it. Clearly, in this situation we would all agree, Milton Friedman included, that P did not give his watch to R voluntarily, that this was a case of coercion or force. Now go back to the neoclassical criterion. What happens in this story is that R gives P a choice: give me your watch (x) or give me your life (y)—that is what the gun is meant to say. P then chooses the option he likes more (in fact, by quite a margin), namely x. By the neoclassical criterion we would say that P was not coerced. This shows that the neoclassical criterion is flawed.

I argued elsewhere (Basu, 2000, 2003) that it is this flaw that tilts neoclassical economics toward a rather pervasive view of voluntariness. From exploited miners working 12 hours a day to women choosing to do all the housework with no help, these are all treated as voluntary and noncoercive. I also pointed out that we find the opposite problem of some schools of thought labeling virtually all relationships as coercive. These are all consequences of flawed definitions.

What needs to be recognized is that coercion is essentially a normative concept (Steiner, 1994; Basu, 2000; Vallentyne, 2000). We have to have a prior position on people's rights. Then if a person is

---

27. I am not quite sure if it was necessary to say children.

deprived of that right, even if he or she is given a choice, we can say that the person has been forced or coerced. Thus, when you go out for a stroll in the evening, you have the right to return home with both your watch and your life. If you are suddenly made to choose between them, you are being coerced since you have been deprived of your right to both. But for this, the baseline of rights is critical.

To develop this idea formally we have to define a game of life more elaborately, not by simply describing the set of choices open to people but by specifying which of these choices are a part of a person's right and so must not be denied, even if the denial is made hard to detect by ultimately making the person choose while acquiescing to the denial. This will open up a richer avenue for defining and analyzing the legitimacy of the law.

CHAPTER EIGHT

Picking Up the Threads

8.1 The Road Ahead

The rise of law and economics in the second half of the past century is one of the great success stories of the comingling of two major disciplines. It has contributed to our understanding of human behavior and the designing of policy instruments. Yet, as with many pioneering intellectual advances, it had its weaknesses, in this case, burrowed quite deep. In this book, I showed that once we scrutinize the foundations of traditional law and economics, we stumble upon internal contradictions. They are so important that once we become aware of them, it becomes impossible to pretend they do not exist. Moreover, it becomes clear that some of the failures of law and economics, such as the poor implementation of laws in developing economies and the persistence of corruption, are aggravated by our failure to address this weakness in the foundation of the discipline.

One big challenge is the non-implementation of the law. There are examples from around the world of laws enacted with the finest intention, written down diligently into the constitution, the nation's statutes, and codes of behavior, and then overlooked or implemented poorly. Not only do civilians ignore and violate the law, but the police, the magistrates, and other functionaries of the state do little to enforce them, at times resorting to taking bribes but also at times seemingly unaware of these laws. Important interventions, such as the rights to basic food, health care, and education, are often enshrined in a nation's law books and then, with the conscience cleared, overlooked. Traditional law and economics is generally at a loss to understand this pervasive phenomenon and therefore unable to amend it.

Even apart from this, the potential of law and economics as a discipline to help us understand economic outcomes and to facilitate policies to improve our living standards remains woefully unexploited, and one reason for this is the fault line beneath the discipline. The aim of this monograph was to highlight these weaknesses and then correct them. Law and economics is an important discipline, but what has been achieved so far is nowhere close to its potential. It is my belief that once its methodological foundations are made stronger, this can be a subject of fundamental importance to society, economics, and polity and can facilitate growth and development and also curb conflict and instability.

Fortunately, the fault lines, once they are properly understood, are rectifiable. We can write down a rigorous way of doing law and economics where these problems are much more clearly addressed. That is what the focal point approach to law and economics tries to do. The move from the traditional or neoclassical approach to the focal point approach is, in some ways, as pointed out earlier, akin to the move from partial equilibrium economics to general equilibrium. As in that case, the new approach that we have on hand is a rigorous usable model but also vastly more complex than the traditional method. It is possible to write up a prototype simply, in the same way that the Edgeworth Box provides an easy representation of general equilibrium. But we know from the work of Léon Walras in the nineteenth century and that of Kenneth Arrow, Gérard Debreu, and Lionel Mackenzie in the mid-twentieth that the task of a full-fledged model is more complex and also open-ended since we can keep adding features from the real world to the model.

Using this analogy of partial and general equilibria, I may point out that the focal point approach should not be thought of as necessarily overriding the traditional or neoclassical approach. After all, economists continue to develop and use partial equilibrium analysis even now, though we are aware of its limits. There are two reasons for this. In many situations, a full general equilibrium analysis is so complex as to be beyond our capacity for analysis. In such situations we do partial equilibrium analysis, while keeping our fingers crossed. The second reason for doing partial equilibrium analysis once we have learned of general equilibrium models is that we now know where and when the economy is sufficiently partitioned for partial equilibrium analysis to be a reasonable approximation of reality. That is, we know that there are no serious feedbacks from the rest of the economy on the sector we are analyzing. In such contexts partial equilibrium analysis is fine. The same logic carries over to the neoclassical approach to law and economics. For reasons of ease we may have to continue to use this approach in analyzing some real-life law and economics questions. But if we do this with an awareness of the generalized focal point approach, we will avoid egregious mistakes. As we saw in Section 5.5, there are situations where the interaction between the civilians can be analyzed by treating the behavior of the functionaries of the state as exogenous—it is in the self-interest of the latter to enforce the law. The neoclassical approach to law and economics would work fine in such contexts.

Again, using the analogy of general equilibrium models and the awareness that these can be made ever more realistic and complex, we have to recognize that there is scope for further development with the focal point approach to law and economics. Several such avenues were explored in the previous chapters, but I nevertheless remain acutely aware of their inadequacy and the fact that this is an agenda that needs much more work. Further, as one spends a lot of time on an approach, as I have done with the focal point approach, one also begins to see open ends, the scope for further elaboration, and new conundrums that need to be dealt with. This is the inevitable fate of all research projects and intellectual enterprises.

This book was essentially about theory and methodology, an effort to create a frame of analysis that can be used to answer practical questions and solve problems that policymakers have to contend with. Answering those questions and solving those problems were not the immediate purpose of the book. This means that in pursuing the rather linear path that this book set itself on, there were many loose ends and leads that arose but had to be abandoned so that I was not distracted from the central purpose. The aim of this final chapter is to draw attention to some of the open ends of the main project, the inevitable incompleteness that I mentioned above, in the hope of encouraging future research, and in the process to pick up some of the threads of ideas that are important but not central to law and economics, and so had to be hushed when they arose in earlier chapters.

There are three particular threads that I pick up in the next three sections, two abstract topics and one practical. We encountered the role of statistical information, or probabilities based on past data, in devising rules and laws. How should we square up such statistical information and hard data with intuition and common sense? I stressed the role of reasoned intuition and the lived experience in several places. It is now time to pick up on this. There are two particular issues. First, a normative matter. How should we use statistical information, for instance, regarding group characteristics or as evidence in a legal case? Some of our unwitting usage can lead to dreadful discrimination against groups and the marginalization of some people with a special boost for others, as we saw in Chapter 5. What should be our moral stand on this? Second, what is the methodological status of statistical information? Is that the only source of human knowledge? How do we square up differences between knowledge acquired, for instance, through randomized controlled trials and other more informal methods? Sections 8.2 and 8.3 answer these two questions, and, in the process, also point to new directions that deserve to be followed in the future.

Section 8.4 is a foray into a pressing contemporary problem, which rose tangentially in the above chapters. To speak of a realistic game involving the state and citizens, it may not be right to treat the boundaries of the game to be defined by the boundaries of the nation-state. Especially in the modern world, what one government does can impact residents of another nation and have their government react. This is an enormously important practical project on which the survival and health of the world depends. Barring a brief mention in Chapter 1, I have stayed away from this debate of our times in pursuing the main agenda of this book—methodology and theory. But, even as I write this book, the world is going through a phase of heightened political convulsion. There is a clear exacerbation of age-old political divides, the hardening of in-group identities, and a sharp rise in conflict and fragility. I believe this has something to do with the failure of our laws and conventions to keep pace with economic globalization. The book sheds some light on this and, though I am in no position to offer a definitive prescription, this last chapter may be a good place to comment on it.

8.2 Statistical Information and Morals

Statistical information and probability play an important role in both the formulation and the implementation of the law. We know from masses of data that wearing seat belts saves lives; it raises the probability of a person in the car surviving a crash. We know from past statistics that smoking cigarettes increases the chance of getting cancer. We also know from studies done by behavioral economists in laboratories and in the field that most people tend to treat low-probability events as having even lower probability. Hence, we have laws that require drivers and passengers in cars to wear seat belts, and taxes that make it more expensive for people to buy cigarettes and laws prohibiting cigarette commercials on television.[1]

In implementing the law as well, though we are reluctant to admit this, we use statistical information. In criminal cases, we often insist that a person should be treated as innocent until proven guilty. In reality, barring logical truths such as the Pythagoras theorem or Arrow's Impossibility theorem, nothing in life can be *proved*. We use past experience and, increasingly, masses of data to decide that from the description of some situation we can take it as "beyond reasonable doubt" that someone is guilty. "Reasonable" doubt is an allusion to probability. And since we cannot imagine too many cases that come up in court where the decision hinges on some logical truth, we are forced to pass judgment based on smoking-gun evidence. In the real world, there is no evidence but that of the smoking gun.

---

1. Such is the irony of economics that there is some evidence that cigarette companies saw their profits rise as a consequence of the ban on advertising. This is because a lot of the advertising turned out to be almost like competitive bidding. Each firm had to advertise to keep its customers, and in the end all firms were worse off.

Alongside all the challenges opened up by the use of statistical or probabilistic information come some moral questions that we encountered in Chapter 5. We are in a strange world where, on the one hand, we are trying to expand the reach of human rights but, on the other hand, are witnessing an exacerbation of group discrimination, and the denial of some basic rights to certain groups.[2] I want to investigate how we can bring reason to bear on this challenge.

We have already seen that the use of certain kinds of information can lead to discrimination against groups, even when there is no malicious intent on the part of the discriminator. We saw that in markets where human productivity has complementarities, race or gender can begin to play the role of a focal point. Suppose we believe that a particular person has low productivity because he or she belongs to a group and we believe that the *average* productivity of people in that group is low. This belief can become self-fulfilling.

Since this outcome can occur without any racism or sexism on anyone's part, it is not evident how to correct it. One possibility is deliberate affirmative action enforced through the use of state power. In India, the government has enacted laws to ensure that a certain percentage of women get to be leaders of village councils. It was a constitutional amendment that was passed in 1993 requiring one-third of village councils, chosen through a lottery, to have the seat of the leader of the council reserved for women. That is, only women can be candidates for these posts. There is also the Women's Reservation Bill, 2008, which is not yet a law, which tries to create a similar one-third quota in the parliament and also in state councils.[3] Further, in India, all colleges and universities and all state-sponsored firms and institutions are required to admit a certain percentage of students or employees who belong to the backward castes.

But, all said and done, the reach of the state is limited. Societies can be partitioned in numerous ways—gender, race, religion, caste, levels of education, body weight, shape of nose, and so on. If

2. See Barkan (2011) for a discussion of some of these issues in the context of some of the most gross rights violations, such as in the context of ethnic cleansing and genocide.

3. This is actually a lapsed bill. The Upper House, or the Rajya Sabha, passed it in 2010; but the Lower House had not considered it when it was dissolved in 2014 as a consequence of the general election, in which the incumbents lost.

the state tries to have all these traits represented in job hiring, the level of intervention will be crippling for the economy. Further, if the market creates the need for discrimination, we can use any of these numerous markers to achieve this. It is almost impossible for any central authority to monitor and correct this. There are also numerous occasions in everyday life when people use statistical information. Pedestrians have been known to cross the road to the other side when they see people of certain races or sizes coming toward them. This is, at times, prejudice but at times a pure use of statistical information. There is a limit to what can be corrected by the state, and it is also not clear that we want the state to be so involved in our everyday lives.

This is where morality comes in. Human beings are capable of using their innate morals to "correct" their own behaviors. What we can do is to show people what the right use of morals happens to be to help them do their moral reasoning better.

Good people, confronted with the problem of discrimination, often take the route of *denying* there *is* any statistical information underlying some of the more objectionable cases, such as crossing the road or not employing members of a group known to be less productive. This, however, is not a good route, for it amounts to tampering with the evidence. Indeed some of the evidence may be wrong and some of the evidence may be cooked up to provide cover for our more base instincts, and also, as I will discuss in the next section, we do often misread the meaning of statistical information or the findings of randomized controlled trials. But with all these caveats in mind, it nevertheless remains true that rejecting information because we do not like its implications is not a good idea, no matter how noble the motivation. This leads to ascientific thinking, and spawns superstition and false truths.

So how should we respond to the challenge? Fortunately, David Hume can once again be marshalled to rescue us, and I am here referring to what is often called Hume's Law, to wit, that a "should-statement" or a normative claim can never be deduced from one or more purely "is-statements" or positive claims. As Hume (1739 [1969]) himself put it, he found that many moralists, after discussing various is or is-not claims moved over, ever so imperceptibly, to normative statements connected with an ought or ought not, and treated this as deduction. This was unacceptable. This impossibility of crossing over from positive statements to normative stands has come to be known, following Black's (1964) paper, as "Hume's guillotine."

What Hume's Law implies is that whenever we reach a normative position—I should not employ a person of a particular gender or I should cross over to the other side of the road when I see a person of a certain group coming—from seemingly positive information, in this occasion statistical information about some group's productivity or crime propensity, there must be some hidden normative priors. In this case, these could be: I should maximize profit or I should not get physically hurt.

This now allows us a way out of some of the more noxious decisions by classifying in our own heads the salience of the hidden normative priors and help us decide when it is not strong enough to justify a certain behavior. Thus we may decide—and this one I would actually urge you to do—not to take account of a person's group identity—race or religious background, for instance—when considering someone to employ, *even though there may be information in it*. We can look into education and previous work experience but not group identity. This may shave off a little bit of our profit, but that is a cost we should be willing to take, because we know that if everybody takes group identity into account, this does make some groups less productive and marginalizes them in society. In other words, I am suggesting that greater profit is not an important enough objective and should be forgone by individuals for the greater social good of nondiscrimination.

To understand this better suppose it has been proved, as well as one can, using statistical information, that people of religion X (the resort to the symbol X here is not for love of mathematics but for fear of controversy) are less productive than others. Suppose it is also true that we like to earn more profit rather than less. What I am suggesting is that, when we decide not to discriminate against people of religion X when choosing an employee, of the two precepts, namely, that (1) people of religion X *are* less productive and (2) we want to maximize profit, we should give up (2). That is, we should not give up the positive or the factual one, which would amount to a denial of reality.

I am aware that we are asking people to do what is not in their self-interest. But that is what being a moral creature is all about, and as we have seen, human beings, once persuaded, can act morally. There is, however, an additional problem here; we are appealing to a morality that is not strictly consequential, since, if you, as an individual, forgo some profit and hire people from a certain group that is currently less productive than others, that, in itself, will have a negligible effect on society and on the productivity of the people discriminated against. So one has to appeal to deontological ethics to make people adhere to such behavior.[4]

Let me take one more example. Consider the statement "Slavery is good for economic growth." This is a purely positive statement. So we should decide whether it is right or wrong based entirely on evidence and reason. Our morals play no role in this decision. To go from this statement to the normative statement "Slavery is good" requires, for instance, another proposition, "Economic growth is good."[5] If I want to reject the claim "Slavery is good," I can do so by rejecting the normative proposition "Economic growth is good." In fact, that is exactly the line I take. If my study shows that slavery

---

4. I am aware that calling this deontological ethics may be questioned since it is not purely a rule-based moral but has an eye on consequences. It behooves everybody to behave in a certain way because everybody doing so has a socially desirable consequence, even though each person's behavior may have no effect. In other words, we are appealing to actions that may be called "individualistic deontology," even though their ultimate justification lies in a collective consequentialism. Individualistic deontology is at the heart of Parfit's moral mathematics (Parfit, 1984). In a different context I made use of this argument to show how one can be a Paretian, and still ban "voluntary sexual harassment" in the workplace, where "voluntary" refers to work contracts where the employer makes it clear at the time of a person's employment that he reserves the right to sexually harass the worker (Basu, 2003). In other words, it is up to the potential worker to weigh the benefits of the relatively good salary and other benefits and deduct the cost of harassment and then make a decision in his or her own interest. Such contracts are individually Pareto improving since the employer and the employee are better off and there is no obvious negative fallout on others. But moral mathematics does get in here and makes it reasonable to argue that even such "voluntary" harassment should be declared illegal. In commenting on sexual harassment in the workplace, it is worth mentioning that it has interesting links with labor market discrimination, discussed in Chapter 5. Before they adopted specific laws to prohibit sexual harassment in the workplace, countries such as the United States used their antidiscrimination laws to punish such behavior. Further, there is evidence that laws that punish and therefore reduce sexual harassment diminish gender inequality in labor supply and wages (Chen and Sethi, 2017).

5. Needless to add, implicit in this statement is the qualifier "under all circumstances."

is good for growth, I would not reject that conclusion but would reject the axiom that economic growth is good.

Finally, when I urge the academic reader, the plaintiff, the lawyer, and the judge not to distort and deny statistical facts because they seem to lead to morally uncomfortable actions, we must recognize that there is a difference between not distorting and accepting uncomfortable facts and talking about them publicly. The latter is speech but it is also an action, with its own consequences, and so one has to weigh those consequences in deciding whether or not one should talk about it. If after analyzing data you reach the conclusion that person X has a low IQ, it is I think wrong to deny this "fact," but that does not make it right to *say* publicly that X has a low IQ, which can be emotionally wounding to X. In fact, there may even be a moral case, based on simple welfare-based consequentialism, to lie in public about X's IQ.[6]

The same problem arises with the slavery example. Suppose your statistical analysis suggests that slavery is good for economic growth. You are invited to speak at the annual convention of the Ku Klux Klan. What should you do? My first advice would be to not accept the invitation. But if you do, it would be advisable not to say that slavery is good for economic growth, because this could trigger morally unacceptable action on the part of those listening to you. There may even be a moral reason to lie and say "Slavery is bad for economic growth."

Statistical facts, useful as they are, deserve to be taken with a dose of skepticism. They must not be denied because we do not like what we take to be their normative consequence (as just argued), but there may be other *positive* reasons for skepticism. That is the subject matter of the next section.

8.3 The Noah's Ark Critique

The previous section dealt with the normative and ethical challenge of using statistical information, especially that pertaining to

---

6. I have to add a word of caution though. I have done a detailed, game-theoretic analysis of this, using the metaphor of M. C. Escher's famous *Waterfall*, in my paper Basu (1994a; see also Voorneveld, 2010). The risk in telling white lies so as not to hurt people is that if it is done too often, it may damage the effectiveness of the spoken word so much that it may be a welfare-lowering behavior.

groups, for decision making. As we saw in Chapter 5, it may be individually rational to use such information, but it can have social consequences that are undesirable. With the normative challenge dealt with in the previous section, I turn here to the positive problem. When is it reasonable to use statistical information on which so much of science is based? I show that the use of such information, even when it is based on perfectly controlled randomized trials, has some pitfalls, which have been commonly overlooked. To give away the final line, I show that inductive and statistical information alone can never give us knowledge; the use of intuition is unavoidable.

Human beings have long suffered by their reluctance to use data and statistics to help create knowledge. One of the most celebrated cases comes from one of humankind's greatest thinkers, Aristotle. Aristotle had lots of opinions on differences between men and women and was quite steadfast in his belief that women had darker blood and fewer teeth than men. While I can see how we can differ on whether or not someone has a soul, since it is not clear what this means and how it can be proved one way or the other, the belief about blood and teeth, and especially teeth, is baffling. All one has to do is make men and women open their mouths and count. Not doing so seems like obstinacy against any form of data and statistics. One, however, has to be cautious in leveling this charge against Aristotle because, elsewhere, he is careful to stress the importance of facts. Thus in his essay *History of Animals* (ca. 350 BCE), he notes, "Males have more teeth than females in the case of men, sheep, goats, and swine; *in the case of other animals observations have not yet been made*" (my italics), thereby revealing a fastidiousness with facts.[7]

Fortunately, this is not a debated matter anymore. We now live in the age of evidence and data. And in this book I have referred in several places to statistical information. The use of such information, especially information that comes from the laws of random numbers, has a long, if somewhat ominous, history in the social sciences. Some of the earliest uses of this happened in parapsychology. In 1884, the eminent French physiologist Charles

7. See http://classics.mit.edu/Aristotle/history_anim.2.ii.html. I am grateful to Michael Singer for drawing my attention to this.

Richet wanted to see if card players could transmit information to others just by looking at their own cards. In his study, one person had to look at a card from a certain subset of cards, and someone else would have to guess which one he saw. Of the 2,927 guesses, if these were completely random, 732 would be right. In his controlled experiment, it so happened, 789 guesses were right. This led him to conclude that there is transmission of knowledge that occurs directly between people's minds (Hacking, 1988), thereby raising some questions about Richet's deductive skills. (It is reassuring to know that Richet's deductive skills were not flawless, since he, an advocate of eugenics, had also deduced that some races were innately superior to others, his own race, needless to add, being part of the superior lot.)

First in medicine and epidemiology and now in economics, the role of statistical information and randomized controlled trials (RCTs) is increasingly recognized. This is as it should be. But in development economics this has at times been taken to an extreme, equating all knowledge with statistical information, for instance, information revealed through RCTs. That is, however, a mistake. In this book, I made several references to the importance of lived experience and of reasoned intuition.[8] How do they square up with data, statistical information, and regularities discovered through RCTs?

First, we must not forget that theory and pure reason are critically important sources of knowledge. To deny this is either not to know a lot or to use unnecessarily cumbersome methods to acquire knowledge. To see the latter, suppose we insisted that Pythagoras could use only empirical methods. It is arguable he would nevertheless have proved his famous theorem. If he collected lots of triangles and measured the squares on the sides he is likely to have reached the conclusion that the two smaller squares together have the same area as the large one. But this would be a very inefficient method and he would also be embroiled in controversies about whether the triangles he picked were really a random selection. His critics would no doubt claim that he had proved this only for the Mediterranean region.

---

8. I discuss the importance of reasoned intuition and why it is important elsewhere (Basu, 2014).

Of course, what can be discovered through pure reason is by definition a tautology, but some of these tautologies are so complex and nonobvious, Arrow's Impossibility theorem being a good example, that their discovery is a huge contribution to human knowledge. But even when we go beyond circular or tautological truths, it is important to recognize the limitations of statistical information and the fact that there are other ways to acquire knowledge.

As for the limitations, even the best-run RCTs are based on random draws from *past* populations. There is no hard reason that the findings will apply to tomorrow. Take the findings of some of the finest RCTs in development economics, such as the Chattopadhyay and Duflo (2004) paper, showing that choosing a woman leader to head a village council improves the provision of public goods in the village. From that finding you cannot however say anything about what selecting women leaders will do tomorrow, especially if you use the rule that randomizers insist on, namely, that you can say something about the population only if you study a properly random sample of that population, since tomorrow's people are not a part of the population from which samples are drawn.

To make a general claim about the impact of women leaders of tomorrow you have to use intuition and common sense. Outside of unearthing tautological truths, in the enterprise of knowledge creation, there is no escape from the use of intuition, based on our lived experience.

As I have argued elsewhere (Basu, 2014),[9] there are numerous ways in which human beings acquire knowledge, and to deny those channels of knowledge acquisition can do great damage. Growing up from birth, a child learns many things—that a friendly smile means good things are to follow, that a grimacing man with a knife is best left alone, that a slap hurts, and so on. If the parent asks the child if these pieces of knowledge were picked up from properly conducted randomized experiments and, if not, insists such knowledge be discarded, it is likely the child will grow up an ignoramus. The share of knowledge that we pick up through these nonscientific

9. There is a large literature on this subject, exploring the power of this method and its ability to unearth causality. Here is a small selection: Banerjee (2005), Mookherjee (2005), Rodrik (2008), Cartwright (2010), Deaton (2010), Rust (2016).

methods is vastly greater than what we learn from journals and scientific studies. It is true that superstitions also come through the same window, but we cannot bolt that window altogether for that reason.

Finally, let me show how there are situations in life where there is a case for rejecting even properly collated statistical information by using experience and reasoned intuition. Suppose a researcher comes to your "town" and does an RCT by injecting a green liquid in a random sample of characters in the town and showing that this causes better hair growth, with no adverse side effects. You want to have better hair. Will you agree to take this injection?

Here is a scenario where you will have good reason not to. Let us suppose your town actually happens to be Noah's Ark. There are you, and maybe another human being, and there are two snakes, two frogs, two toads, and so on—a large population. The injection trial was done by using proper statistical methods with a random draw of sample from the entire Ark.

Next suppose there is a neighboring town where all the inhabitants are human beings, who look and behave similar to you. In that town, it is well known, some people took this same green injection in the hope of getting better hair, but all of them got a racking headache and lost all their hair. This was however not a statistically controlled study. It may have been the case that the injection was given to only those whose last names begin with A, B, and C. This was because the treatment was being administered alphabetically but had to be called off midway through because of an abrupt budget cut.

Most people in such a situation would intuitively feel they will be better off learning from the experience of the neighboring town, despite its failure to randomize, than from the proper statistical study from their own town and population, which happens to be Noah's Ark. It appears to me that they will be eminently sensible in doing so.

The Noah's Ark critique has wide applicability. Consider medicine. Increasingly, and in many ways understandably, we rely on the expert—be it a doctor or a Google search—in deciding when and how to medicate ourselves. It is, however, important to realize that the bulk of this "expert" opinion is based on statistical information, and there may well be a case to overrule some of this by using one's own knowledge of oneself, accumulated over time. Luckily, there are doctors who share this view. Groopman and Hartzband (2011) provide a lot of evidence of the role of the patient's own opinion. As they observe, approvingly (p. 7), "Sir William Osler, an eminent physician of the last century . . . famously said that when trying to unravel a complex medical diagnosis, you should listen carefully to the patient, because he is telling you the answer."

The way to understand this is by using the Noah's Ark paradigm. What the doctors and medical books tell you is what they have found by studying hundreds and thousands of patients, often randomly drawn. This information is useful but should not be used to mechanically overrule all other kinds of information. What you have learned about yourself through many years of observation that may not have been scientifically collected is like the information from the neighboring town, the residents of which are more like you than the inhabitants of your town, Noah's Ark.

If I may go further and offer a piece of medical advice—do use this with caution. In dealing with physical pain and depression, you should be much more mindful of your own experience and use it. Try to figure out what triggers your pain or sadness. If you feel you have found the triggers, try them out a few times by deliberately setting them off and checking if they cause pain and depression (I am assuming these pains and depressions are not too acute for such scientific experiments). One can discover truths about oneself that a doctor or a medical book may not be able to provide, using other people's statistics, no matter how scientifically they are collated.

We live in an age when knowledge is increasingly deduced from statistics. Credit rating agencies classify people's likelihood of repaying debt by correlating behavior patterns with defaults; we collect statistics to form judgments about different people's risk of committing crimes and then take precautionary actions accordingly. As we deal with masses of people across the globe this is a natural tendency, but as the Noah's Ark example warns us, we will also make big mistakes by the increasing banishment of knowledge that comes from reasoned intuition and the lived experience. This is also a warning that some of the group characteristics that we collect statistically and on which we base judgments of productivity of different groups and then discriminate in the labor market could use a shot of skepticism.

It is difficult to pin down why common sense and reasoned intuition are such powerful ingredients of knowledge, but one may conjecture that it has something to do with evolution. What we take to be common sense is what has, in all likelihood, survived many generations of natural selection and so, even though it can misguide us on occasions, it is not something to be dismissed out of hand. Further, since with all the statistical information, we still do not have any foolproof method of carrying over what happened in the past to what may happen in the future, there is a case to add reasoned intuition and common sense in forming opinions and in passing judgment.

8.4 Prologue to a Global Constitution

A "prologue" at book's end is unusual, but in this case it is meant to be a reminder of the fact that the purpose of theory and methodology, the main concerns of this book, is to set the foundation for more applied work. The aim must be to build on this so that we can have more effective policies, better regulation, and more efficient and equitable interventions. Theory thus serves as a prologue to a more active engagement with society in the hope of making a better world.

We live in troubled times. The magnitude of refugees and people moving from their homes in search of safer and economically viable havens is reminiscent of what we read about biblical times. While poverty is on a slow decline, inequality is reaching cataclysmic heights. A recent Oxfam report calculates that the aggregate wealth owned by the world's wealthiest eight persons is equal to the aggregate wealth of one-half of the world's population, 3.6 billion people (Oxfam, 2017). My own calculation, using the wealth database of Credit Suisse, shows that three of the world's wealthiest persons have greater wealth than all the people of three countries, A, B, and C, Angola, Burkina Faso, and Congo (Democratic Republic), with an aggregate population of 122 million. It is not surprising that political divisions within nations are seemingly at an all-time high. There is a resurgence of nationalism and distaste for the other that has not been seen since the end of World War II. It is arguable that as the world has become more globalized and brought people into greater interaction with one another, conflict has increased and is reaching a level where there is anxiety about the viability of society as we know it.[10]

The challenge of inequality will likely fester, spilling into different forms of political instability. For years, the poor and the marginalized were told how their condition was a natural predicament, the will of God, part of nature's design, and just deserts for their past sins, including those committed in previous lives (never mind that no one knows what that means). To this heady brew was added the claim of some neoclassical economists that the inequality we see in the world is an outcome of people's free choice between work and leisure, unmindful of the fact that the bulk of human inequality is determined at birth. Since babies do not choose between hard work and leisure, this has little to do with choice. The myths that were fed to the population to assure them that their poverty was just are beginning to be seen for what they are.

As the law gets more complicated, one new form of deprivation that is beginning to show up is access to legal services. If you cannot afford a lawyer, you may never be able to claim some of your rights. Your rights, enshrined in the law, will remain merely some ink on paper. In a moving essay on legal deprivation, Rakoff (2016, p. 4) notes, "Over the last few decades, ordinary US citizens have increasingly been denied effective access to their courts." And he goes on to catalog its implications: "Individuals not represented by lawyers lose cases at a considerably higher rate than similar individuals who are represented by a counsel. In mortgage foreclosure cases, for example, you are twice as likely to lose your home if you are unrepresented by counsel." These additional deprivations, concomitant of extreme inequality, imply that excessive inequality is not just bad in itself but is an assault on democracy. It takes away some of the basic rights of the poor.

10. This subject matter is addressed in the World Bank's (2017) report on governance and the law. As the report points out (p. 257), "Countries today face an inter-connected, globalized world characterized by a high velocity and magnitude of flows of capital, trade, ideas, technology and people." It then goes on to discuss the special challenges that arise from this situation.

It is the age of inequality combined with the age of information that is creating a dangerous brew. There are many causes behind this phenomenon. As I have discussed elsewhere (Basu, 2016b), the simultaneous advance in two kinds of technology—the age-old, labor-saving one, and the new-age, "labor-linking" technology, enabling people to work for faraway companies and customers—is a major factor and is showing up in the form of a shrinking share of wage bill in the GDP of almost all middle- and high-income countries. It is also possible, and this is pure conjecture, that, as human beings evolve and our brain capacity increases, there will be a rise in the Gini coefficient of IQs, with a small number of individuals seeing a steady rise in their intelligence quotient. This is driving a wedge between the layperson and the expert. The laity is suspicious that, while the experts will give the best advice, it will be the best advice for the experts.

This is not without precedent. Sir William Petty, seventeenth-century English economist and inventor, did some pioneering work on surveying land. Entrusted to survey large quantities of army land in Ireland in 1654, he did an amazing job, in record time, using some truly innovative methods. In addition, he emerged owning large parts of the land he had surveyed. The "Petty problem" is at the root of some of our current political instability. There is a genuine dilemma. The majority in most countries is ever more suspicious of experts. As a result, genuine democratic processes are leading to results that reject expertise and talent, and end up with perverse choices.

The only way to correct this is to take on the problem of inequality directly. We have to think of intelligent policy that limits the gap between the rich and the poor. If there were a cap on how much land Petty could get for himself, that may have served Ireland better. I do not want to jump to suggest actual legislative interventions here because I am acutely aware of the need to design these with great caution, so as not to damage individual incentive and enterprise, while trying to cap inequality.

The need to address this challenge is, however, urgent. The reason this will not be easy is that, for every legal intervention we can think of, there is a market response by virtue of people trying to get around it. Groups, for instance, can get together and keep down

their individual wealth to avoid the tax net but have a disproportionate amount of common property—parks, hospitals, schools—
available for themselves. At the international level this means that
even if individual countries have more equality, we can have hor-
rendous levels of intercountry inequalities. This challenge of global
inequality will require policy interventions at an international level,
raising all the issues mentioned in the previous chapter.

A book concerned with the foundations of the social sciences
may not seem like the right place to go into this topic; nor do I plan
on any comprehensive discussion here. Yet the subject matter of
this book has an important bearing on these practical challenges.
For that reason, I want to make a brief foray into this, with the
warning that it is a merely suggestive discussion, presenting an argument that is speculative and has gaps, in the spirit of a prologue
to future work.

The reason why regulation in a globalizing world is dealt with
so poorly is the presumption that the power of the law derives from
the state and so, as soon as we move beyond the state to the world,
the standard idea of law flounders (see discussion in Dixit, 2004;
Hadfield and Weingast, 2013). As Sarat, Douglas, and Merrill (2011,
p. 3) note, "In the absence of the state, the contract is void, without
prescriptive voice. Thus the social contract, if it is to be binding,
presupposes the very state it calls into question." And, again on the
same page, referring to the Hobbesian view of law, they point out,
"If law is exclusively the creation of the state, then it is impossible to
imagine law *qua* law existing in the state's absence. We can imagine
principles of prudence, maxims of reason, notions of justice existing in the absence of states, but not law as an enforceable code of
conduct designed to solve social disputes." Having noted this, they
go on to examine contrarian ideas, which have some resonance
with what is bring argued here.

The Hobbesian view that the law acquires force only when there
is a state to back it up is what is contested here. This book takes the
view that, in the final analysis, the state is, in an important sense, a
vacuous construct. It is not the exogenously powerful authority that
some take it to be. The state's power, important though it may be, is
the product of the beliefs that ordinary people carry in their heads,
beliefs about how others will behave, beliefs about beliefs, and so

on. There is, of course, a difference between how we conceive of the law in a nation-state and the law across a comity of nations, but the presumption that permeated so much writing in economics and also law, namely, that the law cannot be effective at a supranational level, is wrong. As the focal point approach to law shows, enforcement occurs because of what I expect others to do when I violate the law; and others do that because of what they expect others to do if they do not do so. If we can get appropriate conventions and beliefs in place, we can have the rule of law at the global level, as we have at the national level. This is because the claim that the effectiveness of the law comes from the exogenously given power and authority of the state is, as we saw in this book, flawed.

Going from the state to the global level involves formidable challenges. But they are not insurmountable if we focus attention on collective, self-enforcing agreements. The scope for this is enormous, even though it remains largely unexplored.

As long as we lived partitioned within the confines of different nation-states, it was fine to talk of the law of the nation and leave it at that. The game of life people played was played largely within the confines of the nation. There has, of course, been trade and travel from time immemorial, but we could push those to the margins of analysis and ignore them, with a casual footnote tossed in by way of apology. With the steady march of globalization, we do not have that luxury any more. As Hadfield (2016, p. 129) notes, "Cheap communications and transportation have given us the global supply chains. But flattening production processes with global supply chains requires more than technology and container ships. It requires resolution of that basic problem of how to coordinate and support collaboration and exchange. It requires ways of resolving the externalities and conflict that upheaval in economic life creates."

At some level this problem was always there. For a while, the challenge was met using what is often referred to as "statutist" interventions. The statutist doctrine originated in fourteenth-century Italy and was meant to contend with problems that arose with trade and commerce, which gave rise to multijurisdictional problems. Breyer (2015) discusses this problem by creating an imaginary scenario in the Middle Ages. If a Roman citizen brought a suit in Florence against a Florentine citizen for having damaged his property in Rome, whose law would apply? The statutist system was a simple set of rules about handling such multijurisdictional issues. In this situation, the laws of Rome, where the property was situated, would apply, even if the case was being tried in Florence. But with long-distance travel and capital flows, including across warring nations, deep linkages involving trade and outsourcing, the statutist system is no longer able to handle the challenges that arise. To quote Breyer (p. 96), "Major businesses are often made up of networks, connecting divisions located in many countries. . . . Commercial cases are more complex, with ambiguous jurisdictional boundaries to be determined and their outcome can have a significant impact upon international commerce." It is not hard to see what is happening around us and the origins of some of today's conflicts.

Similar problems, though at a different level, were encountered in traditional, feudal societies. Henry Maine, the nineteenth-century British jurist who had extensive knowledge of ancient European law, and later experienced India when he served as legal adviser to the imperial British government, was acutely aware of the challenges of small communities, ruled by their own village laws. Special problems arose as, with changing technology, local communities, with their own locally evolved laws, came into contact with other communities (Maine, 1871). The larger sovereign clearly had to play a mitigating role when these local communities had conflict, akin to what global bodies have to do across nations today.

The dramatic changes that are occurring in the workplace as a consequence of globalization and the rise of digital technology have taken us beyond what can be solved merely by the statutist doctrine. There are stories galore from around the world. Take Nike. It began in 1964, its early model being that of designing and selling its products in the United States but having them produced abroad. The original production used to take place in Japan. As Japan's labor cost rose and Nike's production expanded, it moved to Korea, and later to Indonesia, Vietnam, China, and Latin America. Today 600 contractors in 46 countries supply Nike with products (Katz, Kochan, and Colvin, 2015, p. 267). With the rise of artificial intelligence it is possible that some of this work will shift back to high-income countries because robots in Germany will sooner or later begin to undercut workers in Bangladesh.

These global linkages are even more visible in the information technology sector. It is arguable that the growth pickup in the Indian economy was because of economic reforms in the early 1990s and the uplifting role played by the IT sector. A good example is India's Infosys Limited. Started in 1981 by seven engineers, with a capital of roughly $250, to do some data and back-office work, initially for American companies, Infosys now has over 1,000 client companies spread over 50 countries. It has nearly 200,000 workers spread over 32 countries. These changes have given rise to hope and opportunity, but also to disruption, with massive movements of jobs around the world, with attendant political problems and dissent. Managed well, this can contribute to a better world, but it requires a level of global rules and laws that we have not seen in the past and how well we will do remains an open question.[11]

To see the kinds of new problems that can arise with globalization, consider the social and the cultural. The coming together of people can lead to challenges that we may not have had to confront before.[12] Consider people of different religions who come to live in geographic proximity. This can result in cultural and religious conflict. Well-meaning people often point to seemingly easy solutions. The way to resolve this, they will say, is to allow each person to practice his or her own religion, without trying to thwart or impose it on others. This will entail, for instance, that I have the right not to eat pork, while you have the right not to eat beef; all we have to do is not to impose one group's eating rules on others. Likewise, we should have the right to worship one God, many gods, or, what is arguably the most rational option, no God. For peace to prevail

---

11. Basu and Stiglitz (2015) discuss a stark example of the opportunities and setbacks that can arise with the coming together of economies with the example of the formation of the European Union, defined by the Treaty of Lisbon, and its predecessor, the Treaty of Maastricht (see also Basu, 2016a). In that paper, we show that by enabling joint liability it is possible for all EU countries to benefit. But what gets in the way is Section 125 of the Treaty of Lisbon. That section has an origin that is understandable because joint liability can create its own hazards, but the full implication of Section 125 was not evident until the European sovereign debt crisis became full-blown in 2011.

12. Quite apart from the challenge of bringing such a large constituency to function in unison, globalization raises contentious issues of what our normative goal should be. Setting collective goals is hard enough in small committees; it is vastly harder for the comity of nations (Posner, 2006).

what citizens have to learn is to treat these practices as belonging to one's private space. Well-meaning people who recommend such behavior are aware that it may not be easy to persuade everybody to adhere to this principle of respecting other people's private practices. What they do not always realize is that, even as a principle, this may not work. The presumption is that, as long as I practice what my religion and culture demands, and let others practice what their religion and culture demands, there will be no conflict. This is true in the case of the two examples just discussed, pertaining to eating habits and worshipping rules. But there are other examples where such normative rules can run into difficulty. Here is an admittedly contrived example. Suppose some people follow a religion that requires them to drive on the left, whereas others follow a religion that asks them to drive on the right. As long as these groups live in separate nations, the principle of letting people practice their own religion is fine. But when they come to live in the same space or region, this principle is no longer viable, at least not without head-on collisions.

Another social and political problem of globalization arises from our inability to empathize with others. When we live within our own cultural space, as most of us do, it is hard to fully comprehend differences. Most people who will be reading this book are people who get baffled by rural folks in poor, Muslim regions in Afghanistan and Pakistan, who run for cover when they see Western volunteers descend on their villages with polio vaccines. If they could do the mental experiment of getting into the shoes of those rural folks, they would have greater empathy. Here is the experiment you need to do. Imagine Kim Jong-un, in a charitable mood, sending volunteers from North Korea to give us a red injection that will enhance our immunity against infections. When we see these people come into our locality, most of us would run for cover the same way as the rural folks of Afghanistan and Pakistan did from the polio vaccine volunteers.

Globalization is increasingly bringing under the same roof such totally divergent cultures. The conflict that we see around us has roots in this. The law of the nation-state is not adequate to take on this new challenge. There are two ways in which we can mediate in today's global conflict. The first is via multilateral organizations, such as ILO, WTO, the World Bank and the International Monetary Fund, which try to work across nations and mediate between them. One good example has to do with labor laws. It was long recognized that nations often cut labor standards, limit trade union rights, and trim minimum wages to attract global capital. This gave rise to the "race to the bottom" literature and different methods were used, such as ILO's labor conventions, which were basically global covenants, to curb such practices.[13] With the rise of outsourcing and multicountry production, the challenge will get harder.

For global conventions and multilateral organizations to do this job well we have to have voting systems within these organizations that are more democratically organized.[14] For the Bretton Woods organizations, for instance, the rule is roughly that you command the share of votes in keeping with the size of your contribution to these organizations. That is about as fair as it would be if the United States had a voting system for its own presidential election in which individuals had vote shares in keeping with the amount of taxes they paid. Jeff Bezos, Bill Gates, Warren Buffett, and a few others would quickly get to have majority say in US decision making under such a system, to wit, the one that the Bretton Woods organizations currently use. This needs reform and redesign because multilateral organizations will play an increasingly important role in the world, and, apart from anything else, people need to perceive these organizations as fair and representative of global opinion.

The second route to mitigating global conflict, one that is increasingly needed in today's world, is to work toward a global constitution, a set of minimal rules that we all agree to abide by.[15] It should play the same role that a constitution within a nation

13. See Engerman (2003), and Katz, Kochan, and Colvin (2015). Moreover, as Mohamed El-Erian points out in his Project Syndicate essay, reform is in the self-interest of these organizations, for they otherwise risk being edged out of their dominant position by the new multilateral organizations being initiated by China (El-Erian, 2017).

14. For an analysis of multilateral agencies, and specifically the Bretton Woods organizations, in today's globalizing world and why they may have failed to deliver, see Stiglitz (2002), who recognizes that globalization in all likelihood expands global GDP. Yet it has been the source of much discontent; and part of the reason is that economic globalization has occurred without adequate structures of global governance.

15. An intermediate step toward this is played by international treaties. Further, customs among nations often evolve into virtual international laws (Choi and Gulati, 2016).

does—by providing a backdrop of basic legal norms to which we all adhere to. Each nation can continue to make its own laws, but it has to respect the world constitution when enacting and enforcing its own laws. The idea of having an *ius commune humanitatis* has been around for a while (Stone, 2011). It may sound idealistic, but it is an idea we cannot give up on. Without this, there is a risk of human extinction by rising conflict and increasing negative externalities across nations, involving not just climate change (that we are all—well, almost all—aware of) but also the fallout of discordant monetary and fiscal policies and the loss of jobs and accompanying conflict.

The aim of such a constitution would be to create space so that nations can formulate their own laws in ways that do not conflict with the laws of other nations. This is not easy. What should the global constitution rule be concerning people like those whose religion requires them to drive on the left and those whose religion requires them to drive on the right? Each ruling will be controversial, but we cannot do without some rule in a globalized world. Likewise, should individuals have the right to wear the hijab and the bikini? To some people it seems axiomatic to assert that each person should have the right to wear what he or she wishes to, no matter where the person lives. My own sympathies are with such a view, but I am also aware that we cannot ignore the fact that what one wears, others have to see. It is not clear where one person's personal freedom ends and another's begins. Is the wearer's right greater than the seer's right?

In Sen's celebrated paper (Sen, 1969) on the conflict between the Pareto principle and what he called the "minimal liberty" axiom, he argued forcefully that individuals have certain recognized personal spheres where the choices of those individuals reign supreme. Others cannot overrule them. The example Sen took was whether or not a person reads *Lady Chatterley's Lover* should be the decision of that person. Someone else's preference for this person reading it or not should be treated as immaterial. Sen's aim was to precipitate a paradox and compel us to think of what should be salient, Pareto or liberty. While most of us would agree with the minimal liberty axiom, namely, the *existence* of a personal sphere, what exactly *constitutes* that sphere is not obvious. Many would argue that a person has the right to wear what she wants—the loudest colors or the most muted colors, for instance. But few would defend a person's right to talk as loudly as she wishes. This difference may have some justification rooted in biology. I am not forced to see the loud colors a person wears, but it is hard not to hear what a person loudly says, since we have eyelids but not earlids (which I have long felt is a major design flaw in the construction of the universe, whoever designed it). So the issue remains that even if we consider the right to have a personal sphere, the content of that sphere and where its boundaries lie will be contentious; and this will be more so if we try to write down some principles that apply to all of humanity, across cultures and nations. But in today's globalized world, where people increasingly cohabit in the same space, we do not have the luxury to look away from this.

There is one more reason why a global constitution is increasingly urgent today. With the rise of globalization there is an inevitable erosion of democracy. One critical element of democracy is for people to have the right to vote in choosing leaders who can affect their well-being. This is what led all democracies to have an electoral system. And this worked well as long as the world economy was largely balkanized into nation-states. Over time, with globalization this has been changing quite rapidly. The policy that one nation adopts can have an effect beyond its boundaries. An injection of money supply in the United States can cause inflation in Vietnam in today's world of easy capital flows. Malaysia's decision to curb trade union rights can cause foreign direct investment to Indonesia to dry up, with greater flows into Malaysia. This is the challenge of governance in an interconnected world, discussed in World Bank (2017).

In such a world, to have a say in the election of only your own nation's leader may not help very much. It is entirely reasonable to suggest that, to Mexicans, the person who becomes US president is more consequential than who gets elected as Mexican president. Since Mexicans have no say in the US presidential election (you could deduce that from the outcome of the US election in November 2016), global democracy is clearly flawed. If you have difficulty in seeing this, consider the United States having a system whereby people in the District of Columbia, and only they, vote to elect the US president. It would not take much effort to persuade a Californian or a New Yorker that the United States does not have proper democracy. It is in the same sense that we can argue that, as the world globalizes, and our voting system remains nation-based, global democracy is in steady erosion.

It is not clear what can be done about this, but having some global rules that curtail the powers of leaders of nations is a reasonable interim step.[16] In other words, there should be prior global rules that place restrictions on what Donald Trump or Xi Jinping or Theresa May may do, just as the governors of states in the United States have restrictions imposed on them by the federal government.

Once a global constitution is specified and we also have accompanying rules of how someone who violates the global constitution will be punished, such a body of global rules can gradually gather strength and be enforced not by any state but by ordinary people around the world, through a web of self-enforcing beliefs. After all, even within the nation-state in the final analysis, it is individuals who do the policing. In the republic of beliefs, where we are all doomed to live, dangers arise from the fact that there is no single, tangible source of power. But this is also a source of hope, hope that the collectivity can bring law and order to regions and domains that may have earlier seemed immune to the rule of law.

The management of inequality and global conflict will require the kind of international effort that we are beginning to put into climate change and the management of the environment. Such interventions will take us into arenas of law and legal activism we have not seen before. With all such intervention comes the risk of negative fallouts, such as damage to individual incentives at levels that cause overall welfare to decline. Legal interventions, without adequate attention to the laws of the market, can spell disaster. This is what makes "law and economics" such an important subject. Just as its success can create new opportunities, its failures can have a disproportionate effect on human lives.

16. I say this in a similar vein to the suggestion from Breyer (2015, p. 92, my italics): "Since there is no Supreme Court of the world, national courts must act piecemeal, without direct coordination, in seeking interpretations that can dovetail rather than clash with the working of foreign statutes." And he goes on to add what would be anathema for many in a powerful nation, "And so our Court does, *and should, listen to foreign voices.*"

Consider communism. Unlike some other -isms, like the many fascisms, where even the founding motivations were ignoble, sectarian, and selfish, communism, from the earliest writings of Karl Marx to the actual experiments in early twentieth century, had aims that were rooted in genuine egalitarianism. But it was a system conceived without a blueprint of how it should be run once it was in place. And the sketchy blueprints that were there paid scant attention to the laws of markets and the economy. Without such a blueprint of how to realistically run the system, what happened was inevitable. The laws of property and trade were changed, and wealth was centralized and brought under state control. Pooled under one command, it was the focus of coveted eyes; and the inevitable happened. It was captured and soon it was evident that the last phase of communism is crony capitalism.

The fault was not in the original ambition but in an intellectual failure, the inability to comprehend the complexities of the laws of society and markets and, as a consequence, the failure to create a viable design.

As we enter the new age of globalization and digital advance, the world's opportunities are rising, creating potential for levels of growth never witnessed before. But with this will come challenges, the headwinds of which we are beginning to feel. If labor productivity continues to rise as steeply as it is doing now, we will have either exponential growth or diminishing wages and vanishing jobs. It is not evident which way we will go. But a lot will depend on our ability to respond to this new challenge, and we will have to attend to this with both our heads and our hearts. Matters that were left to the free market may now need the law and collective interventions; matters that previously had to be managed by the state may now be amenable to the free market and individual enterprise. Much will depend on the right blend of legal interventions and space for individual enterprise and choice.

8.5 Coda

Law and economics as a discipline is critically important for development, and it will no doubt grow in importance. As our economic life gets more complex, as technology hooks up people and corporations across the world, and as robots displace workers, new challenges will arise that will have to be met with new regulations and laws. The invisible hand of the market is important, but its efficacy depends on the regulatory space within which it is made to work.

The one big mistake frequently made is to treat the invisible hand as an ideological matter, with a polarization at the two ends—leave it all to the market or the state can do it all. In reality, as anybody who has pondered the matter recognizes, we need both; but that is also too trite a way to put it. Depending on the state of technology, the level of globalization, and the trends in climate, we may need different kinds of regulations. When people lived in village communities and in small scattered settlements, the main livelihood being agriculture, the environment was a concern but much of it could be handled with rules for the village community, and norms for the use of common lands and the local commons (the classic work being that of Ostrom, 1990). But this is no longer enough in today's world with global warming and environmental spillovers that are massive and carry from one nation to another and even across continents. The regulation that we need today has to involve multicountry agreements and will be much more complex than what was needed in farming communities earlier.

For markets to function, we invariably need a regulatory structure. At times this has to be provided explicitly by the state and its laws; at times this is provided by the social norms and habits that guide our behavior; and at times it needs multicountry agreement and enforcement. That we do not try to run away without paying after every taxi ride is usually because of our internalized norms. The law, even if it were there, would not be needed for this. On the other hand, consider some seemingly free-market operations, such as farmers' markets in the United States. Local consumers, merrily picking up their week's supply of "organic" macadamia nuts, "homemade" caramel candies, and "grandma's" chocolate chip cookies, often treat these places as ultimate havens of the free market, unaware that the well-functioning farmers' markets are underwritten by elaborate rules and regulations.[17]

17. For an analysis of the Dane County Farmers' Market in Madison, Wisconsin, see Basu (2000) and Ferguson (2013).

In today's globalized world, with massive industrial complexes, corporations operating across several continents, and specialized workers engaged in multiple countries, the intervention is needed at a global level. Indeed, this is so critical that whether we are able to create such a global regulatory system is a matter of survival for humankind. What makes this additionally challenging is that the nature of the problem is continuously evolving.

In a celebrated essay, "Economic Possibilities for Our Grandchildren," written in 1930, Keynes predicted that economics would cease to be an important subject in a hundred years because all the important economic problems would have been solved or be within sight of solution. This was a rare bad forecast on the part of Keynes. The mistake he made was to think of the economic problems of humankind to be a fixed set. As research progressed this set would shrink and in fact vanish in a hundred years was Keynes's expectation. We now have 12 years to go for that forecast to be validated, and it seems unlikely that it will be. In reality, economic problems keep evolving. What human beings can do using guile and intelligence is endless. They will keep evolving not just new products but new ways to market to people, taking advantage of human psychological quirks, new ways to price products so that people get tied to buying from the same firm, frequent flyer programs being an example of this, and in many other ways. This means regulation also will have to evolve and change. This is, in all likelihood, an endless process, making law and economics a compelling discipline.

We have come a long way from the antitrust laws of the late nineteenth century. But it is now a race against time. As our economic life gets more complex and the challenges proliferate, we have to marshal all the facts and statistics we have and bring all our powers of reasoning and deduction to bear on them. This is our collective duty. To some this may appear like a collective Sisyphean venture, a task of endless drudgery. My hope is that, as a scientific venture, this will be a task that is, at the same time, a source of intellectual stimulation and excitement.

The aim of this monograph was to straighten out some of the wrinkles in the foundations of law and economics, to make this venture possible. I did this as carefully as I could but cannot be unmindful of the fact that a lot remains to be done. An intellectual enterprise is never finished. You simply have to call it a day at some point, and write it up, if you are so inclined. It is then available to others to discover its weaknesses and loose ends, and carry the agenda forward, if they are so inclined.

REFERENCES

Abbink, K., Dasgupta, U., Gangadharan, L., and Jain, T. (2014), "Letting the Briber Go Free: An Experiment on Mitigating Harassment Bribes," *Journal of Public Economics* 111.

Abbink, K., Freiden, E., Gangadharan, L., and Moro, R. (2016), "The Effect of Social Norms on Bribe Offers," mimeo: Monash University.

Acconcia, A., Immordino, G., Piccolo, S., and Rey, P. (2014), "Accomplice-Witnesses and Organized Crime: Theory and Evidence from Italy," *Scandinavian Journal of Economics* 116.

Acemoglu, D., and Jackson, M. O. (2015), "Social Norms and the Enforcement of Law," mimeo: Harvard University.

Acemoglu, D., Johnson, S., and Robinson, J. (2005), "Institutions as a Fundamental Cause of Long-Run Growth," in P. Aghion and S. Durlauf (eds.), *Handbook of Economic Growth*, Elsevier.

Acemoglu, D., and Wolitzky, A. (2015), "Sustaining Cooperation: Community Enforcement vs. Specialized Enforcement," National Bureau of Economic Research Paper 21457.

Akerlof, G. (1976), "The Economics of Caste, Rat Race and Other Woeful Tales," *Quarterly Journal of Economics* 90.

—— (1991), "Procrastination and Obedience," *American Economic Review* 81.

Akerlof, G., and Kranton, R. (2010), *Identity Economics: How Our Identities Shape Our Work, Wages, and Well-Being*, Princeton University Press.

Akerlof, G., and Shiller, R. (2015), *Phishing for Phools: The Economics of Manipulation and Deception*, Princeton University Press.

Akerlof, R. (2017), "The Importance of Legitimacy," *World Bank Economic Review* 30.

Aldashev, G., Chaara, I., Platteau, J.-P., and Wahhaj, Z. (2011), "Using the Law to Change the Custom," *Journal of Development Economics* 97.

—— (2012), "Formal Law as a Magnet to Reform Custom," *Economic Development and Cultural Change* 60.

Alger, I., and Weibull, J. (2013), "Homo Moralis—Preference Evolution under Incomplete Information and Assortative Matching," *Econometrica* 81.

—— (2018), "Morality: Evolutionary Foundations and Policy Implications," in K. Basu, C. Sepulveda and D. Rosenblatt (eds.) *The State of Economics, the State of the World*, MIT Press.

Ali, S., and Liu, C. (2017), "Laws, Norms, and Authority: Self-Enforcement Against Coalitional Deviations in Repeated Games," mimeo: Pennsylvania State University.

Angelucci, C., and Russo, A. (2016), "Petty Corruption and Citizen Report," Columbia Business School Research Paper 25.

Arad, A., and Rubinstein, A. (2012), "Multi-dimensional Iterative Reasoning in Action: The Case of the Colonel Blotto Game," *Journal of Economic Behavior and Organization* 84.

—— (2017), "Multi-dimensional Reasoning in Games: Framework, Equilibrium and Applications," mimeo: Tel Aviv University.

Ariely, D. (2008), *Predictably Irrational: The Hidden Forces That Shape Our Decisions*, HarperCollins.

Arrow, K. (1973), "The Theory of Discrimination," in O. Ashenfelter and A. Rees (eds.), *Discrimination in Labor Markets*, Princeton University Press.

—— (1998), "What Has Economics to Say about Racial Discrimination?," *Journal of Economic Perspectives* 12.

Arrow, K., and Debreu, G. (1954), "Existence of an Equilibrium for a Competitive Economy," *Econometrica* 22.

Aumann, R. (1976), "Agreeing to Disagree," *Annals of Statistics* 4.

—— (1987), "Game Theory," in S. N. Durlauf and L. E. Blume (eds.), *The New Palgrave Dictionary of Economics*, Palgrave Macmillan.

Austin, J. (1832), *The Province of Jurisprudence Determined*, Cambridge.

Ayer, A. (1980), *Hume: A Very Short Introduction*, Oxford University Press.

Bac, M., and Bag, P. (2001), "Law Enforcement and Legal Presumptions," *Journal of Comparative Economics* 29.

Bacharach, M. (2006), *Beyond Individual Choice: Teams and Frames in Game Theory*, N. Gold and R. Sugden (eds.), Princeton University Press.

Bagenstos, S. (2013), "Employment Law and Social Equality," *Michigan Law Review* 112.

Baird, D., Gertner, R., and Picker, R. (1994), *Game Theory and the Law*, Harvard University Press.

Banerjee, A. (2005), "'New Development Economics' and the Challenge to Theory," *Economic and Political Weekly* 40, October 1.

Banerjee, R. (2016), "On the Interpretation of Bribery in a Laboratory Corruption Game: Moral Frames and Social Norms," *Experimental Economics* 19.

Banuri, S., and Eckel, C. (2015), "Cracking Down on Bribery," *Social Choice and Welfare* 45.

Baradaran, S., and Barclay, S. (2011), "Fair Trade and Child Labor," *Columbia Human Rights Law Review* 43.

Bardhan, P. (1997), "Corruption and Development: A Review of Issues," *Journal of Economic Literature* 35.

Barkan, E. (2011), "Ethnic Cleansing, Genocide and Gross Violations of Human Rights: The State versus Humanitarian Law," in A. Sarat, L. Douglas, and M. Umphrey (eds.), *Law without Nations*, Stanford University Press.

Barrett, C., Garg, T., and McBride, L. (2016), "Well-Being Dynamics and Poverty Traps," *Annual Review of Resource Economics* 6.

Barrett, S. (2007), *Why Cooperate? The Incentive to Supply Global Public Goods*, Oxford University Press.

Basu, Karna (2011), "Hyperbolic Discounting and the Sustainability of Rotational Savings Arrangements," *American Economic Journal: Microeconomics* 3.

Basu, Karna, Basu, K., and Cordella, T. (2016), "Asymmetric Punishment as an Instrument of Corruption Control," *Journal of Public Economic Theory.*

Basu, K. (1977), "Information and Strategy in the Iterated Prisoner's Dilemma," *Theory and Decision* 8.

—— (1980), *Revealed Preference of Government*, Cambridge University Press.

—— (1983), "On Why We Do Not Try to Walk Off without Paying after a Taxi Ride," *Economic and Political Weekly* 18, November.

—— (1986), "One Kind of Power," *Oxford Economic Papers* 38.

—— (1990), "On the Non-existence of a Rationality Definition for Extensive-Form Games," *International Journal of Game Theory* 9.

—— (1993), *Lectures in Industrial Organization*, Basil Blackwell.

—— (1994a), "Group Rationality, Utilitarianism and Escher's Waterfall," *Games and Economic Behavior* 7.

—— (1994b), "Traveler's Dilemma: Paradoxes of Rationality in Game Theory," *American Economic Review, Papers and Proceedings* 71.

—— (1995), "Civil Institutions and Evolution: Concepts, Critiques and Models," *Journal of Development Economics* 46.

—— (1998), "Social Norms and Law," in P. Newman (ed.), *The New Palgrave Dictionary of Economics and the Law*, Macmillan.

—— (2000), *Prelude to Political Economy: A Study of the Social and Political Foundations of Economics*, Oxford University Press.

—— (2001), "The Role of Norms and Law in Economics," in J. Scott and D. Keates (eds.), *Schools of Thought: Twenty-Five Years of Interpretive Social Science*, Princeton University Press.

—— (2003), "The Economics and Law of Sexual Harassment in the Workplace," *Journal of Economic Perspectives* 17.

—— (2005), "Racial Conflict and the Malignancy of Identity," *Journal of Economic Inequality* 3.

—— (2007), "The Traveler's Dilemma," *Scientific American* 2.

—— (2011a), *Beyond the Invisible Hand: Groundwork for a New Economics*, Princeton University Press.

—— (2011b), "Why, for a Class of Bribes, the Act of Giving a Bribe Should Be Treated as Legal," Ministry of Finance, Government of India, http://mpra.ub.uni-muenchen.de/50335/.

—— (2014), "Randomization, Causality and the Role of Reasoned Intuition," *Oxford Development Studies* 42.

—— (2015), *An Economist in the Real World: The Art of Policymaking in India*, MIT Press.

—— (2016a), "The Economics and Law of Sovereign Debt and Risk Sharing: Some Lessons from the Eurozone Crisis," *Review of Law and Economics* 12.

—— (2016b), "Globalization of Labor Markets and the Growth Prospects of Nations," *Journal of Policy Modeling* 38.

—— (2017), "Discrimination as a Coordination Device: Markets and the Emergence of Identity," *Forum for Social Economics.*

———— (2018), "Markets and Manipulation: Time for a Paradigm Shift," *Journal of Economic Literature*, forthcoming.

Basu, K., Bhattacharya, S., and Mishra, A. (1992), "Notes on Bribery and the Control of Corruption," *Journal of Public Economics* 48.

Basu, K., and Dixit, A. (2016), "Too Small to Regulate," *Journal of Quantitative Economics* 15.

Basu, K., and Emerson, P. (2000), "The Economics of Tenancy Rent Control," *Economic Journal* 110.

Basu, K., and Stiglitz, J. (2015), "Sovereign Debt and Joint Liability: An Economic Theory Model for Amending the Treaty of Lisbon," *Economic Journal* 125.

Basu, K., and Van, P. H. (1998), "The Economics of Child Labor," *American Economic Review*, vol. 88.

Basu, K., and Weibull, J. (1991), "Strategy Subsets Closed under Rational Behavior," *Economics Letters* 36.

———— (2003), "Punctuality: A Cultural Trait as Equilibrium," in R. Arnott, R. Kanbur, B. Greenwald, and B. Nalebuff (eds.), *Economics for an Imperfect World: Essays in Honor of Joseph Stiglitz*, MIT Press.

Basu, K., and Zarghamee, H. (2009), "Is Product Boycott a Good Idea for Controlling Child Labor? A Theoretical Investigation," *Journal of Development Economics* 88.

Battigalli, P., and Siniscalchi, M. (2002), "Strong Belief and Forward Induction Reasoning," *Journal of Economic Theory* 106.

Bavly, G. (2017), "Uncertainty in the Traveler's Dilemma," *International Journal of Game Theory* 46.

Becker, G. (1957), *The Economics of Discrimination*, University of Chicago Press.

———— (1968), "Crime and Punishment: An Economic Approach," *Journal of Political Economy* 76.

———— (1971), *The Economics of Discrimination*. University of Chicago Press.

Becker, G., and Stigler, G. (1974), "Law Enforcement, Malfeasance, and Compensation of Enforcers," *Journal of Legal Studies* 3.

Becker, T., Carter, M., and Naeve, J. (2005), "Experts Playing the Traveler's Dilemma," Inst. für Volkswirtschaftslehre, Univ.

Benabou, R., and Tirole, J. (2006), "Incentives and Pro-social Behavior," *American Economic Review* 96.

Ben-Porath, E., and Dekel, E. (1992), "Signaling Future Action and the Potential for Sacrifice," *Journal of Economic Theory* 53.

Berlin, M., Qin, B., and Spagnolo, G. (2018), "Leniency, Asymmetric Punishment and Corruption: Evidence from China," CEPR, Discussion Paper No. DP 12634.

Bernheim, D. (1984), "Rationalizable Strategic Behavior," *Econometrica* 52.

Bernstein, L. (1992), "Opting Out of the Legal System: Extra-legal Contractual Relations in the Diamond Industry," *Journal of Legal Studies* 21.

Bertrand, M., and Mullainathan, S. (2004), "Are Emily and Greg More Employable Than Lakisha and Jamal? A Field Experiment on Labor Market Discrimination," *American Economic Review* 94.

Besley, T., and Coate, S. (1992), "Understanding Welfare Stigma: Tax Payer Resentment and Statistical Discrimination," *Journal of Public Economics* 48.

Besley, T., and Persson, T. (2009), "The Origins of State Capacity: Property Rights, Taxation, and Politics," *American Economic Review* 99.

Bhardwaj, P., Lakdawala, L., and Li, N. (2013), "Perverse Consequences of Well Intentioned Regulation: Evidence from India's Child Labor Ban," National Bureau of Economic Research Working Paper 19602.

Bicchieri, C., and Xiao, E. (2009), "Do the Right Thing: But Only if Others Do So," *Behavioral Decision Making* 22.

Bilz, K., and Nadler, J. (2009), "Law, Psychology, and Morality," *Psychology of Learning and Motivation: Moral Judgment and Decision-Making* 62.

Binmore, K. (1994), *Game Theory and the Social Contract: Playing Fair*, MIT Press.

—— (1995), "The Game of Life: Comment," *Journal of Institutional and Theoretical Economics* 151.

Binmore, K., and Samuelson, L. (2006), "The Evolution of Focal Points," *Games and Economic Behavior* 55.

Black, M. (1964), "The Gap between 'Is' and 'Should,'" *Philosophical Review* 73.

Blattman, C., Jamison, J., and Sheridan, M. (2017), "Reducing Crime and Violence: Experimental Evidence from Cognitive Behavioral Therapy in Liberia," *American Economic Review* 107.

Blume, A., and Sobel, J. (1995), "Communication-Proof Equilibria in Cheap-Talk Games," *Journal of Economic Theory* 65.

Blume, L., and Durlauf, S. (2003), "Equilibrium Concepts for Social Interaction Models," *International Game Theory Review* 5.

Bobbio, N. (1989), *Thomas Hobbes and the Natural Law Tradition*, D. Gobetti (trans.), University of Chicago Press.

Boettke, P., Coyne, C., and Leeson, P. (2008), "Institutional Stickiness and the New Development Economics," *American Journal of Economics and Sociology* 67.

Borooah, V. (2016), "Deconstructing Corruption," *Journal of South Asian Development* 11.

Bose, P., and Echazu, L. (2007), "Corruption with Heterogeneous Enforcement Agents in the Shadow Economy," *Journal of Institutional and Theoretical Economics* 163.

Bourguignon, F., Ferreira, F., and Walton, M. (2007), "Equity, Efficiency and Inequality Traps," *Journal of Economic Inequality* 5.

Bowles, S. (2004), *Microeconomics: Behavior, Institutions, and Evolution*, Princeton University Press.

—— (2014), "Niccolo Machiavelli and the Origins of Mechanism Design," *Journal of Economic Issues* 48.

Bowles, S., Durlauf, S., and Hoff, K. (eds.) (2006), *Poverty Traps*, Princeton University Press.

Breyer, S. (2015), *The Court and the World: American Law and the New Global Realities*, Knopf.

Bull, R., and Ellig, J. (2017), "Judicial Review of Regulatory Impact Analysis: Why Not the Best?," *Administrative Law Review* 69.

Burguet, R., Ganuza, J. J., and Montalvo, J. G. (2016), "The Microeconomics of Corruption: A Review of Thirty Years of Research," mimeo: University of Pompeu Fabra.

Burlando, A., and Motta, A. (2016), "Legalize, Tax and Deter: Enforcement Policies for Corruptible Officials," *Journal of Development Economics* 118.

Cadot, O. (1987), "Corruption as a Gamble," *Journal of Public Economics* 33.

Calabresi, G. (1961), "Some Thoughts on Risk Distribution and the Law of Torts," *Yale Law Journal* 70.

—— (2016), *The Future of Law and Economics: Essays in Reform and Recollection*, Yale University Press.

Cameron, L., Chaudhuri, A., Erkal, N., and Gangadharan, L. (2009), "Propensities to Engage in and Punish Corrupt Behavior," *Journal of Public Economics* 93.

Capra, M., Goeree, J., Gomez, R., and Holt, C. (1999), "Anomalous Behavior in a Traveler's Dilemma," *American Economic Review* 89.

Capraro, V. (2013), "A Model of Human Cooperation in Social Dilemmas," *PLOS One* 8.

Carothers, T. (2003), "Promoting the Rule of Law Abroad: The Problem of Knowledge," Carnegie Endowment for International Peace Working Paper 34.

Cartwright, N. (2010), "What Are Randomized Trials Good For?," *Philosophical Studies* 147.

Chakravarty, S., and Macleod, W. B. (2009), "Contracting in the Shadow of the Law," *RAND Journal of Economics* 30.

Charness, G., and Dufwenberg, M. (2006), "Promises and Partnership," *Econometrica* 74.

Chattopadhyay, R., and Duflo, E. (2004), "Women as Policymakers: Evidence from a Randomized Policy Experiment in India," *Econometrica* 72.

Chen, D., and Sethi, J. (2017), "Insiders, Outsiders, and Involuntary Unemployment: Sexual Harassment Exacerbates Gender Inequality," mimeo: Toulouse School of Economics.

Chernushkin, A. A., Ougolnitsky, G. A., and Usov, A. B. (2013), "Dynamic Models of Corruption in Hierarchical Control Systems," *Game Theory and Management* 6.

Choi, S., and Gulati, M. (2016), "Customary International Law: How Do Courts Do It?," in C. A. Bradley (ed.), *Custom's Future: International Law in a Changing World*, Cambridge University Press.

Cigno, A., and Rosati, F. (2005), *The Economics of Child Labor*, Oxford University Press.

Coase, R. (1960), "The Problem of Social Cost," *Journal of Law and Economics* 3.

Cole, D. (2017a), "Trump's Travel Ban: Look beyond the Text," *New York Review of Books* 64, May 11.

Cole, D. (2017b), "Why Free Speech Is Not Enough," *New York Review of Books* 64, March 23.

Cooter, R. (1982), "The Cost of Coase," *Journal of Legal Studies* 11.

—— (1994), "Market Affirmative Action," *San Diego Law Review* 31.

—— (1998), "Expressive Law and Economics," *Journal of Legal Studies* 27.

—— (2000), "Do Good Laws Make Good Citizens? An Economic Analysis of Internalized Norms," *Virginia Law Review* 86.

Cooter, R., and Ullen, T. (1988), *Law and Economics*, Pearson.

Cotterell, R. (1997), *Law's Community: Legal Theory in Sociological Perspective*, Oxford University Press.

Crawford, V., and Sobel, J. (1982), "Strategic Information Transmission," *Econometrica* 50.

Davis, K. (2016), "Multijurisdictional Enforcement Games," New York University School of Law Working Paper 438.

Deaton, A. (2010), "Instruments, Randomization, and Learning about Development," *Journal of Economic Literature* 48.

Debroy, B. (2000), *In the Dock: Absurdities of Indian Law*, Konark.

Del Carpio, X., Loayza, N., and Wada, T. (2016), "The Impact of Conditional Cash Transfers on the Amount and Type of Child Labor," *World Development* 80.

Deshpande, A. (2011), *The Grammar of Caste: Economic Discrimination in Contemporary India*, Oxford University Press.

Dharmapala, D., Garoupa, N., and McAdams, R. (2015), "Punitive Police? Agency Costs, Law Enforcement, and Criminal Procedure," mimeo: University of Chicago Law School.

Dixit, A. (2004), *Lawlessness and Economics: Alternative Modes of Governance*, Princeton University Press.

—— (2015), "How Business Community Institutions Can Help Fight Corruption," *World Bank Economic Review, Papers and Proceedings* 29.

Doepke, M., and Zilibotti, F. (2005), "The Macroeconomics of Child Labor Regulation," *American Economic Review* 95.

Dreber, A., Ellingsen, T., Johannesson, M., and Rand, D. G. (2013), "Do People Care about Social Context? Framing Effects in Dictator Games," *Experimental Economics* 16.

Dufwenberg, M., and Essen, M. (2017), "King of the Hill: Giving Backward Induction Its Best Shot," mimeo: University of Arizona.

Dufwenberg, M., and Spagnolo, G. (2015), "Legalizing Bribe Giving," *Economic Inquiry* 53.

Durlauf, S. (2001), "A Framework for the Study of Individual Behavior and Social Interactions," *Sociological Methodology* 31.

Dworkin, R. (1986), *Law's Empire*, Harvard University Press.

Edmonds, E., and Schady, N. (2012), "Poverty Alleviation and Child Labor," *American Economic Journal: Economic Policy* 4.

El-Erian, M. (2017), "The Risk of a New Economic Non Order", *Project Syndicate*, September 19.

Ellickson, R. (1991), *Order without Law: How Neighbors Settle Disputes*, Harvard University Press.

Ellingsen, T., and Johannesson, M. (2008), "Pride and Prejudice: The Human Side of Incentive Theory," *American Economic Review* 98.

Ellingsen, T., Johannesson, M., Tjotta, S., and Torsvik, G. (2010), "Testing Guilt Aversion," *Games and Economic Behavior* 68.

Ellingsen, T., Ostling, R., and Wengstrom, E. (2013), "How Does Communication Affect Behavior?," mimeo: Stockholm School of Economics.

Elster, J. (1989), "Social Norms and Economic Theory," *Journal of Economic Perspectives* 3.

Emerson, P., and Souza, A.-P. (2003), "Is There a Child Labor Trap? Intergenerational Persistence of Child Labor in Brazil," *Economic Development and Cultural Change* 51.

Engerman, S. (2003), "The History and Political Economy of International Labor Standards," in K. Basu, H. Horn, L. Roman, and J. Shapiro (eds.), *International Labor Standards*, Blackwell.

Esteban, J., and Ray, D. (2008), "On the Salience of Ethnic Conflict," *American Economic Review* 98.

Farrell, J., and Rabin, M. (1996), "Cheap Talk," *Journal of Economic Perspectives* 10.

Fehr, E., and Falk, A. (2002), "Psychological Foundations of Incentives," *European Economic Review* 46.

Fehr, E., and Gachter, S. (2000), "Fairness and Retaliation: The Economics of Reciprocity," *Journal of Economic Perspectives* 14.

Feldman, Y., and Teichman, D. (2009), "Are All Legal Probabilities Created Equal?," *New York Law Review* 84.

Ferguson, W. (2013), *Collective Action and Exchange: A Game-Theoretic Approach to Contemporary Political Economy*, Stanford University Press.

Field, E., and Nolen, P. (2010), "Race and Student Achievement in Post-Apartheid South Africa," mimeo: Harvard University.

Fish, S. (1994), *There's No Such Thing as Free Speech*, Harvard University Press.

Fisman, R., and Miguel, T. (2007), "Corruption, Norms and Legal Enforcement: Evidence from UN Diplomatic Parking Tickets," *Journal of Political Economy* 115.

Frank, R. (1988), *Passions within Reason: The Strategic Role of the Emotions*, Norton.

Fried, R. (1990), *Nightmare in the Red: The McCarthy Era in Perspective*, Oxford University Press.

Friedman, L. (2016), *Impact: How Law Affects Behavior*, Harvard University Press.

Friedman, M. (1962), *Capitalism and Freedom*, University of Chicago Press.

Funcke, A. (2016), "Instilling Norms in a Turmoil of Spillovers," mimeo: University of Pennsylvania.

Gaertner, W., Pattanaik, P., and Suzumura, K. (1992), "Individual Rights Revisited," *Economica* 59.

Gamba, A., Immordino, G., and Piccolo, S. (2016), "Corruption, Organized Crime and the Bright Side of the Subversion of Law," Department of Economics, University of Naples Working Paper 446.

Gambetta, D. (2009), *Codes of the Underworld: How Criminals Communicate*, Princeton University Press.

——— (2017), "Why Is Italy Disproportionately Corrupt? A Conjecture," in K. Basu and T. Cordella (eds.), *Institution, Governance and the Control of Corruption*, Palgrave Macmillan.

Gard, S. (1980), "Fighting Words as Free Speech," *Washington University Law Review* 58.

Gautier, B., and Goyette, J. (2014), "Taxation and Corruption: Theory and Firm-Level Evidence from Uganda," *Applied Economics* 46.

Geisinger, A. (2002), "A Belief Change Theory of Expressive Law," *Iowa Law Review* 88.

Genicot, G., and Ray, D. (2003), "Endogenous Group Formation in Risk-Sharing Arrangements," *Review of Economic Studies* 70.

Georg, S. J., Rand, D., and Walkowitz, G. (2017), "Framing Effects," mimeo: Yale University.

Gigerenzer, G., and Garcia-Retamero, R. (2017), "Cassandra's Regret: The Psychology of Not Wanting to Know," *Psychological Review* 124.

Gintis, H. (2003), "Solving the Puzzle of Prosociality," *Rationality and Society* 15.

—— (2009), *The Bounds of Reason: Game Theory and the Unification of the Behavioral Sciences*, Princeton University Press.

—— (2010), "Rationality and Common Knowledge," *Rationality and Society* 22.

Gintis, H., Bowles, S., Boyd, R., and Fehr, E. (2005), *Moral Sentiments and Material Interests*, MIT Press.

Giraud, G., and Grasselli, M. (2017), "The Macrodynamics of Household Debt, Growth, and Inequality," mimeo: Centre d'économie de la Sorbonne, Paris.

Glaeser, E., and Goldin, C. (eds.) (2006), *Corruption and Reform: Lessons from America's History*, University of Chicago Press.

Gluckman, M. (1955), "The Judicial Process among the Barotse of Northern Rhodesia," Free Press.

Goeree, J., and Holt, C. (2001), "Ten Little Treasures of Game Theory and Ten Intuitive Contradictions," *American Economic Review* 91.

Goldsmith, W. (1996), "Hobbes on Law," in T. Sorrell (ed.), *The Cambridge Companion to Hobbes*, Cambridge University Press.

Govindan, S., and Wilson, R. (2009), "On Forward Induction," *Econometrica* 77.

Granovetter, M., and Soong, R. (1983), "Threshold Models of Diffusion and Collective Behavior," *Journal of Mathematical Sociology* 9.

Greif, A. (1993), "Contract Enforcement and Economic Institutions in Early Trade: The Maghribi Traders' Coalition," *American Economic Review* 85.

Greif, A., Milgrom, P., and Weingast, B. (1994), "Coordination, Commitment and Enforcement: The Case of the Merchant Guild," *Journal of Political Economy* 102.

Groopman, J., and Hartzband, P. (2011), *Your Medical Mind: How to Decide What Is Right for You*, Penguin.

Habyarimana, J., Humphreys, M., Posner, D., and Weinstein, J. (2007), "Why Does Ethnic Diversity Undermine Public Goods?," *American Political Science Review* 101.

Hacking, I. (1988), *The Emergence of Probability: A Philosophical Study of Early Ideas about Probability, Induction and Statistical Inference*, Cambridge University Press.

Hadfield, G. (2016), *Rules for a Flat World: Why Humans Invented Law and How to Reinvent It for a Complex Global Economy*, Oxford University Press.

Hadfield, G., and Weingast, B. (2013), "Law without the State: Legal Attributes and the Coordination of Decentralized Collective Punishment," *Journal of Law and Courts* 1.

—— (2014), "Microfoundations of the Rule of Law," *Annual Review of Political Science* 17.

Hahn, F. (1980), "Unemployment from a Theoretical Viewpoint," *Economica* 47.

Hall, G. (ed.) (2002), *The Treatise on the Laws and Customs on the Realm of England Commonly Called Glanvill*, Oxford University Press.

Halpern, J. Y., and Pass, R. (2012), "Iterated Regret Minimization: A New Solution Concept," *Games and Economic Behavior* 74.

Han, B. (2016), "The Role and Welfare Rationale of Secondary Sanctions," *Conflict Management and Peace Science*, forthcoming.

Hardin, R. (1989), *Liberalism, Constitutionalism and Democracy*, Oxford University Press.

Harrington, J. E. (1999), "Rigidity of Social Systems," *Journal of Political Economy* 107.

Hart, H. L. A. (1961), *The Concept of Law*, Oxford University Press.

Hart, H. L. A., and Honore, T. (1959), *Causation in the Law*, Oxford University Press.

Hashimoto, T. (2008), "Japanese Clocks and the History of Punctuality in Modern Japan," *East Asian Science, Technology, and Society: An International Journal* 2.

Hatlebakk, M. (2002), "A New and Robust Model of Subgame Perfect Equilibrium in a Model of Triadic Power Relations," *Journal of Development Economics* 68.

Havel, V. (1986), "The Power of the Powerless," in J. Vladislav (ed.), *Living in Truth*, Faber & Faber.

He, Q., Pan, Y., and Sarangi, S. (2017), "Lineage-Based Heterogeneity and Cooperative Behavior in Rural China," REPEC-MPRA Paper No. 80865.

Heilbroner, R. (ed.) (1986), *The Essential Adam Smith*, Norton.

Hindriks, J., Keen, M., and Muthoo, A. (1999), "Corruption, Extortion and Evasion," *Journal of Public Economics* 74.

Hobbes, T. (1668 [1994]), *Leviathan*, E. Curley (ed.), Hackett.

Hockett, R. (1967), "Reflective Intensions: Two Foundational Decision Points in Mathematics, Law and Economics," *Cardozo Law Review* 29.

—— (2009), *Law*, Chicago Review Press.

Hoff, K., and Pande, P. (2006), "Persistent Effects of Discrimination and the Role of Social Identity," *American Economic Review* 96.

Hoff, K., and Stiglitz, J. (2001), "Modern Economic Theory and Development," in G. Meier and J. Stiglitz (eds.), *Frontiers of Development Economics*, Oxford University Press.

—— (2015), "Striving for Balance in Economics: Towards a Theory of Social Determination of Behavior," *Journal of Economic Behavior and Economics* 126.

Hollis, M. (1994), "The Gingerbread Game," *Analysis* 54.

Hovenkamp, H. (1990), "The First Great Law and Economics Movement," *Stanford Law Review* 42.

Hume, D. (1739 [1969]), *A Treatise on Human Nature*, Penguin.

—— (1742 [1987]), "Of the First Principles of Government," in *Essays: Moral, Political and Literary*, Liberty Fund.

Humphries, J. (2013), "Childhood and Child Labour in the British Industrial Revolution," *Economic History Review* 66.

Huq, A., Tyler, T., and Schulhofer, S. (2011), "Why Does the Public Cooperate with Law Enforcement? The Influence of the Purposes and Targets of Policing," *Psychology, Public Policy, and Law* 17.

Ifcher, J., and Zarghamee, H. (2011), "Happiness and Time Preference: The Effect of Positive Affect in a Random-Assignment Experiment," *American Economic Review* 101.

Jain, S. (1995), "The Coherence of Rights," in D. Andler, P. Banerjee, M. Chaudhury, and O. Guillaume (eds.), *Facets of Rationality*, Sage.

Janssen, M. (2001), "Rationalizing Focal Points," *Theory and Decision* 50.

Jha, S., and Ramaswami, B. (2010), "How Can Food Subsidies Work Better? Answers from India and the Philippines," Asian Development Bank Working Paper 221.

Johnson, D. (1976), "Increased Stability of Grain Supplies in Developing Countries: Optimal Carryovers and Insurance," *World Development* 4.

Jolls, C. (2013), "Product Warnings, Debiasing, and Free Speech: The Case of Tobacco Regulation," *Journal of Institutional and Theoretical Economics* 169.

Jolls, C., Sunstein, C., and Thaler, R. (1998), "A Behavioral Approach to Law and Economics," *Stanford Law Review* 50.

Joshi, S., and Mahmud, S. (2016), "Sanctions and Networks: 'The Most Unkindest Cut of All,'" *Games and Economic Behavior* 97.

Kahneman, D. (2011), *Thinking, Fast and Slow*, Farrar, Straus and Giroux.

Kahneman, D., and Tversky, A. (1979), "Prospect Theory: An Analysis of Decision under Risk," *Econometrica* 47.

Kaplow, L., and Shavell, S. (2003), "Fairness versus Welfare: Notes on the Pareto Principle, Preferences, and Distributive Justice," *Journal of Legal Studies* 32.

Karabarbounis, L., and Neiman, B. (2014), "The Global Decline of the Labor Share," *Quarterly Journal of Economics* 129.

Katz, H., Kochan, T., and Colvin, A. (2015), *Labor Relations in a Globalizing World*, Cornell University Press.

Kelsen, H. (1945), *General Theory of Law and State*, Harvard University Press.

Khera, R. (2011), "Trends in Diversion of Grain from the Public Distribution System," *Economic and Political Weekly* 46, May 21.

Klitgaard, R. (1988), *Controlling Corruption*, University of California Press.

Kohlberg, E., and Mertens, J.-F. (1986), "On the Strategic Stability of Equilibria," *Econometrica* 54.

Kornhauser, L. (1984), "The Great Image of Authority," *Stanford Law Review* 36.

Kranton, R., and Swamy, A. (1999), "The Hazards of Piecemeal Reform: British Civil Courts and the Credit Market in Colonial India," *Journal of Development Economics* 58.

Kugler, M., Verdier, T., and Zenou, Y. (2005), "Organized Crime, Corruption and Punishment," *Journal of Public Economics* 89.

Kuran, T. (1988), "Ethnic Norms and Their Transformation through Reputational Cascades," *Journal of Legal Studies* 27.

—— (1998), "Ethnic Norms and Their Transformation through Reputational Cascades," *Journal of Legal Studies* 2.

Lacey, N. (2004), *A Life of H. L. A. Hart: The Nightmare and the Noble Dream*, Oxford University Press.

La Ferrara, E. (2007), "Descent Rules and Strategic Transfers: Evidence from Matrilineal Groups in Ghana," *Journal of Development Economics* 83.

Laibson, D. (1997), "Golden Eggs and Hyperbolic Discounting," *Quarterly Journal of Economics* 112.

Landa, J. (ed.) (2016), *Economic Success of Chinese Merchants in Southeast Asia: Identity, Ethnic Cooperation and Conflict*, Springer.

Larkin, P. (1982), "The Art of Poetry No. 30," *Paris Review* 24.

Lebovic, S. (2016), *Free Speech and Unfree News: The Paradox of Press Freedom in America*, Harvard University Press.

Ledyaev, V. (2016), "Gatekeeping as a Form of Power," *Journal of Political Power* 9.

Leibenstein, H. (1950), "Bandwagon, Snob, and Veblen Effects in the Theory of Consumers," *Quarterly Journal of Economics* 64.

Lessig, L. (1996), "Social Meanings and Social Norms," *University of Pennsylvania Law Review* 144.

Levi, E. (1949), *An Introduction to Legal Reasoning*, University of Chicago Press.

Levine, R. V., West, L. J., and Reis, H. T. (1980), "Perceptions of Time and Punctuality in the United States and Brazil," *Journal of Personality and Social Psychology* 38.

Lewis, D. (1969), *Convention: A Philosophical Study*, Harvard University Press.

Li, X. (2012), "Bribery and the Limits of Game Theory: The Lessons from China," *Financial Times*, May 1, http://blogs.ft.com/beyond-brics/2012/05/01/guest-post -bribery-and-the-limits-of-game-theory-the-lessons-from-china.

Lindbeck, A., Nyberg, S., and Weibull, J. (1989), "Social Norms and Economic Incentives in the Welfare State," *Quarterly Journal of Economics* 114.

Loewenstein, R. (1987), "Anticipation and the Valuation of Delayed Consumption," *Economic Journal* 97.

Lopez-Calva, L.-F. (2003), "Social Norms, Coordination and Policy Issues in the Fight against Child Labor," in K. Basu, H. Horn, L. Roman, and J. Shapiro (eds.), *International Labor Standards*, Blackwell.

Lopucki, L., and Weyrauch, W. (2000), "A Theory of Legal Strategy," *Duke Law Journal* 49.

Lui, F. T. (1986), "A Dynamic Model of Corruption Deterrence," *Journal of Public Economics* 31.

Lukes, S. (1974), *Power: A Radical View*, Macmillan.

Macey, J. (1997), "Public and Private Ordering and the Production of Legitimate and Illegitimate Legal Rules," *Cornell Law Review* 82.

Mailath, G., Morris, S., and Postlewaite, A. (2007), "Maintaining Authority," mimeo: University of Pennsylvania.

——— (2017), "Laws and Authority," *Research in Economics* 71.

Maine, H. (1871), *Village Communities in the East and West*, John Murray.

Makowsky, M., and Wang, S. (2015), "Embezzlement, Whistle-Blowing, and Organizational Architecture: An Experimental Investigation," GMU Working Paper in Economics.

Malinowski, B. (1921), "The Primitive Economics of the Trobriand Islanders," *Economic Journal* 31.

Manapat, M., Rand, D., Pawlowitsch, C., and Nowak, M. (2012), "Stochastic Evolutionary Dynamics Resolve the Traveler's Dilemma," *Journal of Theoretical Biology* 303.

Maskin, E. (2016), "How Can Cooperative Game Theory Be Made More Relevant to Economics? An Open Problem," in J. F. Nash and M. Rassias (eds.), *Open Problems in Mathematics*, Springer Verlag.

Maskin, E., and Sjostrom, T. (2002), "Implementation Theory," in K. Arrow, A. Sen, and K. Suzumura (eds.), *Handbook of Social Choice Theory and Welfare*, Elsevier.

Mauro, P. (1995), "Corruption and Growth," *Quarterly Journal of Economics* 110.

McAdams, R. (1995), "Cooperation and Conflict: The Economics of Group Status Production and Race Discrimination," *Harvard Law Review* 108.

—— (2000), "A Focal Point Theory of Expressive Law," *Virginia Law Review* 86.

—— (2015), *The Expressive Powers of Law: Theories and Limits*, Harvard University Press.

Meade, J. (1974), "Preference Ordering and Economic Policy," in A. Mitra (ed.), *Economic Theory and Planning: Essays in Honour of A. K. Dasgupta*, Oxford University Press.

Medema, S. (1998), "Wandering the Road from Pluralism to Posner: The Transformation of Law and Economics in the Twentieth Century," *History of Political Economy* (supplement) 30.

Menon, N., and Rogers, Y. (2017), "Child Labor and Changes in the Minimum Wage: Evidence from India," *Journal of Comparative Economics*, forthcoming.

Mercuro, N., and Medema, S. (1997), *Economics and the Law: From Posner to Postmodernism*, Princeton University Press.

Mishra, A. (2002), "Hierarchies, Incentives and Collusion in a Model of Enforcement," *Journal of Economic Behavior and Organization* 47.

—— (2006), "Corruption, Hierarchies, and Bureaucratic Structures," in S. Rose-Ackerman (ed.), *International Handbook on the Economics of Corruption*, Edward Elgar.

Moene, K., and Soreide, T. (2015), "Good Governance Facades," in S. Rose-Ackerman and P. Lagunes (ed.), *Greed, Corruption and the Modern State*, Edward Elgar.

Mookherjee, D. (2005), "Is There Too Little Theory in Development Economics Today?," *Economic and Political Weekly* 40, October 1.

Mookherjee, D., and Png, P. L. (1995), "Corruptible Law Enforcers: How Should They Be Compensated?," *Economic Journal* 105.

Morita, H., and Servatka, M. (2013), "Group Identity and Relation-Specific Investment: An Experimental Investigation," *European Economic Review* 58.

Morone, A., Morone, P., and Germani, A. (2014), "Individual and Group Behavior in the Traveler's Dilemma: An Experimental Study," *Journal of Behavioral and Experimental Economics* 49.

Morris, S., and Shin, H. (1998), "Unique Equilibrium in a Model of Self-Fulfilling Currency Attacks," *American Economic Review* 88.

—— (2001), "Rethinking Multiple Equilibria in Macroeconomics," in B. Bernanke and K. Rogoff (eds.), *NBER Macroeconomic Handbook*, MIT Press.

Mukherjee, P. (2015), "The Effects of Social Identity on Aspirations and Learning Outcomes: A Field Experiment in Rural India," mimeo: College of William and Mary.

Mullainathan, S., and Shafir, E. (2013), *Scarcity: Why Having Too Little Means So Much*, Times Books.

Murphy, J., and Coleman, J. (1997), *The Philosophy of Law*, Rowman & Littlefield.

Myerson, R. (1983), "Mechanism Design by an Informed Principal," *Econometrica* 51.

——— (2004), "Justice, Institutions and Multiple Equilibria," *Chicago Journal of International Law* 5.

——— (2006), "Fundamental Theory of Institutions: A Lecture in Honor of Leo Hurwicz," mimeo: Department of Economics, University of Chicago.

——— (2008), "The Autocrat's Credibility Problem," *American Political Science Review* 102.

——— (2017), "Village Communities in Economic Development," mimeo: University of Chicago.

Myerson, R., and Weibull, J. (2015), "Tenable Strategy Blocks and Settled Equilibria," *Econometrica* 83.

Naipaul, V. S. (1961), *A House for Mr. Biswas*, Andre Deutsch.

Nash, J. (1950a), "Equilibrium Points in n-Person Games", *Proceedings of the National Academy of Sciences*, 36.

Nash, J. (1950b), "The Bargaining Problem", *Econometrica*, 18.

Nussbaum, M. (1997), "Flawed Foundations: The Philosophical Critique of (a Particular Type of) Economics," *University of Chicago Law Review* 64.

Oak, M. (2015), "Legalization of Bribe Giving When Bribe Type Is Endogenous," *Journal of Public Economic Theory* 17.

O'Donoghue, T., and Rabin, M. (2001), "Choice and Procrastination," *Quarterly Journal of Economics* 116.

Oleinik, A. N. (2015), *The Invisible Hand of Power*, Pickering & Chatto.

Osborne, M., and Rubinstein, A. (1994), *A Course in Game Theory*, MIT Press.

Ostrom, E. (1990), *Governing the Commons*, Cambridge University Press.

Oxfam (2017), "An Economy for the 99%," January 16, https://www.oxfam.org/sites/www.oxfam.org/files/file_attachments/bp-economy-for-99-percent-160117-en.pdf.

Pace, M. (2009), "How a Genetic Algorithm Learns to Play Traveler's Dilemma by Choosing Dominated Strategies to Achieve Greater Payoffs," mimeo: Institut de Mathématiques de Bordeaux.

Pani, N. (2016), "Historical Insights into Modern Corruption: Descriptive Moralities and Cooperative Corruption in an Indian City," *Griffith Law Review* 25.

Parfit, D. (1984), *Reasons and Persons*, Clarendon.

Paternoster, R. (2010), "How Much Do We Really Know about Criminal Deterrence?," *Journal of Criminal Law and Criminology* 100.

Pearce, D. (1984), "Rationalizable Strategic Behavior and the Problem of Perfection," *Econometrica* 52.

Persson, M., and Siven, C.-H. (2006), "Incentive and Incarceration Effects in a General Equilibrium Model of Crime," *Journal of Economic Behavior and Organization* 59.

Pethe, A., Tandel, V., and Gandhi, S. (2012), "Unravelling the Anatomy of Legal Corruption in India: Focusing on the Honest Graft by the Politicians," *Economic and Political Weekly* 47.

Phelps, E. S. (1972), "The Statistical Theory of Racism and Sexism," *American Economic Review* 62.

Pigou, A. (1920), *The Economics of Welfare*, Palgrave Macmillan.

Pistor, K., Haldar, A., and Amirapu, A. (2010), "Social Norms, Rule of Law, and Gender Reality: An Essay on the Limits of the Dominant Rule-of-Law Paradigm," in J. J. Heckman, R. L. Nelsen, and L. Cabatingam (eds.), *Global Perspectives on the Rule of Law*, Routledge.

Platteau, J.-P. (1994), "Behind the Market Stage, Where Real Societies Exist: The Role of Public and Private Order Institutions," *Journal of Development Studies* 30.

—— (2000), *Institutions, Social Norms, and Economic Development*, Harwood.

Polinsky, A. M., and Shavell, S. (2001), "Corruption and Optimal Law Enforcement," *Journal of Public Economics* 81.

Popov, S. V. (2015), "Decentralized Bribery and Market Participation," *Scandinavian Journal of Economics* 117.

—— (2016), "On Basu's Proposal: Fines Affect Bribes," mimeo: Queens University Management School.

Posner, E. (1996), "Law, Economics and Inefficient Norms," *University of Pennsylvania Law Review* 144.

—— (2000), *Law and Social Norms*, Harvard University Press.

—— (2006), "International Law: A Welfarist Approach," *University of Chicago Law Review* 73.

Posner, R. (1977), *Economic Analysis of the Law*, Little, Brown.

—— (1993), "What Do Judges Maximize? (The Same Thing Everybody Else Does)," *Supreme Court Economic Review* 30.

Rabin, M. (2013), "An Approach to Incorporating Psychology into Economics," *American Economic Review*, 103.

Rahman, D. (2012), "But Who Will Monitor the Monitor?," *American Economic Review* 102.

Rakoff, J. (2016), "Why You Won't Get Your Day in Court," *New York Review of Books* 63, November 24.

Rasmussen, E. (2001), "Explaining Incomplete Contracts as the Result of Contract-Reading Costs," *Advances in Economic Policy Analysis* 1.

Ray, D., and Esteban, J. (2017), "Conflict and Development," *Annual Review of Economics* 9.

Ray, R. (2000), "Child Labor, Child Schooling, and Their Interaction with Adult Labor: Empirical Evidence for Peru and Pakistan," *World Bank Economic Review* 14.

Raz, J. (1980), *The Concept of a Legal System*, Clarendon.

Reny, P. (1992), "Rationality in Extensive-Form Games," *Journal of Economic Perspectives* 6.

Reuben, E., Sapienza, P., and Zingales, L. (2014), "How Stereotypes Impair Women's Careers in Science," *Proceedings of the National Academy of Sciences* 111.

Robson, A. (2012), *Law and Markets*, Basingstoke: Palgrave Macmillan.

Rodrik, D. (2008), "The New Development Economics: We Shall Experiment but How Shall We Learn?," in J. Cohen and W. Easterly (eds.), *What Works in Development?*, Washington, DC: Brookings Institution.

——— (2015), *Economics Rules: The Rights and Wrongs of the Dismal Science*, Norton.

Roemer, J. (1998), *Equality of Opportunity*, Harvard University Press.

——— (2015), "Kantian Optimization: A Micro-foundation for Cooperation," *Journal of Public Economics* 127.

Rose-Ackerman, S. (1975), "The Economics of Corruption," *Journal of Public Economics* 4.

Rose-Ackerman, S., and Palifka, B. (1999 [2015]), *Corruption and Government: Causes, Consequences, and Reform*, Cambridge University Press.

Rothstein, B. (2011), "Anti-corruption: The Indirect 'Big Bang' Approach," *Review of International Political Economy* 18.

Rothstein, R. (2017), *The Color of Law: A Forgotten History of How Our Government Segregated America*, Liveright.

Roy, T., and Swamy, A. (2016), *Law and the Economy in Colonial India*, University of Chicago Press.

Rubinstein, A. (1989), "The Electronic Mail Game: Strategic Behavior under Complete Uncertainty," *American Economic Review* 79.

——— (1991), "Comments on the Interpretation of Game Theory," *Econometrica* 59.

——— (2006), "Dilemmas of an Economic Theorist," *Econometrica* 74.

——— (2016), "A Typology of Players: Between Instinctive and Contemplative," *Quarterly Journal of Economics* 131.

Runciman, W., and Sen, A. (1965), "Games, Justice, and the General Will," *Mind* 74.

Rust, J. (2016), "Mostly Useless Econometrics? Assessing the Causal Effect of Econometric Theory," *Foundations and Trends in Accounting* 10.

Samuelson, L. (2016), "Game Theory in Economics and Beyond", *Journal of Economic Perspectives*, 30.

Sanyal, A. (2015), "Bribe Chains in a Police Administration," in S. Guha, R. P. Kundu, and S. Subramanian (eds.), *Themes in Economic Analysis*, Routledge.

Sarat, A., Douglas, L., and Merrill, M. (2011), *Law as Punishment / Law as Regulation*, Stanford University Press.

Savage, L. J. (1951), "The Theory of Statistical Decision," *Journal of the American Statistical Association* 46.

Schafer, H.-B., and Ott, C. (2005), *The Economic Analysis of Civil Law*, Edward-Elgar.

Schauer, F. (2015), *The Force of Law*, Harvard University Press.

Schelling, T. (1960), *The Strategy of Conflict*, Harvard University Press.

Shleifer, A., and Vishny, R. (1993), "Corruption," *Quarterly Journal of Economics*, vol. 108.

Schlicht, E. (1998), *On Custom in the Economy*, Oxford University Press.

Schrecker, E. (1994), *The Age of McCarthy: A Brief History with Documents*, Bedford Books.

Sen, A. (1969), "The Impossibility of a Paretian Liberal," *Journal of Political Economy* 78.

——— (1973), "Behaviour and the Concept of Preference," *Economica* 40.

——— (1980), "Description as Choice," *Oxford Economic Papers* 32.

——— (1993), "Internal Consistency of Choice," *Econometrica* 61.

——— (1997), "Rational Fools: A Critique of the Behavioral Foundations of Economic Theory," *Philosophy and Public Affairs* 6.

——— (2006), *Identity and Violence*, Norton.

Sen, Arunava (2007), "The Theory of Mechanism Design: An Overview," *Economic and Political Weekly* 42, December 8.

Shih, M., Pittinsky, T., and Ambady, N. (1999), "Stereotype Susceptibility, Identity Salience and Shifts in Performance," *Psychological Science* 10.

Singer, M. (2005), *The Legacy of Positivism*, Palgrave Macmillan.

—— (2006), "Legitimacy Criteria for Legal Systems," *King's College Law Journal* 17.

Smith, A. (1762 [1978]), *Lectures on Jurisprudence*, R. L. Meek, D. D. Raphael, and P. G. Stein (eds.), Clarendon.

—— (1776 [1976]), *An Inquiry into the Nature and Causes of the Wealth of Nations*, R. H. Campbell and A. S. Skinner (eds.), Clarendon.

Spengler, D. (2014), "Endogenous Detection of Collaborative Crime: The Case of Corruption," *Review of Law & Economics* 10.

Starr, W. C. (1984), "Law and Morality in H. L. A. Hart's Legal Philosophy," *Marquette Law Review* 67.

Steiner, H. (1994), *An Essay on Rights*, Blackwell.

Stern, N. (1978), "On the Economic Theory of Policy towards Crime," in J. M. Heineke (ed.), *Economic Models of Criminal Behavior*, North-Holland.

Stiglitz, J. (1973), "Approaches to the Economics of Discrimination," *American Economic Review* 63.

—— (1974), "Theories of Racial Discrimination and Economic Policy," in G. von Furstenberg (ed.), *Patterns of Racial Discrimination*, D. C. Heath.

—— (2002), *Globalization and Its Discontents*, Norton.

Stone, S. (2011), "Law without Nation? The Ongoing Jewish Discussion," in A. Sarat, L. Douglas, and M. Umphrey (eds.), *Law without Nations*, Stanford University Press.

Stoppard, T. (1982), *The Real Thing*, Faber & Faber.

Subramanian, S. (2011), "Inter-group Disparities in the Distributional Analysis of Human Development: Concepts, Measurement, and Illustrative Applications," *Review of Black Political Economy* 38.

Sugden, R. (1989), "Spontaneous Order," *Journal of Economic Perspectives* 3.

—— (1995), "A Theory of Focal Points," *Economic Journal* 105.

Sundell, A. (2014), "Understanding Informal Payments in the Public Sector: Theory and Evidence from Nineteenth-Century Sweden," *Scandinavian Political Studies* 37.

Sunstein, C. (1996a), "On the Expressive Function of Law," *University of Pennsylvania Law Review* 144.

—— (1996b), "Social Norms and Social Roles," *Columbia Law Review* 96.

—— (2016), "Listen, Economists," *New York Review of Books* 58, November 10.

Surowiecki, J. (2004), "Punctuality Pays," *New Yorker*, April 5.

Suthankar, S., and Vaishnav, M. (2014), "Corruption in India: Bridging Academic Evidence and Policy Options," *India Policy Forum* 10.

Swedberg, R. (2005), *Interest*, Open University Press.

—— (2014), *The Art of Social Theory*, Princeton University Press.

Thaler, R., and Sunstein, C. (2008), *Nudge: Improving Decisions about Health, Wealth and Happiness*, Yale University Press.

Thorat, S., Banerjee, A., Mishra, V. K., and Rizvi, F. (2015), "Urban Rental Housing Market," *Economic and Political Weekly* 50.

Thorat, S., and Newman, K. (2007), "Caste and Economic Discrimination: Causes, Consequences and Remedies," *Economic and Political Weekly* 42.

Tirole, J. (1996), "A Theory of Collective Reputations (with Applications to the Persistence of Corruption)," *Review of Economic Studies* 63.

Treisman, D. (2000), "The Causes of Corruption: A Cross-National Study," *Journal of Public Economics* 76.

—— (2007), "What Have We Learned about the Causes of Corruption from Ten Years of Cross-National Empirical Research," *Annual Review of Political Science* 10.

Tversky, A., and Kahneman, D. (1986), "Rational Choice and the Framing of Decisions," *Journal of Business* 59.

Tyler, T., (2006), *Why People Obey the Law*, Princeton University Press.

Tyler, T., and Jackson, J. (2014), "Popular Legitimacy and the Exercise of Legal Authority," *Psychology, Public Policy, and Law* 20.

Vallentyne, P. (2000), "Introduction: Left-Libertarianism—A Primer," in P. Vallentyne and H. Steiner (eds.), *Left-Libertarianism and Its Critics*, Palgrave.

Van Damme, E. (1989), "Stable Equilibria and Forward Induction," *Journal of Economic Theory* 48.

Vanberg, C. (2008), "Why Do People Keep Their Promises?," *Econometrica* 76.

Varshney, A. (2002), *Ethnic Conflict and Civic Life: Hindus and Muslims in India*, Yale University Press.

Veblen, T. (1899), *The Theory of the Leisure Class*, Macmillan.

Velu, C., Iyer, S., and Gair, J. (2010), "A Reason for Unreason: Returns-Based Beliefs in Game Theory," mimeo: Cambridge University.

Vermeule, A. (2016), *Law's Abnegation*, Harvard University Press.

Villanger, E. (2005), "Company Interest and Foreign Aid Policy: Playing Donors Out against Each Other," *European Economic Review* 49.

Voorneveld, M. (2002), "Preparation," *Games and Economic Behavior* 48.

—— (2010), "The Possibility of Impossible Stairways: Tail Events and Countable Player Sets," *Games and Economic Behavior* 68.

Weber, R., and Camerer, C. (2003), "Cultural Conflict and Merger Failure: An Experimental Approach," *Management Science* 49.

Weibull, J. (1995), *Evolutionary Game Theory*, MIT Press.

Weinrib, L. (2016), *The Taming of Free Speech: America's Civil Liberties Compromise*, Harvard University Press.

Wihardja, M.-M. (2009), "Corruption in Public Procurement Auctions," mimeo: Center for Strategic and International Studies, Washington, DC.

Wolpert, D. (2008), "Schelling Formalized: Strategic Choices of Non-rational Persons," mimeo: Santa Fe Institute, Santa Fe, NM.

World Bank (2015), "World Development Report 2015: Mind, Society, and Behavior," World Bank.

—— (2016), "World Development Report 2016: Internet for Development," World Bank.

—— (2017), "World Development Report 2017: Governance and the Law," World Bank.

Worstall, T. (2016), "India's Mistake in Trying to Ban Child Labor," *Forbes*, March 15, http://www.forbes.com/sites/timworstall/2016/03/15/indias-mistake-in-trying -to-ban-child-labour/#21f748714f3e.

Wu, K., and Abbink, K. (2013), "Reward Self-Reporting to Deter Corruption: An Experiment on Mitigating Collusive Bribery," mimeo: Monash University.

Yang, J. (2014), "The Politics of Pai Ma Pi: Flattery as Empty Signifiers and Social Control in a Chinese Workplace," *Social Semiotics* 24.

Yoo, S. (2008), "Petty Corruption," *Economic Theory* 37.

Young, P. (1993), "The Evolution of Conventions," *Econometrica* 61.

—— (2008), "Social Norms," in S. Durlauf and L. Blume (eds.), *The New Palgrave Dictionary of Economics*, Macmillan.

Zambrano, E. (1999), "Formal Models of Authority: Introduction and Political Economy Applications," *Rationality and Society* 11.

Zantovsky, M. (2014), *Havel: A Life*, Grove Press.

Tandel, V., 19n7
Teichman, D., 169
Thaler, R., 20n9, 110, 158
Thorat, S., 96n14
Tirole, J., 20n9, 87n1, 95n10
Tjotta S., 76n3
Torsvik, G., 76n3
Treisman, D., 138n13, 140n17
Trump, Donald, 66–67, 201
Tversky, A., 20n9, 156
Tyler, T., 158n17, 164n23

Ullen, T., 15n1
Usov, A. B., 22n13

Vaishnav, M., 19n7, 138n13, 141n18
Vallentyne, P., 173
Van, P., 54n14, 106, 106n22
Vanberg, C., 76n3
Van Damme, E., 76
Varshney, A., 95n10
Veblen, T., 20n9, 158n20
Velu, C., 150n6
Verdier, T., 138n13
Villanger, E., 105, 124n2
Vishny, R., 137
Voorneveld, M., 64n27, 126n5, 184n6

Wada, T., 107n24
Wahhaj, Z., 109n26
Walkowitz, G., 158n18
Walton, M., 53n12

Wang, S., 139n15
Weber, M., 164n23
Weber, R., 59n20
Webster, Margaret, 130
Weibull, J., 53n13, 54n14, 64, 64n23, 90, 110n28, 149, 157n15
Weingast, B., 49n8, 88n3, 193
Weinrib, L., 134
Weinstein, J., 58
Welles, Orson, 130
Wengstrom, E., 75
West, L., 90
Weyrauch, W., 66
Wihardja, M., 138n13
Wilson, R., 78
Wolitzky, A., 112, 121n1, 124n2
Wolpert, D., 31n26
Worstall, T., 108n25
Wu, K., 141n18

Xi, Jinping, 201

Yang, J., 105n21, 124n2, 131
Yoo, S., 138n13
Young, P., 43, 157n16

Zambrano, E., 75n2, 90n4
Zantovsky, M., 125
Zarghamee, H., 108n25, 158n20
Zenou, Y., 138n13
Zilibotti, F., 106n22
Zingales, L., 96n14

A NOTE ON THE TYPE

THIS BOOK has been composed in Miller, a Scotch Roman typeface designed by Matthew Carter and first released by Font Bureau in 1997. It resembles Monticello, the typeface developed for The Papers of Thomas Jefferson in the 1940s by C. H. Griffith and P. J. Conkwright and reinterpreted in digital form by Carter in 2003.

Pleasant Jefferson ("P. J.") Conkwright (1905–1986) was Typographer at Princeton University Press from 1939 to 1970. He was an acclaimed book designer and AIGA Medalist.

The ornament used throughout this book was designed by Pierre Simon Fournier (1712–1768) and was a favorite of Conkwright's, used in his design of the *Princeton University Library Chronicle.*